The Great Expectation

The Great Expectation

The Promised Saviour and Our Coming King

by

Ivan A. Beals

Beacon Hill Press of Kansas City
Kansas City, Missouri

ISBN: 0-8341-0419-9

Printed in the United States of America

Unless otherwise indicated, all scriptures quoted are from the American
Standard Edition of the Revised Bible, 1901.

Permission to quote from the following copyrighted versions of the Bible
is acknowledged with appreciation:

Revised Standard Version of the Bible (RSV), copyrighted 1946 and 1952.

The *New English Bible* (NEB), © The Delegates of the Oxford University
Press and the Syndics of the Cambridge University Press, 1961, 1970.

Contents

FOREWORD

For Martin Luther, the Bible is the cradle in which Christ is found. As we approach a crib to catch a glimpse of a newborn child, so we should read the Holy Scriptures to discover the Saviour. The written Word points beyond itself to the Living Word. Jesus Christ is indeed King of the Scriptures.

Such is the conviction of the author of this fascinating study of Jesus the Messiah. He is concerned that we grasp what the Bible means by ascribing Messiahship to the Son of Mary. Those who would press beyond threadbare ways of thinking and merely formal concepts about Jesus' messiahship should find this book a treat and joy. This is a work to be studied with the Bible open at its side. In its pages the author penetrates to the very core of the Holy Scriptures and shows us Jesus Christ as its true Subject.

One of the heartening signs of the times is the new place serious Bible study has made for itself on the agenda of the Church. Both small groups and individuals are searching the Word of God with new enthusiasm. This magnificent study of the Messianic idea, from its very roots in Gen. 3:15 to its flowering glory in the Book of Revelation, should find its place in the library of every serious student of the Bible.

The mood of this study is devotional. Both the first and second advents of our Lord are considered by the author as he traces all the strands of prophetic thought and imagery through the Old Testament and then demonstrates how these find expression in the New. His acquaintance with the scholars and literature of the subject is impressive, but his writing is not pedantic.

—WILLIAM M. GREATHOUSE, *President*
Nazarene Theological Seminary

PREFACE

One might well ask why this book was written. To a certain extent, it is our reply to a question once asked by Seneca, the noted Roman philosopher. His time-penetrating question was: "Where shall He be found whom we have been seeking for so many centuries?"

We have endeavored to trace the scriptural answer to this typical inquiry throughout both the Old and New Testaments. Both the question and the answer have special significance for us today.

There is a distinct similarity between the expectation of Christ's first coming and our present expectation of His return. In both instances, God has been faithful to reveal His Word to men of faith. The focus of Bible prophecy, from Genesis to Revelation, is concentrated upon the coming of Christ. This is the Great Expectation, whether it be in anticipation of His birth or of His return. Upon the specific fulfillment of all the prophecy of Christ's birth, we now confidently base our expectation of His coming again.

Tragically, although God's chosen people were expecting the Messiah of divine promise, they failed to recognize the sign of His birth, and they ultimately rejected His kingdom. According to God's Word, our generation may well experience the spectacular event of Christ's return. By unbelief, many are likely to miss the salvation presently offered through faith in Him. Our overwhelming concern is that mankind will recognize the truth and certainty of His promise and be ready when King Jesus comes for His own.

In expectation,
—IVAN A. BEALS

Chapter 1

A Concept of the Messiah

On the surface, the anticipations of mankind seem clouded in mystery. We must inevitably turn to the Scriptures to gain a clear concept of the revelation of the Messiah.

The Old Testament records the beginnings of human history and the development of religious life. It tells of the unique creation of Adam and Eve, of their close relationship to the Creator, and eventually of the transgression which broke their fellowship with God. Then it relates how God began seeking man out, revealing himself in awe-inspiring experiences.

Thus, in spite of the separation of sin, man began to expect God to intervene on his behalf. He had been given a glimmer of hope at the time of his expulsion from the garden of God. There was the divine pronouncement to the evil one that enmity would be placed between him and the woman, between his seed and her seed (cf. Gen. 3:15).

From that time, humanity has looked expectantly for the coming of the Anointed One of God to deliver them from a destiny of destruction.

Although some scholars reject this divine edict as being the first gleam of hope for a coming Messiah, there seems to be repeated indication that salvation was expected through childbearing. Such a view is confirmed by the testimony of Eve (Gen. 4:1, 25), the divine covenant with Abraham (Gen. 12:3; 22:18), the prophecy and expectation of Jacob (Gen. 49:10, 18), and the promise to David (2 Sam. 7:12-13). These prophetic promises regarding the Messiah progressively refer to the "seed of woman," to the seed of Abraham, and to the seed of David, of the tribe of Judah.

Therefore, looking back from a Christian perspective, we view Gen. 3:15 as the dawn of hope for man's salvation from the curse of sin. As the Seed of the woman, the Messiah is to be the Conqueror of Satan and his evil works among men. As the Seed of Abraham, He is to be the World Blesser, the Redeemer of all mankind. As the Seed of David, He is to be the King of glory, the One who shall rule forever in righteousness. Indeed, it is the belief of Christians that such Messianic prophecies converge on Jesus Christ, and that all prophecy will be fulfilled by Him "to confirm the promises made unto the fathers" (Rom. 15:8, KJV).

Considering the development of Messianic expectation from the "seed of the woman," we note that God particularly revealed His will and way to chosen individuals. Jehovah *(Yahweh)* thus became known as the God of Abraham, the God of Isaac, and the God of Jacob (Israel). He eventually made a covenant with the children of Israel, saying, "I will take you to me for a people, and I will be to you a God" (cf. Exod. 6:3, 7-8).

In this manner, the scriptural record gives an account

of the progressive divine revelation. Generally speaking, it manifests the great operation of God in bringing about His kingdom on earth through His chosen people, Israel. Jehovah not only made himself known unto them, but He declared His will for man's whole life by the giving of the Law to His people.

Historically, the development of the Messianic expectation in Israel was largely influenced by their basic concept of God's moral rule overshadowing the affairs of mankind. Jewish monotheism was not reached from reflections on the unity of nature or of being, but from Jehovah's sovereignty in the world. There does, however, appear to be a "gap" here, for God and the world were held separate in the mind of the Israelites.

Although Jehovah caused the natural processes, He was considered quite distinct from them. God is *supra*-mundane. He is above the world; His abode is in heaven —indeed He is the Lord of heaven. But God is not *extra*-mundane; He is not excluded from His world because He is exalted above it. God is everywhere. He knows everything, and His providence embraces all His creatures— especially His chosen people. Jehovah is the sole Creator and Sustainer of the world, which He brought into being by the word of His power, according to a wise and unchanging plan. It is thus Jehovah's own operation and His own presence in the midst of the people which is essential in the development of Messianic concepts.[1]

However, this gives rise to an important issue: How can a transcendent God manifest His presence to men? How can a transcendent God become involved in world affairs? This gap must be bridged if a hope for man's ultimate deliverance is to be developed.

The transcendence of God—His independence of the world and superiority to it—and the opposite truth of

13

God's presence in the world—must be spanned by a mediary, the Messiah, the Anointed One, sent of God. This focal point of Jehovah's work and presence proceeds throughout the movement of Israel's history.

For instance, Jehovah appears and manifests himself to the patriarchs in the form of heavenly messengers. The references in the Pentateuch which relate to the "angel of Jehovah" (cf. Gen. 16:7 ff.; 22:11 ff.; Exod. 3:2; Num. 22: 22 ff., etc.) have been thought by some to bear direct reference to the Messiah.

Then, as a tribal nation, the Israelites became recognized as the chosen of God particularly because of His apparent presence in their midst. In leading them, He appeared as a pillar of cloud by day and a pillar of fire by night (cf. Exod. 14:19-25).

This manner of divine revelation was instrumental in Israel's deliverance from their enslavement in Egypt, leading them to the land promised to their father Abraham. Also, the ark of the covenant, which was made according to divine instruction (cf. Exod. 25:10 ff.), was symbolic of God's continuing presence. It not only contained the testimony of God to His people, but it was the place of meeting and communion with Him.

Furthermore, the following establishment of the priesthood, by the anointing of Aaron and his sons (Exod. 28:1), becomes particularly significant. This meant that the people had a consecrated representative before Jehovah, and that Jehovah had a representative amongst the people. Eventually the tribe of Levi was set apart for the holy service of maintaining the covenant relationship between God and Israel.

The development and progress of the idea of the Messiah is closely related to such a relationship. Israel's growing conviction was that God had especially chosen and related himself to them as a nation. Certainly, of His own

14

gracious, free choice, God entered into a relationship with Israel in which He uniquely took them for His people, and in which He offered to be their "living" God. In turn, the Israelites pledged themselves to keep and to obey His laws (cf. Exod. 24:1-8). This covenant relationship conveyed the idea of special privilege and honor with regard to the destiny of all mankind.[2]

As Stanton puts it, the Israelites were convinced that "the condition of the nation which would adequately correspond to God's covenant with them must at length be realised." Because they were God's covenant people, the Jews believed that someday their nation must enter into the visible glory and supremacy which, as at least in popular thought they conceived it, were the right of the covenant people. Indeed, the expected Messiah was to bring about that consummation. He was to be the agent of God through whom the destiny of the nation was to be fulfilled.[3]

To some, the Messianic expectation became rather simple. It was nothing more than a dream of peace and prosperity to be realized under a king of David's line. For, during the time of the monarchy, it is the Davidic king who is the anointed one, the representative of Jehovah.

It should be noted that sometimes the Messianic ideal centered, not so much in any single individual, but rather in a succession of kings of the line of David. Then, when the Davidic line was threatened with extinction during Isaiah's and Micah's prophetic ministry, the Messianic hope in Israel became mainly connected with the end time, the ultimate period of Israel's perfection, peace, and blessing.

As such, the Messianic hope belongs to the eschatology, the new age of the nation and of the peoples of the world. So, whether the Messiah is considered to be a person or a corporate personality, it is Jehovah in him that is Saviour. It is thus evident that Jehovah's own operation and His own presence make up the essential Messianic element. This is true if we view it in the state and conduct of the people as a whole. Also, it applies when the theocratic King is idealized, as He shall be in the latter day when the kingdom of God is perfected. For He is the Representative of Jehovah, and the destinies of the kingdom are in His hand.[4]

This Messianic hope, as it is called, obviously differs considerably in different periods of history. There is a sense in which the prominent agent of a particular time will be idealized. Perhaps this is most notable during the monarchy, when the prominent personage was the Davidic king.

However, at all times, Jehovah's work and presence is emphasized. Also, in any given time, the condition of the people of Israel is an important factor in relation to the manner of their expectation of the coming Messiah.

Dividing Old Testament history into periods, the prominent figures seem to be these:

1. Jehovah is present and at work in His world at all times. This is of absolute importance, because it lays the foundation for the work and the person of the Messiah. Whoever he is, it is Jehovah in him that is Saviour.

2. In the premonarchial period it is chiefly the people or mankind that is involved, as in the Protoevangelium (Gen. 3:15), the promises to the patriarchs, particularly Abraham and Jacob (Gen. 12:3; 22:18; 49:10, 18), where it is specified, "In thee and in thy seed," from whence Shiloh should come. Also, there is the poetic prophecy of Balaam about the Star out of Jacob (Num. 24:17-19).

3. During the monarchy it is the Davidic king who assumes the role as Messianic king, as the anointed representative of Jehovah. Even so, David himself looked for the ideal king to come from his line. This thought became

amplified when the Davidic monarchy was threatened with extinction in the days of the prophets Isaiah and Micah. Whereas the Davidic king is mainly intra-Israel, the enlarged prophetic concept of the Servant of the Lord becomes much broader, even intranational. The widening ideas created a larger subject, giving the expected Messiah a more inclusive scope of the entire world.

4. After the destruction of the monarchy in both portions of the divided kingdom of Israel, which David and Solomon had ruled in splendor, the Messianic or eschatological hopes seem to shift toward the action of God's people as a whole, as in the second half of the Book of Isaiah. However, the idea of the Davidic kingship and the concept of the Messiah as the Son of David were never totally lost. In fact, this remained the underlying hope.

5. At the restoration of the captured Jews to their land, the priest, or the union of the priestly and kingly figure, comes into prominence. This would be expected because the great sense of sin, following the defeat and captivity of Judah by the Babylonians, brought into focus the necessity of atonement for their sin against God. Indeed, this was the message of the prophets of the Restoration, of Zechariah, Haggai, and Malachi.[5]

Throughout every period, the one underlying hope which runs through the Old Testament is that Jehovah is present in person, coming to the aid of His people. However, His coming is not always represented as being accomplished in the same way. Sometimes the visible appearance of Jehovah in person is asserted, and the question of how His appearance shall be realized is immediately answered. Then, the Divine Presence is sometimes accomplished in the line of the Messianic hope, where Jehovah comes down among His people in the Messiah. As Isaiah put it, the Messiah is "Immanuel—God with us"; He is *"El Gibbor,"* "mighty God" (cf. Isa. 7:14; 9:6).

17

Thus, God is fully present, for the purposes of redemption, in the Messianic king.[6]

Such a concept of the expected Messiah hinges upon its interrelation with three complementary ideas: (1) the Messiah and anointing, (2) the Messiah and sin, and (3) the Messiah and prophecy. It seems that any discussion of a concept of the Messiah would be incomplete, at least from the Christian viewpoint, without considering His coming in the light of these contributing ideas. They all join together to formulate the reason why a personage such as the Messiah was expected. Certainly, the clear, abiding concept of this great expectation did not just happen.

The Messiah and Anointing

The Hebrew word for Messiah is *Mashiach,* which means "anointed." This is applicable in its first sense to anyone anointed with holy oil, consecrated to the service of God. It comes from the Hebrew verb *mashach,* which means "to anoint"; and, therefore, the Messiah is "the Anointed One." In the New Testament the equivalent Greek word is *Christos,* translated "Christ" in English, which also means "anointed, the Messiah."[7]

Thus, according to the very meaning of the title "Messiah," the person must be anointed. Perhaps the original idea of anointing was the actual communication of supernatural or divine qualities through contact with the unguent used. In Hebrew practice we find that anointing with holy oil was particularly connected with three special offices, that of priest, prophet, and king.

The first scriptural reference to anointing connects it with the office of priest. God's command was that the priest should be anointed, consecrated, and sanctified so that he should minister to Him (Exod. 28:41). Anointing oil was to be taken and poured on the head of the priest

(Exod. 29:7). It is also specifically applied to the high priest (Lev. 4:3, 5, 16).[8]

Then, we find that anointing was similarly connected to the office of prophet. Elijah was instructed to anoint Elisha as prophet in his place (1 Kings 19:16). It is Isaiah's claim that the Spirit of the Lord is upon him, because God has anointed him to preach good tidings to the people (Isa. 61:1). In respect to the prophets, as with the priesthood, the ceremony of anointing was to indicate their qualification for the office by virtue of this symbolic, divine approval and enabling.

Above all, anointing was applied to the office of king. The kings of Israel were called anointed, from the specific mode of their consecration. For example, in Jotham's parable it is told how the trees went forth to anoint a king (Judg. 9:8). When the prophet Samuel saw young David, the Lord said to him: "Arise, anoint him, for this is he." Then Samuel took a horn of oil and anointed him in the midst of his brothers (cf. 1 Sam. 16:12-13).

Also, God is recorded as saying of David: "With my holy oil I have anointed him" (Ps. 89:20). Significantly, in 1 Kings 1:45, we read that Zadok the priest and Nathan the prophet anointed Solomon king in Gihon. Thus, all three offices initiated by anointing are brought into single focus.

It is therefore a fact of interest and importance that from the beginning the Messiah, the Anointed One, was considered Prophet, Priest, and King. Apparently the development of the figure of the Messiah was especially from the idea of the Hebrew king as "Yahweh's anointed." Specifically, it was from the idealized kingship of David, to whom the promise of perpetuity is given: "I will set up thy seed after thee . . . and I will establish the throne of his kingdom for ever . . . and thine house and thy kingdom shall be made sure for ever before thee; thy throne shall be established for ever" (2 Sam. 7:12 ff.).[9]

This points to a succession of "kings and princes sitting upon the throne of David," so that "David shall never want a man to sit upon the throne of the house of Israel" (Jer. 17:25; 33:17). But the "righteous branch," or "shoot," to be raised unto David is conceived as the beginning of a new line of Davidic kings: "He shall reign as king and deal wisely, and shall execute judgment and justice in the land" (Jer. 23:5-6).

So the anointed king of David's line gave foundation to the expectation of the Messiah as God's gracious manifestation in the world—even the establishment of His kingdom on earth. The future Davidic ruler became idealized and recognized as the Prince of the kingdom of God. Indeed, the prophets foretold of the expected Prince of the chosen people who was to complete God's purposes for them and redeem them (cf. Isa. 9:6 ff.). The divine purpose was, so to speak, individualized, and the Kingdom was expected to be actually established through the Anointed One.

Thus, both the basic and progressive relationships of the Messiah are revealed as that of God towards man, and of man towards God, all because of man's sin. The former relational aspect is expressed by the word "Father"; the latter by that of "Servant"—as well as by the combination of the two ideas: "Son-Servant." This was first implied in the so-called Protoevangelium (Gen. 3:15), following the fall of our racial head. As the preexistent Anointed One, the words of Jesus thus apply: "Before Abraham was born, I am" (John 8:58).[10]

So, by the ritual of anointing, God's plan was to have a representative among the people to bring them back to His will and way for their lives. It points specifically to the Anointed One, the Messiah, who is actually sent of God to be "God with us," saving us from our sins. Only He can truly establish the kingdom of God in righteousness. There can be no doubt that the underlying purpose of anointing was not just for secular power, but rather for spiritual guidance in bringing wandering humanity back to the original plan of Almighty God.

The Messiah and Sin

Despite the strong sentiment attached to the kingly characteristics of the Anointed One, we need to consider the practical purpose of His coming. A clear concept of the Messiah is inseparably related to man's recognition of sin.

In the Old Testament, we readily see that the sense or thought of sin corresponds to the conception and fear of Jehovah. Moreover, as the thought of the spirituality and purity of Jehovah developed, so did the sense of what was required of man to be in fellowship with Him. This also deepened the sense of sin in humanity.

At its beginning, the Scriptures lay down the categories of good and evil: "God saw everything which he had made, and, behold, it was very good" (Gen. 1:31); "It is not good that the man should be alone" (Gen. 2:18). Here, there is a distinction made between the "good" and the "not good." Opposite to good, the Scriptures place the category of "evil." Good and evil are so irreconcilable that they are given as the two poles of human thought and experience: "Ye shall be as God, knowing good and evil" (Gen. 3:5). Even the Almighty himself is bounded by these two realms.[11]

In fact, the distinction between good and evil is so radical that the prophet Isaiah is divinely moved to denounce those who confound the two as sunk to the lowest stage of perversity. He says: "Woe unto them that call evil good, and good evil; that put darkness for light, and light for darkness; that put bitter for sweet, and sweet for

21

bitter!" (Isa. 5:20). Such evildoers did not question the evident distinction, but only inverted the things, saying as one said in Milton's *Paradise Lost,* "Evil, be thou my good."

The Old Testament has a variety of terms for moral evil which, though figurative, tell us something of how its nature was conceived. For instance, God spoke to Cain, when he was angry because of the rejection of his sacrifice, saying, "If thou doest well, shall it not be lifted up? and if thou doest not well, sin *[chattath]* croucheth at the door" (Gen. 4:7).

Here sin is named for the first time. It is personified as a wild beast crouching at the door, ready to spring upon any man who gave entrance to it. The Hebrew root word for sin is *chata,* which means "to miss," as the mark by an archer, or the way by a traveler, and even to find "wanting" in enumerating. Thus there is the definite idea of a goal not reached, a mark not struck.[12]

Again, sin is conceived as transgression (cf. Num. 14:41), which describes it as a personal, voluntary act. It also implies something rebelled against, something which is of the nature of a superior or an authority. Further, it implies the withdrawal of one's self by an act of self-assertion from under this superior or authority. For instance, it is said that Israel "rebelled against" the house of David (1 Kings 12:19). Similarly, Jehovah says: "I have nourished and brought up children, and they have rebelled against me" (Isa. 1:2).[13]

It was thus along such lines of meaning which men thought of what is called sin. In the one case it was failure to hit or to correspond to an objective standard. In the other, it was an attitude taken by a person in reference to another who was his superior. So, in the former instance, "sin" is the opposite of righteousness, for righteousness is seen to be conformity to a standard. It is in this sense that

God is called righteous when He acts in a way corresponding to the covenant relation. This relation would lead Him to forgive and save His people from their sins—even to the extent of sending His Anointed One.[14]

Certainly, the Old Testament teaching regarding sin does not differ from the New Testament. *First,* it teaches that all individual men are sinners. "There is no man that sinneth not" (1 Kings 8:46). *Second,* the sinfulness of each individual is not an isolated thing, but is an instance of the general fact that mankind is sinful. "Before thee no flesh living is righteous" (Ps. 143:2). Then, *third,* the sin of man can be taken away only by the forgiveness of Jehovah: "Who is a God like unto thee, pardoning iniquity?" (Mic. 7:18). This forgiveness is of His mercy, but it necessitates the sending of a Saviour as well as the setting of a clear covenant standard such as the Ten Commandments.[15]

From this, we may say that the individual Adam was guilty of his own sin, as was Cain, etc. But the sin of Adam was also the sin of the ensuing human race, and both the displeasure of God against the race and the penalty for sin followed. There is ever the sense in which the person who committed the sin is individually guilty, and the judgment that befalls him is as an individual.[16]

However, there is also a twofold treatment of sin as a unity. Each individual, being part of it and acting as part, involves not only himself but the whole race. The consequences of his acts fall upon the whole human family. Even though there is treatment of sin as individuals, when the individual is dealt with for himself, there is no escaping the infectious quality of his sin.

In this manner, the Old Testament clearly teaches what may be specifically called "original sin," the corruption of man's whole nature. It is also thought that this sin is inherited by every successive generation. However, no

23

explanation is given of the rationale of this inherited corruption beyond the apparent assumption that the race is a unity, and each member of the race is sinful because the race is sinful.[17]

Such teaching eliminates both the hope and the possibility of man ever saving himself. And it therefore establishes the necessary connection requiring God's Messiah to cope with the problem of man's sin.

Thus, remembering that the priests were anointed to minister, to serve Jehovah in worship as representatives of the people, we see that it was the sin of the chosen people that made the priesthood necessary. Indeed, it was as Ewald says:

> In the sacred community of Jahveh the original purity which, strictly speaking, ought always to be maintained there, is constantly receiving various stains, noticed or unnoticed, expiated or unatoned for . . . and the whole community, while it felt the necessity for strictest purity, felt also that Jahveh's sanctuary dwelt in the midst of the countless impurities of the people, and was never free from their defilement. Between the sanctity of Jahveh and the perpetually sin-stained condition of the people there is therefore a chasm which seems infinite. All the offerings and gifts which the members of the community bring are only like a partial expiation and payment of a debt which is never entirely wiped out. To wipe out all these stains, to bear the guilt of the nation, and constantly to restore the Divine grace, is the final office of the priest (*Antiq.,* Solly's trans., p. 271).[18]

It is at this very point of desperation and inability of the human priesthood to sufficiently deal with the problem of sin that the Anointed One sent of God is seen to intervene. Although recognition of the kingly office of the Messiah was perhaps more popular, the recognition of His priestly office, offering sacrifice (even himself) once for all for the sins of the people, is most necessary.

24

Considering the burden of man's sin, it cannot be justifiable to explain the Jewish concept and expectation of a Messiah merely on the basis of the expectation of a glorious earthly king. Indeed, the rule of such a king would soon come to naught unless there was also atonement provided for the sins of the people, so they could be reconciled unto God.

The priestly office of the Messiah cannot be overemphasized, for it serves to remove the barrier of sin that exists between man and his God. It is the business of the Messiah as Priest to set the people free from the dominion of sin, and to teach them the ways of God.

For instance, in various passages of scripture, the work of such a priest is anticipated (Psalms 22; 40; 110; Isaiah 2; 9; 53). Furthermore, in these and other places, the power of the coming Anointed One reaches beyond the Jews and embraces all mankind. As such, both the kingly and the priestly offices of the Messiah are interrelated with that of prophet. Hence, a concept of the Messiah must also include divine revelation through prophecy.

The Messiah and Prophecy

Following the earliest prophetic gleam of the gospel in the Protoevangelium (Gen. 3:15), Noah indicates remarkable blessings in store for the children of Shem. In Gen. 9:26, Noah prophesies, "Blessed be Jehovah the God of Shem." Next follows the divine promise to Abraham, wherein the blessings of Shem are turned into the narrower channel of one family (Gen. 12:2-3). The prophetic promise is still indefinite, but it tends to the undoing of the curse on mankind through Adam's sin. As death had come on the whole earth through Adam, life and blessing were to come to all the earth through the seed of Abraham.

At this point, let us narrow our survey to where the prophetic history of the kingdom of God becomes enjoined to the life and progeny of Abraham. In retrospect, Jesus said to the Jews: "Your father Abraham rejoiced to see my day; and he saw it, and was glad" (John 8:56).

The line of human history that ensued from Abraham to the Messiah bore a twofold impress: heavenwards (that of Son) and earthwards (that of Servant). In a very distinct sense, Israel, the descendent of Abraham, was God's Son—His "firstborn." Their history is that of the children of God; their institutions were of the family of God; their prophecies were particularly of the household of God.[19]

However, Israel was also recognized as the Servant of God—"Jacob my servant." Again, its history, institutions, and prophecies are those of the Servant of the Lord. Thus, Israel was not merely Servant, but Son-Servant—"anointed" to such service. As previously mentioned, this idea was crystallized in the three important institutions of Israel—king, priest, and prophet. The "Servant of the Lord" in relation to Israel's history was kingship in Israel. The "Servant of the Lord" in relation to their ritual ordinances was the priesthood in Israel. And, the "Servant of the Lord" in relation to prediction was the prophetic order in Israel. All of these institutions generated from the same fundamental idea: that of the "Servant of Jehovah."[20]

So, within the prophetic stream, the origin and development of a Messianic concept is closely related to the idea of the covenant relationship between God and His chosen people. Because of the previous covenant relationship with their forefathers, Abraham, Isaac, and Jacob (Israel), it was the conviction of the people of Israel that they were thus specially chosen and related to God.

According to His purpose, and of His own free choice, God entered into a relationship with Israel in which He took them to be His unique people, and in which He offered to be their God, and in which the Israelites pledged to obey His laws (Exod. 24:1-8).

This covenant relationship conveyed the idea of special responsibility as well as special privilege and honor. Therefore, Israel was convinced that as their nation obeyed, God's covenant with them must be eventually realized. Because they were God's chosen people, the Jews believed that some day their nation must enter into the visible honor and supremacy which seemed to attend the right of the covenant people. Certainly, this was included in the divine promise.

The Messiah was expected to come and bring about this glorious consummation. He was to be the Agent of God through whom the prophetic destiny of Israel would be fulfilled. Indeed, as Moses had prophesied, "Jehovah thy God will raise up unto thee a prophet from the midst of thee" (Deut. 18:15; cf. v. 18). The New Testament reference to Moses in John 5:45-47, where Jesus said, "He wrote of me," may well refer to this passage.

Despite popular belief, the Messiah and His history are not recorded in the Old Testament as something separate from, or superadded to, Israel. The history, the institutions, and the prophetic predictions of Israel run up into Him as He is further revealed in the New Testament. For example, according to Jewish legend, all the miracles which God had shown to Israel in the wilderness would be done again to the redeemed Zion in the "latter days." Needless to say, the miracles performed by Christ during His earthly ministry fulfilled, at least to some degree, this expectation.[21]

Thus, prophetically, the Messiah is seen to be both the Son of God and the Servant of the Lord. As He was "anointed" to be the "Servant of the Lord," if not with the typical oil, then by "the Spirit of Jehovah" upon Him, so also was He the "Son" in a unique sense.

27

The Messiah's organic connection with Israel is marked by the designations "Seed of woman," "Seed of Abraham," and "Son of David." In a sense, He is viewed as the typical Israelite, and again, as typical Israel—alike, the Crown, the Completion, and the Representative of Israel.

All at the same time, He was essentially what Israel was subordinately and typically, fulfilling the pronouncement of the Psalmist: "Thou art my son; This day have I begotten thee" (Ps. 2:7).[22] Therefore, with absolute truthfulness, the Evangelist Matthew could apply to Jesus Christ what referred to Israel, and see it fulfilled in His history: "Out of Egypt did I call my son" (Matt. 2:15).

The other correlate idea, of Israel as the "Servant of the Lord," is also focused on the Messiah as the Representative Israelite. In Isaiah, where a series of predictions are given in which the Messiah's portrait is most fully outlined, He is particularly characterized as "the Servant of Jehovah."

In this manner, as the Representative Israelite, the Messiah combined in himself as "the Servant" the threefold office of Prophet, Priest, and King. Consequently, the two ideas of "Son" and "Servant" are similarly joined together in the New Testament (cf. Phil. 2:6-11). The ultimate combination and full exhibition of these two ideas not only looks to the fulfillment of the typical mission of Israel, but to the actual establishment of the kingdom of God among men.[23]

Thus, in its final, as in the initial stage (cf. Gen. 3:15), the divine intent is to establish His kingdom on earth. This was to be brought about by the "Servant of the Lord," who came to sin-stricken humanity as the God-sent "Anointed Comforter" *(Mashiach ha-Menachem)*. The Messiah comes in the twofold sense of "Comforter" of individuals ("the friend of sinners"), and "Comforter" of

Israel and the world, reconciling both, and bringing them to the salvation of God.[24]

This brings the mission of Israel through three stages. The first, or *historical stage,* was the preparation of the kingdom of God. The second, or *ritual stage,* was the typical presentation of that Kingdom. Then, the third, or *prophetic stage,* brought that Kingdom into actual contact with the kingdoms of the world. Accordingly, the prophet Daniel enlarges upon the designation "Son of David" (typical Israel) to envision the "Son of Man" (the Head of redeemed humanity) (cf. Dan. 7:13-14).

Scores of scripture references could be given wherein God is shown to be the true King, and the expected Messiah sent of God is revealed as the prophetic climax and destiny of all history. After the time of David, the predictions of the Messiah ceased for a time until other prophets were inspired to renew the declaration of His coming. But they continue to affirm that the Messiah is a King and Ruler of David's house, who should come to reform and restore the nation of Israel and purify the people of God (cf. Isa. 11:40-66).

However, the blessings of the Restoration will not be confined to Israel; the Gentiles will also share in them (cf. Isaiah 2; 66). The hope of the entire world hinges on the Messiah's coming. Successive prophets are given further revelation. Micah clearly identifies the birthplace of the Messiah to be in Bethlehem (Mic. 5:2; cf. Matt. 2:6). Again, the royal lineage of David is designated by Zechariah (12:10-14) to be the stock from whence the Anointed One is to come. The prophet Haggai views the time of the rebuilding of the Temple as the signal for the Messiah's coming (2:9). Then, the coming of the Forerunner and of the Messiah himself are specifically revealed in Mal. 3:1; 4:5-6.[25]

So far, we have merely indicated some of the more prominent scripture references in the ladder of Old Testament prophecy leading up to the coming of the Messiah sent of God. We shall be dealing particularly with those passages that seem to be the most outstanding in their message of the Expected One.

It is also our affirmation that the New Testament properly records the fulfillment of these prophecies in the birth and ministry of Jesus Christ. Certainly, the impact of the Scriptures as God's Holy Word is best experienced as we consider the purposeful, prophetic light which finally comes to focus on the manger.

However, from our point in time, we may well say that Christ is still the Expected One. Although Israel as a nation does not yet believe that the Messiah has come, Christians now look for His return. This vital expectation makes a concept of the Messiah a living issue today.

The very nature of our expectancy will dictate the direction of our hope. If we are of the opinion that the promised Messiah has not yet come even the first time, we find our faith strained to the breaking point. On the other hand, if we accept Jesus Christ as the One sent from God, we rejoice in the fact that the same God who kept His Word in the fullness of time, will also return to completely fulfill His promise.

For this reason we trace the promise of God throughout the Scriptures to discern the progressive revelation and the successive reinforcement of that first spark of hope for mankind. The same body of evidence that says: "Christ is come!" also indicates that He *must* come again. Again, the same words which said, "He is coming," are presently echoed to us in living truth. So, in a very real sense, that beginning promise of hope of the coming Deliverer now reiterates to us that He must come again to consummate victory over sin and Satan.

Chapter 2

The First Promise of Hope

> *And I will put enmity between thee
> and the woman, and between thy seed and
> her seed: he shall bruise thy head, and
> thou shalt bruise his heel.*
>
> (Gen. 3:15)

From the beginning of time, man and the world have been embraced by the eternal plan of God. Things are not left to mere chance, to fate, to the impersonal forces of nature, or to the whims of mankind. Rather, they are guided by the steady, creative hand of Divine Providence so that the process of events do not disrupt God's eternal purpose.

Whatever God wills will be accomplished in His own good time. The Holy Scriptures that affirm, "In the beginning God . . ." (Gen. 1:1), also declare that as the eternal God, the Planner of the ages, He is the supreme moral Ruler of the universe. This includes the affairs of the kingdoms of this world (cf. Dan. 4:3-32).

Divine intervention became necessary the instant Adam and Eve disobeyed God. That sin interrupted their hallowed fellowship with Him. It broke the connection with His life, and their lives were polluted with evil corruption, making them vulnerable to the curse of death.

Thus man, the crowning achievement of divine creation, was in jeopardy. Salvation and deliverance must be provided for a race of sinners. Otherwise, God would not be almighty, and good would be hopelessly subordinate to evil. God's holy will and purpose was not to be thwarted by Lucifer's diabolical plan to ruin all creation.

Mankind had been gloriously created by God, fashioned in His very image, after His own likeness. Then he was placed in the ideal surroundings of earthly paradise. Obviously, God's creative plan was that the planet Earth might become populated with obedient, holy people.

Until the blight of sin upon the affairs of man, there was joy and peace, and Adam and Eve had constant communion with their Heavenly Father. In their innocency, that first human pair knew nothing of sin or death or separation from God. They only knew that God had warned them of the potential peril of disobedience.

Breaking into this tranquil scene, the tempter deceitfully displayed his perverse power. The loyalty of man to the righteous commands of His Creator was diverted by whetted selfish appetites. He was fascinated by the cunning suggestions of the serpent. Adam and Eve became more concerned with their own wisdom and glory than with obeying God's will and multiplying His glory.

As their self-interest and desires were captivated, the tempter's trap was laid. Siding with Satan, Adam and Eve woefully found themselves rebels against the Father's command. This set the stage for human misery and destruction, for sin's deadening power soon numbed their whole beings.

Too late, Adam and his helpmate realized the folly of disobedience. Too late, they were concerned with the horrible consequences of transgression. Too late, they became aware of the dreadful meaning of separation from God. Too late, they recognized the devil as the liar he is. Too late, those first parents faced up to the futile prospects of a lost human race.

Instead of becoming as God, they experienced an existence without the glory of holy relationship with their Maker. Thus they found themselves without God and without hope. Only One sent from God could brighten their destiny.

With the disastrous fall of the racial head, all humanity was subjected to the penalty of sin. Only divine intervention could change the course of man's fate. There can be no true life apart from God. Somehow, according to the satisfaction of justice, the redemption of hell-bound humanity must be accomplished by the infinite love and mercy of God. This challenge could be met only by the birth of a heaven-sent Saviour. Sin and death are conquered only as man is born anew through faith in the Saviour's name.

It is still appropriate for us to consider why Christ must come. There seemed to be little doubt in the Old Testament as to why a Deliverer must come. And presently, there should be little doubt as to why Christ must return. However, all too often the plague of sin is overlooked, and its guilty stain is hidden by the pretentious dignity of man. Humanity habitually hurries through life indifferent to God, ignoring that dark blot as though it never occurred.

Yet Christmas, the holiday we so often gaily celebrate

33

and the Advent we so casually observe, is of utmost significance to our own personal destiny. So let us not avoid the issues nor cover our spiritual poverty with "angel hair." The problem of sin has been with mankind from the beginning of time. This fact has not changed, and our desperate need of a Saviour remains.

This important Old Testament text stands as a pillar of divine promise in founding a salvation which would reach men of all generations. God issued it immediately following the fall of that first pair, not only pronouncing judgment, but also promising redemption. To the serpent, the beguiling agent of Satan, God declared, "And I will put enmity between thee and the woman, and between thy seed and her seed: he shall bruise thy head, and thou shalt bruise his heel" (Gen. 3:15).

Theologians call this the Protoevangelium because historically this promise seems to be the base and source of all the succeeding promises of the Anointed One. This appears in type and prophecy throughout the Old Testament and eventually is found fulfilled in Jesus Christ in the New Testament.

Despite the fact that Adam led the human race into sin and rebellion against the Creator, it is here revealed that God proposes to establish the basis for reconciliation. Clearly, the prophecy of a coming Deliverer is given. Three things stand out: (1) The promised Deliverer was to be of the seed of the woman, one of her children; (2) The mission of the Deliverer would be in conflict, temporarily hindered; (3) The Deliverer would finally be victorious over Satan and his evil works.

Admittedly, those who adopt the approach of historical criticism to theology see no allusion in this passage to the devil, or to Christ as fulfilling the promised "seed of the woman" by being "born of a woman." Rather, it is taken simply to be a general statement about mankind

34

and serpents and the struggle between them which continues as long as the earth exists. Thus, "the poisonous serpent strikes at man's foot whenever he is unfortunate enough to come too near to it; and always and everywhere man tries to crush the serpent's head when he has the chance."[1]

On the other hand, we should consider that the ancient Jews, as well as the New Testament writers and the primitive Christians, held the serpent tempter to be the devil. There can be no doubt about the manner in which Jesus viewed the association. To those who were rebelling against God, He said, "Ye are of your father the devil, and the lusts of your father it is your will to do. He was a murderer from the beginning, and standeth not in the truth, because there is no truth in him. When he speaketh a lie, he speaketh of his own: for he is a liar, and the father thereof" (John 8:44).[2]

Obviously, the above refers to this passage in Genesis. It is absurd to suppose that the words of blame, inflicting punishment upon the serpent, were addressed to an irrational animal and not to an intelligent, accountable being. Although the figurative language obscures the definiteness of meaning, some degree of certitude is conveyed. It seems hardly possible for anyone who believes in the existence of "that old serpent, called the Devil, and Satan, which deceiveth the whole world" (Rev. 12:9, KJV), to reject the idea that there is a promise given here which laid the foundation of the hope of future deliverance from the doom of sin.[3]

Thus it seems that the underlying issue is not only a matter of scriptural interpretation, involving a human dislike for snakes, but it is whether or not such a viewpoint recognizes the impact of sin and man's need for a Saviour. It is also noteworthy that humanity actually has not been so unanimous in their dislike of poisonous serpents as historical critics have presumed.

The fact is that there have been and are instances where people have deified serpents. For example, some of the people of India regard the poisonous cobra snake as a sacred object. Every culture where all life is held sacred stands in contradiction to the supposition of human conflict with serpents. Whether mankind likes to admit it or not, his warfare is with sin and Satan (the serpent personified), and not simply poisonous snakes.

Again, although some scholars emphatically reject this passage as having any spiritual or prophetic significance, Adam and Eve apparently viewed it otherwise. The unfolding scriptural account definitely shows that they were concerned with their sin and not the threat of deadly vipers. The testimony of Eve at the birth of Cain was "I have gotten a man with the help of Jehovah" (Gen. 4:1). After Cain had murdered his brother, Abel, and departed to the land of Wandering, we read that "Adam knew his wife again; and she bare a son, and called his name Seth: for, said she, God hath appointed me another seed instead of Abel" (Gen. 4:25). This certainly suggests that the expectation of divine salvation by Adam and Eve was centered upon God's prophecy concerning the seed of the woman. Eve's words indicate that she regarded the event of childbirth as in some way connected with the fulfillment of the promise.

The Targums of Onkelos and Jonathan both bear this interpretation out, for they give the passage a distinct Messianic interpretation. There is an evident allusion to this promise in the apostolic expressions, such as: "God sent forth his Son, born of a woman" (Gal. 4:4); "And the God of peace shall bruise Satan under your feet shortly" (Rom. 16:20; cf. 1 Tim. 2:13-15).

It is also of interest to know that in the primitive

Church this passage (Gen. 3:15) was definitely regarded as a prophecy of Christ. For instance, Irenaeus said, "He [Christ], the sole of whose foot shall be bitten, having power also to tread upon the enemy's head; but the other, biting, killing, and impeding the steps of man, until the seed did come appointed to tread down his head, which was born of Mary."[4]

Thus, the entire history of redemption takes its start from the fall of man, and begins with a judgment governing his whole state of life. But amidst the curse, a gleam of grace unmistakably shines through the gloom of divine retribution, giving fallen humanity hope. As such, this redemptive hope includes the Promise, the Conflict, and the Victory. Its message involves the destiny of the whole human race.

The Promise

In the midst of man's damning transaction—the unholy alliance of Adam and Eve with Satan—a loving Father made a promise to His straying children. Man could not retrace his erring steps away from God nor avoid the imposed curse, so the Almighty determined to provide the means whereby sinful humanity might be reconciled unto himself.

Not only is God able to provide salvation—He is also willing. From His love flows grace—favor to the unworthy; patience—favor to the obstinate; mercy—favor to the miserable; and pity—favor to the poor.

From the moment that sin entered into the world by disobedience to curse the earth with havoc and ruin, God promised the work of redemption through a Deliverer whom He would send. Specifically, sin's destructive work can be catalogued as follows: (1) It robbed man of the moral image of his Creator, in which he was stamped in creation. (2) It separated mankind from communion and fellowship with his God. (3) It brought a curse, a blight upon man's earthly inheritance. (4) It eventually brought death, as God had previously warned (Gen. 2:17).

Since these are the experienced effects of sin, the promised Messiah must necessarily undo sin's wreckage if He is to be a Deliverer. This, then, is included in His promised work of redemption: (1) He must return the Creator's moral image to man. (2) He must bring man back into communion and fellowship with God. (3) He must remove the curse from man's inheritance. (4) He must conquer death and hell in behalf of mankind. Certainly, the maximum destruction of sin marks the minimum purpose of the work of the Redeemer that is to be sent.[5]

Thus, notwithstanding the condemnation of sin, a wonderful promise is given—the promise of a Saviour from the woman's seed. This message of the First Advent is uttered by the voice of God himself. At the time, the words perhaps failed to ease the fearfulness of Adam and Eve concerning their expulsion from the shelter of God's holy Eden. Now they would have to struggle to survive in uncertain and violent surroundings. They would be faced with pain and suffering. Death would eventually claim their mortal bodies—even though they lived almost 1,000 years. Yet, in their gloom, the promise that God made to that guilty pair became the foundation for faith. It was the dawn of hope for a world lost to the dominion of sin and Satan.

From the tragic point of deceit and transgression, the divine covenant proclaims the doom of Satan and promises a Deliverer to release mankind from the tyranny of evil. This prophecy of hope tempers the just judgment of God with loving mercy. It foils the devious attempt of the evil one to seize undisputed control of God's earthly kingdom.

Although man became separated and lost from God, he is not hopelessly so. Here is promise of One who will overcome the vile despotism of Satan—One who will deliver the captives from the serpent's destructive snare.

Though the promise of a Deliverer is divinely given, it shall be fulfilled by the seed of the woman. Whenever a child is born, so is hope. Eventually there will be, by a special act of God, a man born of a woman to be the Saviour of the world. In the fullness of time, God will provide the fruition of the seed, Deity clothed in human flesh. A progeny of woman shall accomplish the divine purpose, becoming the Head of a holy race.

Indeed, this is the promise of Christmas. It is the pledge that humanity would not be left mired in the depths of moral degradation and shattered in the clutches of satanic will. It meets the enemy's subversive assault head on in mortal combat, engaging his lies with truth. Wonder of wonders, the mighty Deliverer is sent in the weak frame of a helpless babe.

At once, the redemptive promise of God becomes the forefront of the conflict of right against wrong. God so involves himself with man's sin that He banks His holy purpose and kingdom on the outcome of the struggle.

The reason for God's consuming concern is because the personal destinies of mankind are at stake. They hover between everlasting life and eternal damnation. God has no intention of allowing the creatures of His image to be lost to the malicious disposal of Satan.

Significantly, through the conflict, the promise remains the glowing signal of God's ultimate victory by the seed of the woman whom Satan deceived. The very person Satan used to introduce the human race to sin, God selects to be the instrument through whom the Son of righteousness would be born.

The Conflict

God's program not only embraces human history throughout time, but also, in its progress, it involves a long and fierce conflict with Satan and his forces of evil. Looking back, we realize that the advent of Christ not only meant peace and goodwill towards men, but it also meant conflict—the conflict of the Seed of the woman with the seed of the serpent. It came to mean the conflict of the manger-born Son of God with the wicked sons of Satan.

However, this warfare, involving humanity, did not begin with King Herod's vicious plot to assassinate the heaven-sent King in His infancy. It began upon the fall of Adam, way back in a sin-polluted garden, back when God pronounced sentence upon sin and Satan, when He proclaimed the means of man's deliverance to be through the childbearing of the woman. Moreover, this conflict will continue until Satan and all who are in league with him are finally cast into "the lake of fire" (cf. Rev. 20:10, 14-15).

Thus, although they were together under the condemnation of God's righteousness at the Fall, enmity soon arose between the devil and humanity. A man-child was to be born who would crush the tempter's evil power. The promise of a Deliverer blocked the total cooperation of Adam's race with the archenemy's treason against God.

Also, it immediately curtailed the serpent's expectation of an unchallenged reign over humanity, preventing the headlong rush of the race to ultimate ruin. The germ of faith implanted by the promise would flourish in the hearts of believers.

Following the promise of hope in Gen. 3:15, in verse 21 we read: "And Jehovah God made for Adam and for his wife coats of skins, and clothed them." Here is the preliminary suggestion of the whole plan of redemption through the shed blood of a substitutionary victim. The "coats of skins" could not have been made without the death of an innocent animal. What, then, was that to which Abel had "faith" (cf. Gen. 4:4; Heb. 11:4), if not in this previous revelation of the necessity of a sacrificial victim and a mediator through whom to approach God?[6]

So, amidst the bleakness of his degradation and despair, man would consider God's way and look for a Saviour. In spite of the conflict with rejectors, men of faith would pursue a renewed relationship with God, awaiting expectantly the promised Deliverer. By doing so, they once again would become allied with God against the onslaught of sin and the evil one.

This conflict on earth, that began with the fall of Adam, is seen to continue with Cain and Abel. We read that "Jehovah had respect unto Abel and to his offering: but unto Cain and to his offering he had not respect" (Gen. 4:4-5; cf. vv. 1-8). Because of his faith, Abel was in the line of the Seed, but he was murdered by his brother Cain, who followed the rebelliousness of the devil. Although Abel was slain in the conflict, Seth took his place in the line of the faithful (cf. Gen. 4:25).

Still, the conflict raged on to the days of Noah (Genesis 6—8), who withstood the scoffers of his day, obeyed God, and was saved from the destruction of the Flood. Except for this remnant of faithful humanity, the judgment of God meant annihilation. Because of the faithful, the tempter failed to bring about the total destruction of the human race.

Also the conflict involved the patriarchs: Abraham, Isaac, Jacob, and Joseph (cf. Genesis 12—45). The warfare is then extended to include the children of Israel while they were in Egypt (Exodus 1—14). The infanticide perpetrated by the Egyptian Pharaoh at the time of Moses' birth was a part of Satan's plot to suspend the appearance of a deliverer for God's people.

Eventually, the conflict intensified during the time of the kingdom of Israel. The people of God are led astray with little hope for return, and the royal line of David is threatened with obliteration.

Finally, from the New Testament viewpoint, the attack of evil is concentrated upon Jesus Christ. It began with Herod's inhuman slaughter in an effort to prevent Christ's coming, and it culminated in His ignominious crucifixion.

Since Pentecost, it has intermittently raged against the followers of Jesus Christ. We may well expect that the future will also unfold embittered conflict against the faithful and against God's chosen nation, Israel (cf. Rev. 6:9-11; 12:7-17; 20:7-9).

In every conceivable manner, the kingdom of God and the usurping kingdom of Satan among men are engaged in perpetual hostility, bounded by the limits of time. War is waged between the Seed of the woman and the seed of the serpent. Under the beguiling cover of the serpent, Satan was sentenced to abasement and eventual destruction.

But the divine seal of doom did not deter the arch-fiend's continuous action to spoil and damn the careless souls of men. With many devious means, he blinds their eyes to the truth, fomenting unbelief and inciting rebellion against God. Then, to those who would believe God's salvation, he suggests doubt and discouragement, arousing foolish questions concerning God's ability to keep His Word.

In his unfallen state, Satan was one of the most glorious and intelligent of all the created beings. Typical of his fall is one Lucifer, son of the morning (cf. Isa. 14:12). This passage is undoubtedly a prophetic and symbolic representation of the king of Babylon in his splendor and his fall. Its application, from Jerome on, to Satan is represented in the Scriptures as the type of tyrannical and self-idolizing power. It is thus especially connected with the empire of the evil one in the Revelation.[7]

Certainly it would be an error to limit the reference in this passage to Satan, or to regard it as referring primarily to him. Yet it is improbable that the Church, through the centuries, has erred in believing that he is somehow directly or indirectly concerned in the prophetic message. Throughout the Scriptures, monarchs and rulers of the great empires antagonistic to God or to His people are regarded as analogic representations of Satan.[8]

Dr. W. B. Godbey made an even more specific connection between the personages of Satan and Lucifer. He used the middle portion of Rev. 9:1, translating it thus: "I saw a star having fallen from heaven." He asserted that Satan is that star; his angelic name being Lucifer, according to Isa. 14:12. Thus, John's vision is considered to be retrospective of Lucifer's apostasy and fall from heaven.

The name Lucifer is a Latin compound which means "light-bearer," indicating that Satan was one of the brightest of all the heavenly host. Further, Rev. 12:4 suggests that one-third of the angels followed his defection from divine authority. Calling him the dragon, it says, "And his tail drew the third part of the stars of heaven, and did cast them to the earth."[9]

Apparently, all created intelligences were originally probationers. Unfortunately, Satan, with many others, forfeited his probation and was cast out. This seems to be the first origin of sin. The full account remains shrouded in mystery. The Scriptures only reveal brief indications of what transpired.

For instance, Jude, in verse 6, writes about "the angels which kept not their first estate." Peter also writes

43

about "the angels that sinned" and that were cast down to be reserved unto judgment (2 Pet. 2:4).

During His earthly ministry, Jesus made an interesting statement about Satan's fall. Jesus' disciples came to Him, rejoicing that even the devils were subject unto them through the power of His name. Instead of registering surprise, Jesus told them, "I beheld Satan as lightning fall from heaven" (Luke 10:18, KJV). The indication seems to be that Jesus' power over devils stemmed from His triumph over Satan's rebellion in the dim prehistory of man.

It also seems noteworthy that we compare the statement of Jesus in Luke 10:18 with other scriptural references such as Isa. 14:12 and Rev. 9:1 and 12:4. Although our scriptural information on Satan's fall is not extensive, and some of its interpretations are debatable, it is nonetheless significant. It seems we may obviously assume that because of his willful and rebellious apostasy, Satan and other angels were cast out of God's heaven.

From this defection originated all the evil spirits in earth and hell. Opposing God, the evil one set his depraved ambition on the earth. He thus determined to possess it and all mankind, expanding the limited dominion of hell. Because of Satan's perversion, the conflict between the forces of good and evil has consequently raged from the lofty streets of heaven to the lowly plains of earth.

In Rev. 12:7-9, we read specifically that there was war in heaven. Michael and the faithful angels fought against the dragon and his angels. "And the great dragon was cast out, that old serpent, called the Devil, and Satan, which deceiveth the whole world: he was cast out into the earth, and his angels were cast out with him" (v. 9, KJV). This attempted overthrow of God's heavenly domain by the devil and his angels may be alluded to in John 1:5, where it is declared, "The darkness has not overcome it" (RSV).

44

The name Michael signifies "Who is like to God?" In Daniel, Michael is the prince who stands up for the people of Israel (Dan. 12:1; 10:13, 21). Again, Michael, "the archangel," is alluded to in Jude verse 9 as the great opposer of Satan. It is therefore appropriate that the Revelator ascribes Michael as the chief of those who remained loyal to the cause of God in the rebellion of Satan and his angels.

Indeed, Michael is symbolic of the power of the excarnate Christ who, with His faithful host, conquered the devil and his evil horde. The rivalry is not simply that of opposing principles, but it is that of opposing personalities. Thus the hostility between the Seed of the woman and the seed of the serpent is a continuation of the war in heaven between Michael and the dragon.

As the prince of darkness and his rebel angels were driven out of heaven, so shall they be defeated in this earthly conflict. The victorious Captain of heaven's righteous forces is born of a woman to assure the triumph of God's kingdom here on earth. He becomes the Embodiment of the covenant that God made with Adam, persevering as the Archfoe of Satan's malicious designs for this world. Following the tempter's conquest of Eden, he remained constantly on the watch for Immanuel, his previous Opponent, who had triumphantly led his banishment from heaven.

Hence, the birth of the Messiah was involved in a conflict—the war of the ages. The entrance of the Anointed One into the defeated human scene signifies the eventual repulsion of the forces of evil and the destruction of sin. But the promise of God to man to provide full salvation did not assume the stigma of a never-ending battle. Rather, it asserts a victorious end with the total triumph of the Saviour, shared by those who will believe on Him.

From the time of Adam's transgression and God's

gracious covenant, the final doom of Satan has been sealed. This promise of hope indicates that the divine victory of man's salvation has been provisionally accomplished. Therefore, this initial redemptive hope not only speaks of conflict and the abolition of evil, but it also prophesies of the victory that is to be attained through the woman's Seed.

The Victory

Now we are able to look back on some of the major aspects of the victory God promised. Before the birth of Jesus Christ, man had to exercise a faith that God would act according to His word. However, since the time of Christ, man must believe that God did indeed fulfill His promise of hope. If the advent of Christ means anything, it certainly means victory—the actual fulfillment of the ancient covenant of God with man.

From our vantage point, we may say that the long-expected occasion of the Saviour's coming did arrive. It was fitting that the angels announced His holy birth. They were aware of the glad tidings they bore to earth. They were heralds of the divine message that a sin-darkened earth was to share heaven's victory over the evil foe. The Lord of hosts had come himself to bring deliverance to mankind.

Although generations from Adam would live and die, the time came when God launched His purging offensive against the entrenched dominion of sin. The promise of hope had been kept alive until it was at last realized.

Satan failed to prevent God from finding a chosen people; he failed to prevent the selection of the honored tribe; and he failed to prevent God from finding the woman that would be the proper holy vessel to give birth to the Deliverer.

The devil and all of his demons could not deter the

triumphant fulfillment of the divine covenant in any way. Despite all of his attempts to obstruct Him, the Christ child came as expected.

Actually, the serpent's time of evil influence and deceit is limited. The Son of God is sent in power to crush the serpent's destructive bondage—not simply from a throne—from a painful cross. There, the serpent bruised the Saviour's heel. But death could not hold Him fast. Soon Christ shall return in power to fatally bruise the serpent's head.

Such complete victory is divinely signified even as the covenant was given to our first parents. Those merciful words of God represent the dawning of the gospel day. No sooner had the disease of sin begun its awful contamination than the glorious remedy was revealed.

God's loving plan of salvation was not an afterthought of the tragic fall of man. By faith in this victorious promise, Adam and Eve found release from the dread curse of sin. Moreover, the patriarchs, before and after the Flood, were justified and saved by their faithful worship of God, looking to the benefits of the covenant.

God's promise to man certified the birth of a mighty Deliverer who would free the human race from the grip of corruption and death. Undoubtedly, this divine utterance was passed on from father to son in the hope that they would one day behold the salvation of the Lord.

But as generations passed on, most people forgot. The world became overwhelmingly wicked. Only an ark, built by a man of faith, saved his family and the race by obedience to the revelation of God. This again preserved the immutable character of God's saving word, projecting divine grace beyond the catastrophe of the Flood.

Certainly the victory of the promise is not only a divine accomplishment. It is also the vindication of womanhood. Though the woman was first in the transgression against God, she became the channel through which the victory over the works of the devil would be attained. Although she was to suffer in childbirth as a consequence, she would be saved through childbearing by the promised Seed who would descend from her (cf. 1 Tim. 2:14-15). Once an instrument of the serpent to sin, she became the chosen means of God's salvation. Hence, the divine edict set in motion the victorious redemption of the human race that Satan so viciously sought to damn.

The Saviour was to be the progeny of the woman—specifically, of a virgin—so that He would not be personally tainted with the corruption of depraved human nature. (At this point, we simply indicate the direction of the Scriptures in the light of a New Testament example.) The Apostle Paul looked back and wrote: "But when the fulness of the time was come, God sent forth his Son, made of a woman, made under the law" (Gal. 4:4, KJV).

Thus, not only is the victory divine, but also it is human. How encouraging for sinful humanity to know that their Saviour was to be the offspring of the woman, clothed in human flesh, bone of man's bone.

Indeed, the victorious event occurred when the Christ child was born. All the hopes of man's history and destiny were fulfilled in His holy birth. The Child of the victim becomes the Victor. He vicariously saves all who will "continue in faith and love and holiness with a sober mind" (1 Tim. 2:15, NEB).

Before His triumph over the sinful works of the devil can be effected, the Redeemer must take upon himself our sins and become accursed for our sakes. The prophet Isaiah declares, "But he was wounded for our transgressions, he was bruised for our iniquities: the chastisement of our peace was upon him; and with his stripes we are healed" (Isa. 53:5, KJV).

The sufferings and death of Jesus Christ signify the

bruising of His heel by the devil. However, through His sacrificial death and glorious resurrection, the power of sin and death is broken, and the satanic control over humanity is abolished. Speaking of the sacrificial, yet victorious, work that Christ performs, Heb. 2:14 states: "Since therefore the children share in flesh and blood, he himself likewise partook of the same nature; that through death he might destroy him who has the power of death, that is, the devil" (RSV).

So, by the Saviour's sustaining grace, His people may tread Satan, the serpent, under their feet (cf. Rom. 16:20). The devil's overthrow will ultimately be completed when God calls an end to time. "And the devil that deceived them" shall be "cast into the lake of fire and brimstone, where the beast and the false prophet are, and shall be tormented day and night for ever and ever" (Rev. 20:10, KJV).

God's redemptive promise extends from the beginning day of man till the "last day." Its scope reaches from the depths of sin and hopelessness to the heights of deliverance unto everlasting life. By the promise of the Anointed One, God deigned to provide a Saviour through human vessels of faith. Man's future depended on it.

Chapter 3

The Covenant Established

> *Now Jehovah said unto Abram, Get*
> *thee out of thy country, and from thy kin-*
> *dred, and from thy father's house, unto a*
> *land that I will show thee:*
> *And I will make of thee a great nation,*
> *and I will bless thee, and make thy name*
> *great; and be thou a blessing:*
> *And I will bless them that bless thee,*
> *and him that curseth thee I will curse:*
> *and in thee shall all families of the earth*
> *be blessed.*
>
> (Gen. 12:1-3; cf. 22:17-18)

According to the scriptural record of Moses, Adam lived to be 930 years old (Gen. 5:5). His life spanned at least seven generations. Now, at the setting of this textual passage, at least 19 generations had passed (from the birth of Seth to the birth of Abram) since God first promised that the woman would one day bear the seed of salvation. Indeed, Eve was the only mother whose son was certain to be either that promised child or in the line of descent.

After Cain is brought conspicuously before us by the murder of his brother Abel, his issue is traced for a little way until his record closes with another murderer, Lamech, his great-grandson (Gen. 4:25-26). So it was Eve's third son, named Seth (or Sheth), who became the ancestor of the Expected One. "For, said she, God hath appointed me another seed instead of Abel" (Gen. 4:25).

But as the population multiplied through the successive generations, the iniquity of humanity also increased. The evil of mankind became so overwhelming that God purposed to destroy their wickedness from the face of the earth. Yet the Lord found a righteous man of the line of Seth, the eighth from his generation. It was Noah, who "found grace in the eyes of the Lord" (Gen. 6:8, KJV).

Thus, Noah and his family bore the prospects of the promise across the intervening judgment of the Flood. For Noah knew people that knew Adam, particularly Methuselah, who was apparently living during the last 243 years of Adam's life. By surviving the catastrophic flood, Noah, his three sons, and their wives, maintained the connecting tie of faith and obedience to God.

Of the three sons of Noah—Shem, Ham, and Japheth—God selected Shem as the one from whose line the Anointed One was to come. Although it seems Japheth was the eldest, Shem received the special prophetic blessing from his father. "And he said, Blessed be Jehovah, the God of Shem; and let Canaan be his servant. God enlarge Japheth, and let him [he shall] dwell in the tents

51

of Shem; and let Canaan be his [their] servant" (Gen. 9:26-27).

According to this prophecy, Japheth was to be enlarged—his numbers and his borders. His posterity was to people all Europe, a great part of Asia, and eventually America. Ham, with Canaan his son, became the forebears of the Canaanites, the Phoenicians, the Carthaginians, the Egyptians, and other African peoples. But Shem is said to be "the father of all the children of Eber" (Gen. 10:21), the father of the Hebrews.[1]

Eber, Shem's great-grandson, was evidently himself a man eminent in the worship of God in a time of general apostasy. It is probable that he retained the holy tongue, being commonly called from him the "Hebrew," in his family during the confusion of Babel as a special token of God's favor to him. Because he was a great example of piety, from him all the professors of true religion were called "the children of Eber."[2]

All too soon, in spite of the divine judgment of the Flood and the lessons entailed, the contagion of infidelity and idolatry again threatened to banish the knowledge of God's plan of salvation from the earth. Beginning with the intemperance of Noah, the impudence and impiety of Ham (apparently also involving Canaan, his son), the corruption of depravity resumed at a rapid rate. The general immorality even infected the Shemite branch of the human family, and it became clear that a second divine interposition would be necessary if any of Adam's race should be saved.

In the succeeding centuries after the Flood, man's departure from the Lord increased until it was consummated in his idolatrous, devilish self-exaltation at Babel. The Tower of Babel was apparently an idolatrous temple, such as the ziggurats of Mesopotamia.[3] There is a vivid scriptural account in Genesis 11:1-6:

And the whole earth was of one language and of one speech. And it came to pass, as they journeyed east, that they found a plain in the land of Shinar; and they dwelt there. And they said one to another, Come, let us make brick, and burn them thoroughly. And they had brick for stone, and slime had they for mortar. And they said, Come, let us build us a city, and a tower, whose top may reach unto heaven, and let us make us a name; lest we be scattered abroad upon the face of the whole earth. And the Lord came down to see the city and the tower, which the children of men builded. And the Lord said, Behold, they are one people, and they have all one language; and this is what they begin to do: and now nothing will be withholden from them, which they purpose to do. (Cf. Rom. 1:21-28.)

Yet, despite the rapid and seemingly total degeneration of Noah's descendants, God was able to find a man. He was the ninth generation from Shem, selected to be the founder of a new and chosen nation. We thus see three great beginnings in Genesis: (1) the human race in Adam, (2) the postdiluvian generations in Noah and his sons, and (3) the chosen nation in Abraham. The repeated failure of man to return unto the Lord brought about a narrowing of God's elective grace from (1) the seed of the woman, (2) to the line of Shem, (3) to the seed of Abraham.[4]

In this people, the light of gospel truth was to be deposited for preservation until the fullness of the times. The chosen patriarch was to conduct the promise of hope forward so that it might come to its ultimate realization in the eventual birth of the woman's Seed. So, Abram, son of Terah, son of Nahor, son of Serug, son of Reu, son of Peleg, son of Eber, son of Salah, son of Arphaxad, son of Shem, was selected for this distinct honor.

As we have already noted, the divine choice of Abram marks an important turning point in God's dealing with sinful man. What was previously declared concerning a suffering and victorious Seed of the woman, and the coming of the Lord into the tents of Shem, is now brought into greater focus and detail by stating the special seed of blessing and the appointed place of blessing. And, in turn, it is indicated how the chosen seed of Abraham will be related in blessing to the entire seed of the woman, mankind in general.

Heretofore, God had administered His truth to the Adamic race as a whole. Noah had carried it and preserved it beyond the destruction of the Flood, and it was eventually entrusted to the line of Shem. But from the time of man's general rebellious effort in the building of the Tower of Babel (cf. Genesis 11), the Lord became primarily engaged in preserving a righteous witness in the midst of universal idolatry. Indeed, the idolatry of the Tower of Babel had even entered the line of Shem, the family of Abraham. This is clearly indicated by the words of Joshua:

> *And Joshua said unto all the people, Thus saith the Lord, the God of Israel, Your fathers dwelt of old time beyond the River, even Terah, the father of Abraham, and the father of Nahor: and they served other gods. . . . And if it seem evil unto you to serve the Lord, choose you this day whom ye will serve; whether the gods which your fathers served that were beyond the River, or the gods of the Amorites, in whose land ye dwell: but as for me and my house, we will serve the Lord* (Josh. 24:2, 15).

This was the responsibility with which God confronted Abram: that out of the background of confused languages, polluted religious beliefs, and exalted family

54

allegiances, he should separate himself and become the patriarch of the one true and living God. There at Babel were human presumption, disobedience, defiance, and arrogance, forsaking the true God for other gods. The inference is that idolatry is always linked with the worship of demons (cf. Deut. 32:17; 1 Cor. 10:20). The choice of Abram was to forsake the turmoil of Babel and accept the grace of God.

Thus, in this personal manner, the covenant of God's salvation for all mankind was established in a world made precarious by universal iniquity. Its success depended upon the vital roles of God-called men and women, hinging on their faith and obedience.

God never in the least indicated that His promised salvation was unconditional. Faith, love, and obedience were prime factors which motivated Abram to become heir to divine promise. Even now, before we may receive the benefits of the Christ who was sent, we must heed the divine call and its conditions, as did Abram.

Although man's fall and continued disobedience had seemingly blocked the way of our being benefited by God's love and salvation, He still loved us. Now a new and blessed way is opened by which God's love might be poured forth on the children of men.

As Dr. Turnbull has shown in his study *Christ in History,* it became the providential choice of a "central nation" to receive and lift up the torch of truth amid the surrounding darkness. Such a people were the ancient Hebrews, specifically the family of Abram. Turnbull aptly writes:

> As in society at large we find a central power, in religion a central principle, and in philosophy a central idea, it may be presumed that in the succession of human affairs, we shall find among the nations, in a more or less perfect form, a central or chosen people, whether

named church, or theocracy, or kingdom of God. We may expect not only a succession of divine facts, maintaining religion in the world, but a succession of individuals, families, and communities, perhaps some one community differing from all the rest in gifts, attainments, and usages, fitted to retain and transmit to all generations, and finally to the whole world, the principles and hopes of a perfect religion.[5]

Note, then, that the call of Abram, and the descendant nation of Israel of which he was the founder, was for the purposes of blessing through them upon the whole world. A nation, through Abram, is chosen as a repository of God's truth and a channel through which the promised Seed of the woman, the Redeemer of the world, could be born and identified when He came.[6]

The divine plan of redemption, in taking this new thrust, was pronounced to Abraham in the form of a covenant no less than five times, under varying circumstances. This was done in order that there might be no doubt in Abraham's mind, or ours, as to the certainty of God's plan.

The Call of God

Whether spoken in a dream or distinctly articulated by a human form, the voice which first called upon Abram to pack up his belongings and move away from Ur was recognized by the patriarch to be divine. It seems that Ur in Chaldea was then a city of some repute, situated on the right bank of the Euphrates River. Its name, which signifies "fire," was probably taken from the type of worship practiced there. This ancient form of the worship of fire evidently originated in honor of the element of fire, the acknowledged symbol of the Supreme Being by the inhabitants of this region.[7]

So it was that the divine summons which Abram

received was both distinguishing and selective. It came specifically to him of all the members of Terah's household, of all the descendants of the line of Shem, of all the citizens of Ur, and of all the inhabitants of the earth. Abram was the youngest son of Terah, but the Grace that chose Seth and Shem, both younger sons, also chose him.

At the time, Abram was an idolater, serving other gods, along with the common practices of his family and the people of Ur (cf. Josh. 24:2). Yet, according to the foreknowledge of God, Abram was chosen from among them all, amidst the evil, an acceptable vessel to carry the seed of promise.

Thus, the divine call issued to Abraham was also separating and dividing. It required the patriarch to disentangle himself from the idolatrous practices of his homeland. Moreover, his ties with relatives and friends must be severed, rather than imperil his vital association with God by conforming with unbelievers there in Chaldea. As the distinction was clear, the break must be complete.

Although there seems to be no definite command that none of Abram's relatives could make the pilgrimage with him, it is evident by the very nature of God's call that the unbelievers would soon exclude themselves. Only one motivated by faith could share Abram's call to inhabit the Promised Land.

We should note, however, that the full functioning of his own faith did not occur until his father had died and he had eventually separated himself from his nephew Lot. Abram alone was entrusted with maintaining humanity's role in the "word of hope" which looked to the birth of God's Anointed One.

As it happened, of Abram's immediate family, Haran, his oldest brother, died in Ur; Nahor, another brother, was left behind; and Terah, his father, apparently died en route from Ur, in the land of Haran. So, aside from

Abram, and Sarai his wife, only his nephew Lot, son of the deceased brother Haran, continued on the divinely inspired journey.

Ultimately, because of strife between their herdsmen, Lot was separated from Abram. Because of their faith and obedience, God's call was particularly intended for Abram and Sarai, that they should be the pair to establish the family line of the promised Son, the Messiah.

Since God had narrowed His choice, the unbelieving of Abram's family could not very well share in the divine purpose. All of the ensuing separation and division was for the distinct purpose of establishing the national and family genealogy of the promised Saviour derived from the selected household of Abram and Sarai. So long as any detracting connections existed between them and their old life with their relatives and friends, there could be no differentiation from God's chosen ones and the unbelieving idolaters. In this manner, God's call to Abram was severe and demanding, but it was certainly rewarding with promise.

However, in order to inherit the promise, the patriarch had to heed the commands and directions of the divine call. Abram was enjoined to make this long and arduous pilgrimage, "not knowing whither he went" (cf. Heb. 11:8). He only knew the way he should take, step by step, as God revealed it to him.

Such a journey, accompanied by sorrow, many difficulties, and dangers, required heroic fortitude and enduring patience. This purposeful pilgrimage could only be accomplished as Abram minutely followed God's instructions, taking each new step in faith. Abram's destiny, as well as that of the human race, depended upon his faithful answer to God's call.

The call of God remained clear and encouraging in spite of the many uncertainties along the way. Abram dared to follow the leadings of Jehovah God simply because he relied on the word of God. The outstanding promises which were assigned to the patriarch more than compensated for any sacrifice or deprivation that should befall him as he complied with the heavenly vision. His was to be a pilgrimage that not only led to the promised land of Canaan, but through it all, Abram was to receive a goodly inheritance, a great posterity, a blessed salvation, worldwide renown, and a lasting influence.

The call of God required much from Abram, but it also signified the great and wonderful blessings in store for him and all mankind. Again, God's call was for Abram and Sarai to receive the age-old promise, to be the means of establishing a select lineage for the promised Deliverer. Although this call was distinguishing, separating, directing, and encouraging, it remained absolutely conditional.

The establishment of the divine word of hope was vitally dependent upon Abram's faith and obedience along the way. Since the promise depended on human instrumentality, it became a covenant between God and His chosen ones. Thus, in the final analysis, God's call was just as much a call to faith in Him as it was a call for Abram to leave his own people and homeland. God indeed called Abram to meet the conditions of the covenant.

The Conditions of the Covenant

God's call would have been rendered useless and His promise inoperative had Abram failed to respond to the tests of his life and meet the conditions of faith and obedience. God's offer of salvation to mankind has never been unconditional, for man's relationship to God has always been dependent upon obeying His commands. Thus the heavenly injunction to Abram demanded an obedient response, even though it meant a forsaking of familiar idols and a breaking of close family ties.

Indeed, submission to the call of God necessitated travel on strange and trying pathways, often contrary to human instinct. But the prompt and unhesitating attitude of Abram to God's call demonstrates a birth of love and faith which ultimately claimed the promise by prevailing obedience.

Whenever the divine testimony contains both precept and promise, a sincere faith will obediently submit to the precept as well as cling to the promise. Certainly, it is a wonder that one so steeped in the practices of idolatry and fire worship could make such a favorable response and recognize the difference between true and false religion so readily.

Without any recorded complaint or question, Abram, the Chaldean flockmaster, put Jehovah's initial order into execution. He willingly departed from his old religious practices and from the beloved land of his fathers. He commenced on the journey which God required, unto a land which God had promised to give him. Although he was undoubtedly charged with folly because of going forth, "not knowing whither he went," Abram wisely obeyed the express command of God. He gladly traversed unknown trails under the sanction and the supervision of God and thus became known as "the father of the faithful."

The patriarch came to know not only the will of God, but also the comforting strength and guidance of God's love. We do not know to what extent human knowledge of God had been preserved through the pollution of sin and the degeneration of mankind from the time of the Flood. In any event, the spiritual insight of Abram rose far above his contemporaries who had forgotten the true God. He faithfully and obediently responded to the conditions of the covenant with awe. His persevering conduct was continuously molded by the requirements to inherit the promise.

Abram had taken God at His word. He reckoned that, although he had no tangible security, he would not be the loser in leaving his own people and country to follow God. Such implicit faith was necessary, for those who would deal with God must do so in absolute trust. They must leave the things that are seen behind in order to apprehend the things of hope and promise that are only visualized through eyes of faith. Thus God called Abram to a land which He would show him. He taught the patriarch to live in continual dependence upon Him and in faithful obedience to Him.

All of God's precepts are attended with "precious promises" to the obedient. Whenever God makes himself known as our righteous Commander, He also makes himself known as a faithful Rewarder. If man will obey His commands—meet the conditions—God will not fail to fulfill the promise. This was the faithful activity of God in selecting Abram to be the progenitor of the Anointed One sent to redeem Adam's race. Although salvation for mankind has always been initially dependent upon the mercy and grace of God to provide a Saviour, it has also been dependent upon man's personal response in faith and obedience.

It was the responsible position of Abram to observe the conditions of the covenant so that the promise of a Deliverer might be personally established in him. Through Abram's faith and obedience, his own salvation was secured, and the divine salvation blessing was passed on to all the peoples of the earth. It became the great privilege of that patriarch to inherit the promises, not only in his day, but throughout the ages. Because Abram had such faith and obeyed God, men since have looked to his example. For there is a particular sense in which every man must meet the conditions of salvation for himself.

Since the commands of God are inevitably punctuated with promise, man does well not only to consider His requirements, but also to appraise the divine promises. The blessings of God far outweigh any sacrifice man may need to make in order to inherit the promise. It is unreasonable to endeavor to bargain with God. He has already most graciously provided the only possible solution to man's problem of sin, undeserving as man is. Thus Abram, idolater though he had been, by continual faith and obedience became heir to the promise of the covenant of God.

The Promise of the Covenant

For the patriarch, the trials and tests of faith were infinitely rewarded as the covenant was multiplied in blessing and benefit upon his life and future. The Lord of all creation proved himself faithful in all of His dealings with Abram. Because of Abram's determination to do the will of God, the covenant was increased to contain a sevenfold promise which he could claim as his rightful inheritance.

First, since the Lord had called him away from his own homeland, *Abram was to possess the new land* which God was to show him. Although he was not immediately told what kind of land it was, nor where it was located, Abram was eventually led by God to a place called Canaan. It was already inhabited, but this did not disturb the "friend of God." There was also the disappointing fact that much of the territory did not appear to be very promising for Abram's grazing flocks and herds. Even so, the patriarch claimed the land of the Canaanites for his own inheritance, and God prospered him (cf. Gen. 13:14-18).

The second promissory aspect of the covenant was the divine declaration that *God would make of Abram a great nation.* When the Lord took him from his own people, He promised to make him the head of a chosen people. God, as it were, had cut Abram off from being the branch of a wild olive shoot to make him the root of a good and flourishing olive tree. It was mysterious comfort to the patriarch to be told that he would be the father of a great nation, for as yet, he and Sarai were childless.

This remained a troublesome trial to Abram's faith. The older he and Sarai became, the less likely seemed the prospects that his seed would exist at all, let alone be innumerable. Yet Abram chose to believe God against all apparent hopelessness. He built his faith simply upon the mighty power of "the most high God, possessor of heaven and earth" (Gen. 14:19, KJV).

Because he was to be the father of many nations, God changed Abram's name to Abraham (cf. Gen. 17:5). Sarai became anxious over the seeming impossibility of her fulfilling the role, so she interjected her handmaid, Hagar, to bear Abraham's children. Yet, although it had become a laughing matter for a 100-year-old man and a 90-year-old woman to have a son, the patriarch continued to walk before the God of promise.

Not only had the Lord promised to make Abraham the father of a great nation, but *He also pronounced an extensive accompanying blessing upon him,* saying, "I will bless thee." This is the third portion of the promise-laden covenant. With this implied benediction, all manner of prosperity is proffered. In substance, God said, "Leave your father's house, your homeland, and I will give you a father's blessing, far greater than that of your progenitors." As the Lord God looked after Adam and Noah, so He would provide abundant blessings for His servant Abraham.

As the fourth part of His promise, God also assured Abraham that *He would make his name great.* When Abraham had departed from his old familiar country, the patriarch's name had become lost there. But God said, "Do not regret that; only trust Me, and I will make you a far greater name than you could ever have had there." Again, without any children yet, Abraham feared he should have no continuing name at all. Somehow God would make of him a great nation, and He would pour out all blessings upon him. Abraham would indeed be a great name for all generations (cf. Gen. 17:1-9).

Then, in the fifth place, God declared that *Abraham himself would be a blessing.* In substance, the divine promise implies that the patriarch's happiness and prosperity would be such an ideal example that those who would bless their loved ones would simply pray for God to be with them as He had been with Abraham. Also, the direct indication is that the very life of Abraham would be a blessing to those with whom he dwelt, to those with whom he came in contact, unto prosperity in the years to come.

The sixth portion of promise contained in the covenant was *a kind of alliance, both offensive and defensive, between God and His servant Abraham.* God had said, "I will bless them that bless thee, and curse him that curseth thee" (Gen. 12:3, KJV). Because Abraham accepted the responsibilities of God's purpose and will, God, in turn, promised to be a Friend to the patriarch's friends and to manifest a continuous protective interest in Abraham's welfare. God would take kindnesses done to Abraham as done even to himself, and He would recompense them accordingly. Any service performed for the benefit of God's chosen people would not go unrewarded.

Also, God promised to take Abraham's part against his enemies. There were those who desired Abraham's ruin, who hated and even cursed him. But their ill wishes, their evil designs and deceits could not defeat this "friend of God." Instead, God's righteous judgment was sent to overtake and destroy Abraham's opposition. This was a wonderful comfort to the patriarch who was a pilgrim and a stranger traveling amidst unfriendly and hostile peoples. The God who called him forth likewise gave him support during the conflicts.

Finally, the seventh and climaxing promise of the covenant was that *in Abraham, "all the families of the earth" would be blessed* (cf. Gen. 12:3b). This promise crowns all the rest. It points to the Expected One, the coming Deliverer, in whom all the promises are "yea and amen." It is thus through Abraham that the original promise of redemption is renewed and established. It is here that the family of Abraham is proclaimed to be the appointed bearer of the promised Seed of deliverance. The Man-child, born of a woman, would be the Saviour of the world, releasing sinners everywhere from the stranglehold of evil.[8]

Only the Anointed One sent of God could be such a great and universal blessing. He is to be the greatest Blessing with which this sin-cursed world could ever be blessed. At this time, in Abraham, the expected Messiah became a family blessing, for by Him salvation is brought to the household of faith.

It became the high honor of Abraham to be the human means of relating the promised Son of God to the erring sons of men. Man's hope was still that by the birth of a child sent of God, He would bring salvation and redemption to all who would believe on Him.

So, the Abrahamic covenant is not only the "by-faith" covenant, it is also the "by-birth" covenant. Such is the assertion of the Apostle Paul, as he wrote centuries later in the New Testament:

> *Even as Abraham believed God, and it was reckoned unto him for righteousness. Know therefore that they that are of faith, the same are the*

*sons of Abraham. And the scripture, foreseeing
that God would justify the Gentiles by faith,
preached the gospel beforehand unto Abraham,
saying, In thee shall all the nations be blessed. So
then they that are of faith are blessed with the
faithful Abraham* (Gal. 3:6-9).

In this manner, the New Testament revelation proceeds from the Abrahamic Covenant and affirms the fact
that Jesus is the Expected One, the promised Messiah.
He is the promised Seed of the woman, the promised Seed
of blessing whom God established with Abraham in covenant. Indeed, Christ is the One for whom the patriarch
looked in faith. The apostle thus verifies the unfolding of
the divine covenant of redemption; he declares it to be a
matter of divine grace and of faith in Christ, not of the
law. For Paul goes on to say:

*Christ hath redeemed us from the curse of the
law, being made a curse for us: for it is written,
Cursed is every one that hangeth on a tree: that
the blessing of Abraham might come on the
Gentiles through Jesus Christ; that we might receive the promise of the Spirit through faith. . . .*

*Now to Abraham and his seed were the prom-
ises made. He saith not, And to seeds, as of many;
but as of one, And to thy seed, which is Christ. . . .*

*And if ye be Christ's, then are ye Abraham's
seed, and heirs according to the promise* (Gal. 3:
13-14, 16, 29, KJV).

In many respects, the covenant did not live for Abraham until after the birth of Isaac, his own divinely
promised seed. Yet, there can be little doubt that the patriarch did indeed behold the salvation of the Lord.

The Scriptures contain an interesting record of the
progressive revelation of God unto Abraham. Following

his remarkable victory in delivering Lot from the captivity of four enemy kings, Abraham recognized God as *"El Elyon,"* "the most high God, possessor of heaven and earth" (Gen. 14:18, KJV). He therefore gave Melchizedek, the kingly priest of God, tithes of all the spoils.

Then, when Abram was 99 years old, and his name was changed to Abraham, God was revealed as *"El Shaddai,"* the Almighty God. It was on this occasion that the Abrahamic Covenant was confirmed and made everlasting.

Here, in a particular way, God becomes the Nourisher, the Strength-giver, and the Satisfier, who pours himself into believing lives. God declares that in spite of Abraham's and Sarah's advanced age, He has made Abraham the father of many nations. Moreover, God reaffirms the promises that would forever establish the covenant of redemption with mankind, saying:

> *And I will make thee exceeding fruitful, and I will make nations of thee, and kings shall come out of thee. And I will establish my covenant between me and thee and thy seed after thee throughout their generations for an everlasting covenant, to be a God unto thee, and to thy seed after thee. And I will give unto thee, and to thy seed after thee, the land of thy sojournings, all the land of Canaan, for an everlasting possession; and I will be their God* (Gen. 17:6-8).

> *And God said, Sarah thy wife shall bear thee a son indeed; and thou shalt call his name Isaac: and I will establish my covenant with him for an everlasting covenant, and with his seed after him* (Gen. 17:19, KJV).

Following the instruction of God, Abraham instituted the rite of circumcision as the established sign of the everlasting covenant of God with his promised descendants. Thereafter, it is recorded that Abraham called upon "the name of Jehovah, the Everlasting God" (cf. Gen. 21:33). This meant that God himself was not only everlasting, but also that He is God over everlasting things, such as His covenant with mankind in general, and with Abraham in particular.

Thus when Abraham was sorely tested by God's instruction to offer up Isaac, his only son, the son of divine promise, as a sacrifice, he clung to the everlasting covenant. From all appearances, this seemed to be a disastrous requirement from God. Yet, when Isaac asked his father about the lamb for the burnt offering, Abraham by faith replied, "God will provide himself the lamb for a burnt-offering, my son" (Gen. 22:8). The patriarch had his eyes fixed upon the everlasting God and the everlasting covenant. If necessary, Abraham believed that God would indeed restore Isaac even though he were a slain sacrifice. It was following this incident that God declared, "And in thy seed shall all the nations of the earth be blessed; because thou hast obeyed my voice" (Gen. 22:18; cf. vv. 17-18).

This ultimate expectation that God would provide the lamb of salvation is undoubtedly the pinnacle of Abraham's experience with the Lord. The resultant divine provision certainly served to verify his faith in every aspect of the covenant, including the great expectation of the Anointed One that was to be sent of God, born among men. It was upon faithful men such as Abraham that the covenant of redemption was established in a rebellious world.

Despite all of the sinfulness of mankind, it was possible for God to find obedient and faithful human instruments that would carry the promise of deliverance from sin into fruition. Eventually it would be fulfilled through the miraculous birth of a Saviour. Because of the faith and obedience of Abraham, the divine word of hope was established, not merely as the seed of the woman, but the promised Son was to be of Abraham's lineage.

Chapter 4

Look for Shiloh

The sceptre shall not depart from Judah, nor a lawgiver from between his feet, until Shiloh come; and unto him shall the gathering of the people be.

(Gen. 49:10, KJV)

A 147-year-old father was lying on his deathbed. This was Jacob, divinely named Israel, son of Isaac, son of Abraham. Even as God had personally made the covenant with Abraham, his grandfather, and had confirmed that covenant with Isaac, his father (cf. Gen. 26:1-5), so had God confirmed the Abrahamic Covenant with Jacob.

It had been many years ago during his youth. Jacob had stopped at Bethel for the night to rest amid his flight from his brother Esau. He had deceived his father Isaac into bestowing the birthright to him instead of to Esau, the older twin. There, at Bethel, the Lord appeared to Jacob in a dream. He dreamed that a ladder was set up on earth, reaching to heaven, and the angels of God were ascending and descending (cf. Gen. 28:12). God stood above the ladder, and said:

> *I am Jehovah the God of Abraham thy father,*
> *and the God of Isaac; the land whereon thou liest,*
> *to thee will I give it, and to thy seed; and thy seed*
> *shall be as the dust of the earth, and thou shalt*
> *spread abroad to the west, and to the east, and to*
> *the north, and to the south: and in thee and in thy*
> *seed shall all the families of the earth be blessed*
> (Gen. 28:13-14).

Time and again, Jacob returned to Bethel to meet with God, to have his confidence in the promise restored. This sacred place was finally called El-bethel by Jacob because of his progressive relationship with God. At first Jacob called the place "the house of God," until at last he recognizes God as the God of Bethel, "the God of the house of God." Throughout the many adversities of his life, Jacob maintained his contact with the God of his fathers, in obedience and sacrifices. Even en route to Egypt, to be reunited with his son Joseph, God spoke reassuringly unto Israel in the visions of the night:

> *And he said, I am God, the God of thy father;*
> *fear not to go down into Egypt; for I will there*
> *make of thee a great nation: I will go down with*
> *thee into Egypt; and I will also surely bring thee*
> *up again: and Joseph shall put his hand upon*
> *thine eyes* (Gen. 46:3-4).

Now, after living for 17 years in Egypt, Jacob realized that the time of his death was near. He therefore called his sons together to give them his final blessing.

71

As his father before him, Jacob had the parental duty and the sacred privilege of passing the Abrahamic Covenant of divine blessing on to his 12 sons. Thus Reuben, Simeon, Levi, Judah, Zebulun, Issachar, Dan, Gad, Asher, Naphtali, Joseph, and Benjamin were to form the 12 tribes of Israel and become the chosen people of God. Here is the beginning of the great nation that God would make out of Abraham. From their midst, the "everlasting covenant" was to be carried forth to bless all peoples.

According to the text, in Gen. 49:10, Jacob's words of blessing were mostly prophetic in nature, for they pointed to the future, particularly to the coming of Shiloh. A great deal of controversy has swirled around the word "Shiloh." Perhaps the most plausible of the anti-Messianic interpretations is that which regards Shiloh as the name of the town in Ephraim, where the ark was deposited after the settlement in Canaan (cf. Josh. 18:1, 8-10; 19:51; Judg. 18:31; 1 Sam. 1:3, 9, 24; 2:14).

This sense explains the meaning of the prophecy that the leadership of Judah over the other tribes of Israel should not cease until he came to Shiloh. For example, Rabbi Adler supposes that the reference is to the revolt of Jeroboam and the 10 tribes, which took place at Shechem, not far from Shiloh, when Judah lost the sovereignty over the tribes of Israel.[1] (So also say Rabbi Lipman, Teller, Eichhorn, Delitzsch, and others.)

However, the tribe of Judah had no historic connection with the place of Shiloh that would give any rational meaning to the grave prophetic forecast of the passage. Judah's real eminence and leadership continued even into a later period. Moreover, it seems improbable that so obscure a locality, whose existence at that time is doubtful, should be mentioned by Jacob. Zidon, the only other name occurring in the prophecy, was a city of renown, existing long before the days of Jacob (Gen. 10:19). Thus, to interpret "Shiloh" as a place would seem to render the statement inaccurate, since the supremacy of Judah was in no way diminished by the events at Shiloh.[2]

Again, "Shiloh" has been regarded as an abstract noun. In such a sense, the import of the prophecy has been expressed as asserting that the sceptre should not depart from Judah, either until he (Judah) should attain to rest, or until tranquility should come. Of course, this rest would come when Judah's enemies would all be subdued. (Variations of this interpretation are held by those who follow Hofmann, Kurtz, and Gesenius.)[3]

Others derive "Shiloh" from the Hebrew verb *shalah*, meaning to be safe, to be at rest, to be at peace, and they render it "rest" or "tranquility." This is perhaps the most natural derivation, and this is the meaning adopted by such learned Hebraists as Vater, Gesenius, Kurtz, De Wette, Knobel, and Hofmann. Thus Gesenius, in his dictionary, renders the passage: "The sceptre shall not depart from Judah until tranquility shall come."[4]

Such an interpretation may take on an anti-Messianic slant, and it has been considered as a prediction of, or reference to, the peaceful reign of Solomon. But it may also fitly represent the peace to be enjoyed in Messianic times. Indeed, the term "Peace" is itself one of the titles of the Messiah given later by the prophets (Mic. 5:15).[5]

Perhaps the word "Shiloh" may be best understood as meaning "rest" or "rest-giver," but such a meaning obviously does not fulfill the supposed significance of Jacob's words. It seems necessary to go further and say that Shiloh is a proper name of the Messiah, denoting a peacemaker, or the Prince of Peace—"Until Shiloh, [that is, the Messiah or Prince of Peace] come."

Because of the difficulty of this passage, some feel that there is a possibility of error in the original text. Thus, when Jerome translated the word *qui missus est,* it seems that he did not read it as Shiloh, but as some form of *shalach,* meaning "to send." It is also felt that the translator in the Septuagint did not read the word as it stands in our Bibles, but rather as *shelloh* or *shello.* With such a translation the meaning would be, "The sceptre will not depart from Judah . . . till the things reserved for him come."[6]

However, we may view the early translations with even more interest. An early Aramaic translation reads "until the Messiah comes," and this interpretation has greatly influenced Jewish and Christian understanding of the text. For instance, the Targum Onkelos reads: "One having the principality shall not be taken from the house of Judah, nor a scribe from his children's children, until the Messiah come, whose the kingdom is."

The Targum Jerusalem reads: "Kings shall not fail from the house of Judah, nor skillful doctors of the law from their children's children, till the time when the King's Messiah shall come." The Syriac translation is: "The sceptre shall not fail from Judah, nor an expounder from between his feet, till He come whose it is" (that is, the sceptre).

The Arabian translation is: "The sceptre shall not be taken away from Judah, nor a lawgiver from under his rule, until He shall come whose it is." The Samaritan translation has it, "Until the Pacific shall come." Then, the Latin Vulgate reads: "Until He shall come who is to be sent."[7]

Nevertheless, in spite of the strong Messianic import of the early translations, some have interpreted the blessing of Jacob about "Shiloh" or "the ruler" of Judah in a much different manner. In a sense, it follows other anti-Messianic interpretations which we have already noted.

For example, Mowinckel simply interprets Shiloh to be fulfilled in David. For David is the one who is to make

Judah the ruling tribe among the children of Israel, and thus he is the one to whom the sceptre will always belong. Because it was David who made Judah the ruling tribe, and it was his house that won an enduring right to the throne of Israel, history itself indicates that David fulfills the personage referred to by Jacob.[8] (Those who hold this position follow the translations of Dathius, and Gulcher before him.)

For the most part, evangelical Christians have been quite united in seeing Christ as the ultimate fulfillment of Jacob's prophetic blessing. When this extent of the message is recognized, his dying words include not only the tribes of Israel, but that the people of the world would become obedient to the One who was to come.[9] Thus the title "Shiloh" is uttered for the first time, pointing to the future, apparently to One yet unborn.

The focus of Jacob's prophetic promise is significantly beamed on this "Shiloh," and not on the personal or collective accomplishments of his 12 sons. Shiloh is obviously a person, and he is characterized as the Expected One who is to come, bringing hope and peace to a troubled world.

Even though the exact words are not spoken, the watchword becomes: "Look for Shiloh!" Certainly, Shiloh is envisioned as the Messiah, the promised Deliverer sent of God. From this great distance, dying Jacob anticipated Christ's day, and it was his comfort and support in crossing from time to eternity.

There is undoubtedly a definite connection between the anticipation of Shiloh's coming and the promised "seed of the woman" (cf. Gen. 3:15). Moreover, there is also an evident relationship between the Abrahamic Covenant of "everlasting" proportions and the coming of Shiloh. As the covenant of redemption was first pronounced by the voice of God to man's sinful parents under

75

the curse of death, and as it was spoken again to Abraham in more specific tones, it is now further proclaimed to humanity through the inspired lips of a dying man.

It is in this fashion that we may observe the development of Messianic truth. At first He is simply expected as the Seed of the woman, which is rather indefinite and undetermined. Next, the range is narrowed to a particular race of the woman, from the line of Abraham. Now, here the line is drawn still closer to include only the tribe of Judah. Thus far in the Scriptures, the three chief Messianic references are: (1) The Seed of the woman; (2) The Seed of Abraham, and (3) The Seed of Judah.[10]

Thus, because of the peerless character attributed to Shiloh, he was not just a meaningless symbol of hope. He was to be the personal answer to man's great need of divine salvation. Once again, God revealed His own involvement with human history. The light of His truth is placed upon a pedestal for all to see. The expected child, anointed and sent of God, now has a name. By the name "Shiloh," the personality and righteous character of God's salvation are declared to come unto mankind through the tribe of Judah.

The Name

In believing Shiloh to be the name of a person, the majority of commentators, both Jewish and Christian, agree that the Messiah is the Person to whom Jacob refers. They also understand Jacob as fore-announcing that the time of his appearance would not be till the staff of regal power had dropped from the hands of Judah. There is, however, a wide diversity of opinion among those who see a Messianic reference in the prediction as to the exact significance of the name Shiloh.[11]

Some render Shiloh to be Jacob's son, or progeny, or

great descendant (as do Kimchi, Calvin, and Ainsworth). Others compare it with Siloam (John 9:7) and Shiloah (Isa. 8:6), and interpret it as *Qui mittendus est* (from the Vulgate, "he that is to be sent"), as does Grotius. Still another group of expositors view the name as an appellation signifying the Pacificator, the Rest-giver, the Tranquilizer, the Peace (as does Luther, Hengstenberg, Keil, etc.). Then the fourth class of scholars conjecture Shiloh to signify "he to whom it [the sceptre or the kingdom] belongs," or he whose right it is (as in Ezek. 21:27: "This also shall be no more, until he come whose right it is; and I will give it him"). (As we have already indicated, the Targums of Onkelos and of Jerusalem, along with the Syriac translation, give support to such a consideration.) It would seem that the preponderance of authority is in favor of the last two interpretations, especially that of the Tranquilizer.[12]

Whatever the most accurate interpretation might be, we must remember that it was out of the void of despondency of death that the name "Shiloh" sounded forth. Certainly, the utterance of that name was divinely inspired. Scriptural harmony will not allow us to view it as the mere token of an imaginary descendant, or simply as a little-known point of divine confrontation.

Rather, the name definitely bespeaks the signal of God's help, of God's salvation for destruction-bound humanity. This divine revelation was somehow beheld by the dimmed sight of Jacob, and it was heard by his aged ears. By faith, the unknown "seed of the woman" is confirmed through the Abrahamic Covenant; and now, further by faith, Shiloh is seen as the One who shall appear in due time, out of the royal line of Judah.

The name itself bears a peculiar significance. It seems there can be little doubt that Shiloh is indeed a proper name of the Messiah. Perhaps the full meaning of the name can easily accommodate the various interpretations and translations without contradiction. Shiloh is no less than the Tranquilizer that is to be sent, the One to whom the kingdom belongs. Hence, the very name "Shiloh" refers to the One who is to be sent in the fullness of time. It was given and identified on this solemn occasion to remind the children of Israel to continue to look for Him who was to be sent of God, born out of their nation.

Shiloh is a sweet and mighty name because it represents the One who is to be sent of God. The character of the name appears as a balm, a healing ointment supplied for all of man's diseases. Its pronouncement voices the cure for the hopelessness of sin and uncleanness. Its healing, saving power reaches deeper than the evil stain has gone in human nature. This name entitles the provided remedy to rescue the dying from certain separation from God.

Thus the sound of the name is a relief to the listening ear. It is like hearing the name of a great physician who has consented to take over a desperate, hopeless case, with the sure promise of recovery. Now the deadly grasp of sin is shaken, for Shiloh signifies the coming of the only Specialist who can provide the salvation which man must have.

The might of the name is not only implied in its healing power over the pollution and curse of sin, but it is a name above every other name. Notice that every name of Jacob's sons became secondary to the name Shiloh. In spite of the special preeminence that is promised to Judah, it is obvious that the success and the survival of the children of Israel depends on the might of this name.

Furthermore, all other human names become secondary, for Shiloh is the Benefactor to all the peoples of the earth. No other name represents such purpose and ability to alleviate the lost condition of humanity. No other name reveals the riches of God's goodness to a straying, fallen creation. No other name possesses the dignity and the righteousness to purchase man's redemption from sin, to establish reconciliation with God.

Shiloh is expected to come to hold converse with mankind, to enter this wicked world situation, and to bring divine grace to this rebellious race. He is seen as a mighty Ally to stem the tide of the forces of evil. He is recognized as coming fearlessly because He is sent by Almighty God to deliver those who will believe and receive a glorious freedom from the bondage of sin.

So the name Shiloh becomes the early banner of triumph over sin and the devil, hell and the grave. Shiloh therefore brightens the prospects of man in the midst of despair and death, directing sin-burdened humanity unto God's salvation. In this unlikely manner, Divine Love pronounces the name long before the personal appearance, and promises its embodiment as the Revelation of divine grace to all who would hear and believe.

The divine mission of Shiloh is apparently remembered by Moses when God declared His desire to send Moses as His ambassador to the Pharaoh of Egypt. At first Moses declined the difficult task of seeking the deliverance of the children of Israel and of leading them out of slavery. He reminded God of the promised Shiloh: "And he said, O my Lord, send, I pray thee, by the hand of him whom thou wilt send" (Exod. 4:13). Evidently, Moses plainly understood the prophecy of Jacob regarding this name to mean that a Deliverer was to be sent by God to help His chosen people.

Then, again, while establishing Israel as a mobile nation, Moses declared, "Jehovah thy God will raise up unto thee a prophet from the midst of thee, of thy brethren, like unto me; unto him ye shall hearken" (Deut. 18:15).

79

A continued reliance upon the name Shiloh is indicated by Moses' final blessing given to the Israelites. It is parallel to the blessing of Jacob, as he prayed that God would sustain Judah and be the Source of his deliverance (cf. Deut. 33:7). But the Israelites was not merely to place their trust in the hollow sound of a name; they were to look for the coming of a personal Messiah.

However, as we have noted previously, some have suggested that the reference of Shiloh is not necessarily in the Messianic sense, but rather that it is more likely a reference to David or Solomon. Such a likelihood is considered plausible because of the supposed late composition of this oracle, set to be about 960 B.C.[13] Although such a view verifies the specific personage of Shiloh, it does not harmonize or fulfill the overall history of expectation and human need. The point is that sin and separation from God require more than the success of kings.

It would appear that the ultimate extent of the attention of devout men was directed to the covenant of redemption. They recognized that their deliverance, their salvation from the curse of sin, was to come from the Seed of the women. Hence, the birth of every male child was a time of expectant rejoicing. Jacob's vision thus further extended the boundaries of knowledge, through eyes of faith. Mankind is thereby informed that the Saviour shall be of selected lineage, of Abraham, Isaac, and Jacob. Here, it is passed to Judah, one of the 12 sons of Jacob, answering the prevailing question "Whose son shall he be?"

In accordance with the special promise to Judah, we now know that Judah indeed became the leader among the tribes. We know that from that tribe, David arose and established the royal line of his successors. We know that according to the prophet Isaiah, it is foretold that the Messianic King was to come out of the tribe of Judah, "a shoot out of the stock of Jesse" (Isa. 11:1). Clearly, the projected prophetic understanding of the Expected One to be sent was that He was to come as a son, out of the tribe of Judah.

Whose Son?

This was no new question. It had been the wonder of humanity for generations, both before and after the Flood. Nevertheless, it was accounted a proper question because of the progressive covenants and blessings extended to Adam and Eve, to Seth, to Noah, to Shem, to Abraham, to Isaac, to Jacob, and now to Judah. Out of all his sons, Jacob designates that Shiloh is to come from Judah's tribe.

Because of the sin of Reuben, the firstborn, and the disobedience of Simeon and Levi, the next two sons in line, the birthright is given to Judah. It is interesting to recall that Jacob received the blessing from his father, Isaac, even though he was younger than his twin brother, Esau. The reason was not only because of Jacob's deception, but it was also because Esau had despised the birthright. Once again, the elder sons are passed over in divine preference for the younger, who is a proper son to carry the promise.

According to the scripture test which relates Jacob's prophecy concerning Judah, it is apparent that Judah's tribe is to be the royal progenitor from which the Anointed One should come. In his prophetic vision, Jacob foresees and foretells that the ruling sceptre should be given unto Judah.

Although Israel's first king was Saul, of the tribe of Benjamin, this was indeed fulfilled when David, son of Jesse, of the tribe of Judah, was eventually crowned king in Saul's stead. Then it was the family of David that established the continuing royal line.

Moreover, it is not only told that Shiloh should be of the tribe of Judah, it is also indicated that He was that promised Seed, through whom all the earth should be

81

blessed. Indeed, He comes to be the Deliverer of the children of Israel, but even more, to be the Saviour of all mankind. After the coming of the ruling sceptre into the tribe of Judah, it was to continue in that tribe until the coming of God's Messiah. The Kingdom is thereby reserved for Shiloh.

Remember, the faith of Jacob has rightfully taken an expanded view. As his fathers before him, Jacob necessarily includes the action of God in the human picture. So, in answer to the question "Whose son?" he not only speaks of the seed of Judah, but also of the One "that is to be sent."

It is evident that the hope of Jacob rests upon his son, Judah, and upon the faithfulness of his tribe, but Jacob's faith was fixed on God. Shiloh, the promised and expected Seed, is not merely the Son of Judah's tribe, the Son of Man, but as the One sent of God, He may be said to be God's Son as well. Both humanity and deity are implied here for this Anointed One.

Obviously, the faith of Jacob looked beyond the insufficiency of the sons of men to the Son sent of God, who would be born as the Son of Man. Despite the incompleteness of the revelation to Jacob, a peak of wisdom was certainly reached. There is no greater realization of the advent of Christ than the fact that the Son must be divinely sent if the world is to be saved.

As Jehovah's Son, Shiloh becomes the Light of salvation's firmament, and the Keystone to salvation's arch. He is the One with the Father—One in nature, One in essence, One in every perfection. In every sense, He is coequal and coeternal with God. From everlasting to everlasting, He is the Almighty God. Before all the created worlds, the world without end, and all the created creatures, He is God over all.

He is the One who is to be sent. There is no hope for

fallen humanity unless the Messiah is God. True, He may not have always been reckoned as such, nor consistently expected as such. But what mockery to say, "Look for Shiloh!" if He were not divine.

If Shiloh were not divine, He could not be the Deliverer that would transform sin-impoverished men by removing the destructive iniquity from their sin-soiled souls. It must be remembered that every sin of man is an infinite evil, and it therefore requires the holy expiation of infinite merit to accomplish personal salvation.

Such infinitude is surely possessed by Shiloh. He comes in power to bring deliverance and to remove with cleansing the countless sins of all who will believe unto redemption. He comes all-sufficient to clothe them with righteousness acceptable to God's heaven. He is all-glorious to present them in glory before the throne of God, surrounded with blessing forever. Shiloh can do all of this only because He is the Son of God.

Thus, in uniting deity with manhood, Shiloh becomes the Mediator between God and all mankind. Without the prospects of Shiloh, man is irreconcilably lost from God. the depth of man's fall was immeasurably below the holiness of the Almighty. But Shiloh comes to unite God and man in fellowship and harmony. Every faculty and property of man is joined to every power of God. This is the wonder of heaven, of earth, of hell, throughout endless ages. With Shiloh was born the unity of God and man. With Him humanity's ultimate deliverance from sin and death is come. In this wondrous manner, faith is satisfied and cries, "My kinsman, my Lord, my God, my complete Salvation!"[14]

Certainly, the answer to the question "Whose Son?" reveals the holy purpose of His coming. Moreover, it establishes the righteous character of His relationship to both God and man. The divine mission of Shiloh clearly implies that not only is He man's Deliverer, but that He is also the sole means of man's reconciliation with the Father.

From the time of the Fall, sin generated increasing enmity between God and His human creation. Sinful man was powerless to take the initiative in returning to the holy kingdom of God. Therefore, Shiloh comes as the wonderful Peacemaker, providing the elements whereby sin-stained humanity might be restored and have peace with God.

The Peacemaker

Such a title sounds conciliatory. But Shiloh will not come waving a white flag to make a truce with the rebellious forces of evil. Rather, He will come to destroy the power of sin, and to meet the disobedience of mankind with convicting, convincing love. This is no sign of compromise with the devil. Indeed, it is the mighty action of God to bring redemption and peace to a sin-troubled world.

Thus, Shiloh is the promised Emissary of the Father who assumes full responsibility for the return of humanity to the holy will of their Creator. He comes as the heralded Prince of Peace who will gather the people unto himself. Both as their Example and Leader, He will reestablish the human race in the way of righteousness originally intended by the Father.

Since Shiloh is the Revelation of divine love and mercy, by believing on Him, the penitent sinner avoids the wrath of God. The awful chasm of condemnation is bridged with the coming of Shiloh, for He appears, not as Judge, but as man's Peacemaker with God. His banner is holiness and truth, so the very promise of His birth restores divine direction to an estranged human race.

There should no longer be any doubt as to the intention of God that all mankind should be saved. The "One who is to be sent" provides both the example and the saving virtue whereby peace is made. There is no other way that peace between sinful man and holy God can be righteously promoted. Man by himself cannot silence the terrible struggle perpetuated by Satan and his own sinfulness.

The situation demands that One must be sent from outside the defeated human scene. Yet He must come to take the bitter dregs of human degradation as a man, bearing humanity's guilt of rebellion with personal innocence and holiness. Only such a person can plead the cause of all men and possess the power to rectify every sin with forgiveness and cleansing. The awful reason for the enmity between God and man must be eliminated if peace is to reign supreme—"on earth, as it is in heaven." Thus, man's only hope for peace with God, as well as peace in this world, is to "Look for Shiloh!" He alone fulfills the qualifications for peacemaker.[15]

To a comforting degree, Shiloh was envisioned by the dying patriarch. Looking at Judah, Jacob saw in this son the shining of the brilliant hope of all Israel. He therefore described him as of the lion nature, the perpetual type of kingship. In the distant future, he saw the glory of Another, One whose name signified peace. It was toward that ultimate Prince of Peace that he looked with longing desire, rejoicing in Judah because through him Shiloh would come.[16]

We cannot say with certainty to what extent Jacob understood what he saw. But perhaps we may say with assurance that Jacob did view Shiloh as the One sent to establish man's peace with God. This is indicated by his further word, "I have waited for thy salvation, O Lord" (Gen. 49:18). Jacob knew that by the very nature of man's predicament, any salvation and significant peace which the world would enjoy must come from God.

Morever, such peace has ever been recognized as dependent upon the redemption of mankind from the rule of sin. Surely, Jacob rejoiced at the knowledge of the divine tidings of peace and salvation. No wonder this dying father instructed his sons to "Look for Shiloh!" His coming would mean everything to the welfare and destiny of all humanity.

How the brightness of redeeming love radiates from Shiloh, the name, the Son, the Peacemaker. Later a prophet is to remind the children of Israel: "O house of Jacob, come ye, and let us walk in the light of Jehovah" (Isa. 2:5). Shiloh thus remains the Light of hope, the Source of confidence, and the very Means of man's salvation. His name was uttered in faith, and its sound has been voiced abroad because an aged patriarch had faith in God.

It is on this basic premise that we reject the conclusion of those scholars who say that Jacob was simply prophesying the coming of David or Solomon and their victorious kingdoms. Indeed, these events were undoubtedly included in the substance of the prophecy. But if Jacob was a religious patriarch as well as a political one, then we must go further to declare that the ultimate hope was fixed on the God of Jacob, and not his future progeny.

By divine intervention, Shiloh is linked with believing men, of the tribe of Judah, the son of Jacob, Isaac, and Abraham. His coming is more glorious than any earthly king, for He comes with healing in His hands to provide the remedy for the sinful plight of mankind. He comes with power to deliver His people from the wrath of God and the curse of sin. Indeed, He comes to establish peace— peace on earth and peace with God. This is the Blessing that shall be unto all peoples, flowing from Abraham to Jacob, through Judah and his chosen tribe.

In coming from the tribe of kings, Shiloh, sent of God, will be peculiarly God's anointed King. This continues to be the divine revelation which is clearly set forth during the time of the judges of Israel, even before a king had been enthroned.

Chapter 5

The King Messiah

> *They that strive with Jehovah shall be broken to pieces; against them will he thunder in heaven: Jehovah will judge the ends of the earth; and he will give strength unto his king, and exalt the horn of his anointed.*
>
> (1 Sam. 2:10; cf. vv. 1-10)

Hannah's prayerful song of praise is very significant. Her thanksgiving to God is dictated, not only by the spirit of prayer, but by the spirit of prophecy. The last word in her song is the first place in the Scriptures where the word "anointed" is used to indicate the Lord's Anointed, the Messiah, the Christ. Since there was no king in Israel at the time, it seems that the most likely interpretation is to refer "his anointed" to the Messiah.[1]

This expressive phrase, "his anointed" (the Hebrew word is *"mashiach"*), from which "Messiah" comes, is first used here in an expectant manner. In the New Testament this became both title and name for Jesus (*Christ* is the Greek term for the Hebrew *mashiach*).[2] Thus, Hannah's language seems to be a direct prediction of the appointment of a theocratic King.

There is indeed a striking resemblance between Hannah's song and that of the Virgin Mary (Luke 1:46-55). Like Mary's "Magnificat," Hannah's hymn of thanksgiving begins with the temporal mercies of God extended to her as an individual. However, she rises immediately into the realm of prophecy, foretelling the Messiah's kingdom and His attending triumphs. In this respect, the theme of both songs is one and the same; that is, they both focus on Christ, the Anointed One, and His ultimate glory as King. Then, underlying the theme is God's action in government, which raises up the meek and casts down the proud.

When we consider Hannah's song in relation to the circumstances, as well as its general nature, there are revealed at least seven significant facets:

1. *Gratitude.* Her prayer had been answered in the divine gift of a son. She thus looked from the gift to the Giver and praised Him with words of joy. So her heart rejoiced not only in the birth of Samuel, but in the Lord who had answered her prayer.

2. *Dedication.* After she had weaned the child, she gave him back to God, saying, "For this child I prayed; and Jehovah hath given me my petition which I asked of him: therefore also I have granted [lent] him to Jehovah; as long as he liveth he is granted to Jehovah" (1 Sam. 1:27-28). So doing, Hannah herself participates in the act of dedication.

3. *Triumph.* She remembers how she had been de-

livered from the scorn of her adversaries during her past barrenness.

4. *Faith.* She thus had an inner confidence in Jehovah's continued help.

5. *Patriotism.* Hannah discerned in her own individual experience the general laws of the divine economy, and its significance in relation to the entire history of the children of God in the establishment of the kingdom of God.

6. *Prophetic hope.* She beheld the dawn of a new day brought about by God's anointed King, and she was glad.

7. *Joy in the Lord.* "My heart exulteth in Jehovah" (2:1). God is the Object and Source of her joy—in communion with Him and in contemplation of His will and way.[3] She thus declares: "I rejoice in thy salvation" (2:1).

The term "salvation" (Hebrew *yeshuah,* meaning "safety, ease, salvation") is very common in the Old Testament. Its application covers a broad scope, being inclusive of deliverance from evils and a realization of good. It may be applied to an episode in personal experience, as in the case of Jacob (Gen. 49:18), of David (2 Sam. 22:47), of Job (Job 13:16), as well as of Hannah and others. Such an experience may refer to a person's reconciliation and restoration to God through the Anointed One.[4]

Again, the term "salvation" may be applied to a people's rescue from calamity and their elevation to relative influence, as when Israel was delivered from the bondage of Egypt and from the threatening waters of the Red Sea. Later, the term referred to Israel's victory over her enemies, ranging from the Philistines to the Assyrians. So throughout the Bible, *yeshuah* ("salvation") is used in many ways to indicate the help of God in achieving military or political victory, or relief from suffering or disease. However, the chief use of "salvation" is to denote deliverance from sin.[5]

Here, it seems that this episode in the life of Hannah is typical of all other salvations to be wrought by the same merciful and Almighty God. The elements of all salvations are found in the blessing granted to this "woman of sorrowful spirit" (1:15). For there was in her case, as in all, a deep human need, arising from the pressures of a heavy burden. There was apparently no realization of the end for which life was supposed to be given.

Moreover, there was utter despair of human resources for the removal of the evil and the acquisition of the good. But we see here divine energy graciously acting directly on the hidden forces by which sorrow may be overwhelmed by joy. Divine patience is evidenced as God worked out the processes by which the want and sorrow were made to pass away. At last, there is the completeness of the result in the bestowment of the very request so long desired and awaited. And with the immediate fulfillment, there was the connection of that result with an issue of broader benefit, the coming King.

This meant the employment of both visible and invisible causes throughout history in bringing about the purposes of divine mercy. Every element of salvation found reality in Hannah's experience, reflecting deliverance from trouble, in the restoration of a lost soul, in the rescue of a nation from destruction, and in the completion of the desire of those who from travail of soul peer through the ages, behold the One who is to come, and are satisfied.[6]

Indeed, salvation in every form brings joy. It is the greatest event of life. It means freedom, peace, rest, enrichment, the full favor of God. Hannah could not help but sing for joy. But we should note that her joy awakened by accomplished salvation was not a mere selfish delight in her own happiness. It was joy in Jehovah. In "thy salvation" did she rejoice. "In the Lord" was her "horn exalted."

Hannah's heart was not simply set on the bliss of Samuel's love; it rejoiced in the salvation of God. Specifically, it was joy in God saving through His anointed. It is joy to recognize God's salvation in preparation unto fulfillment.

Time of Preparation

Apparently the "promised seed," the foreordained Anointed One, was the original Source of all inspired Hebrew expectation of divine salvation. It was indeed Jehovah's founding word with regard to His plan of redemption for mankind. We have no accurate means of discerning how long the divine promise had been moving toward fulfillment. We can only say that at Hannah's point in time the process of preparation was revealed to be one step closer.

In this instance, the birth of a son, in answer to prayer and help from God, evoked Hannah's projected vision. Since it was the woman's Seed that would destroy the power of sin and the domain of Satan, it is appropriate that the Holy Spirit should now use the lips of a woman who had been humiliated to first frame the divine title, "his anointed." Thus the message of Hannah's hymn echoes forth, reminding us of a Child more holy than even Samuel.[7]

Throughout the severe but beneficial discipline of years, the spirit of Hannah had surely been trained to anticipate a salvation more perfect than what Samuel would be able to effect for Israel by a devoted judicial rule. She beheld a Child not only given of God, but sent of God. Her song of faith and fulfillment found inspiration in God's coming King. Here, the relationship to God's Messiah grows closer and clearer. The condition of sharing in Hannah's joy is twofold: (1) being a personally saved one, and (2) anticipating God's anointed, His king.[8]

Israel had no king for many years after Hannah's prophetic words were spoken. However, the idea was familiar, for the people had previously desired Gideon to become their king (Judg. 8:22). Many undoubtedly felt that their nation needed a strong centralized government, which it rarely attained under the judges. Israel fared badly for a time, not only because of their disobedience and weak leaders, but because they were surrounded by aggressive kingdoms.

Even so, God was working out the situation, even amidst the defeat of Israel by the Philistines, and the death of the judge-priest Eli and his sons. Samuel had answered the call of God early in life, and now he was to lead the people to return unto righteousness. Thus Samuel judged Israel under divine direction for a number of years. He eventually became the chief agent in establishing a line of kings.

Meanwhile, the Israelites increasingly manifested their desire for a king, because they wanted to be like all the nations (1 Sam. 8:5). So it was that "Jehovah said to Samuel, Hearken unto their voice, and make them a king" (8:22).

Samuel reluctantly obeyed the Lord and anointed Saul of Kish, a Benjamite, to be the first king of Israel. This was difficult for Samuel to accept for he was getting old and he felt that the movement for a king was a rejection of him and of his sons.

Apparently Samuel had already associated his two sons with him in judging the people. Their very names express the devotion of Samuel's heart to God: Joel means "The Lord is God," and Abiah means "The Lord is Father" (cf. 1 Chron. 6:33). Unfortunately, his sons did not live up to the hope expressed in their names (8:3), for they coveted wealth and took bribes, perverting justice. Moreover, the Scriptures further indicated that an underlying reason the people wanted a king was because they were increasingly rejecting God's rule over them (8:7). Even so, this was not to say that God did not have a king and a kingdom in mind for His people.[9]

Obviously, Hannah's prediction concerned God's King, specifically the One who had long been expected, the Lord's Anointed. As we have indicated, that expectation stemmed from the promised "seed of the woman" (Gen. 3:15); the covenant of God with Abraham (Gen. 12:1-3; 22:17-18); Jacob's vision of Shiloh, "He that is to be sent" (Gen. 49:10); Balaam's prophecy of the star that should come forth out of Jacob (Num. 24:17-19, which will be discussed in a later chapter); and the Prophet which Moses indicated God would raise up (Deut. 18:15-19).

It is evident that Hannah's unfolding prophecy was certainly not fulfilled when Saul was anointed king of Israel. The previous prediction of Jacob cited Judah to be the tribe of rulers. Thus, although Saul's reign began well, it took a disastrous turn because of his own disobedience, and it ended in his suicide and the curtailment of his royal line.

At the time of Saul's anointing by Samuel, God seemed to give approval to his coronation. However, it is evident that Israel got ahead of God's time schedule in the establishment of a kingdom. It was not until David's ultimate succession to the throne, anointed of God by Samuel out of the tribe of Judah, that we are able to detect the unreserved approval of God.

When the reign of David was established, the preceding promises and prophecies were brought into clearer focus. Yet, to a great degree, the expectation looks to an even greater King than David. It is evident that Hannah's prediction was directed toward David, but her focus beams beyond David to One greater than David, to the King Messiah. Let us therefore consider His appointment, His office, and His exaltation.

His Divine Appointment

The prophetic foresight of Hannah looked beyond the material disorder of Eli's day to an ideal king. She particularly was made aware of the fact that God is the moral sovereign of His creation, and that He specifically directs His providential acts among men with a view to establishing a kingdom of righteousness upon this earth. The government of Israel at the time of Hannah could be described as a commonwealth, so far as human administration was concerned. Yet, it had been a theocracy from the time of the exodus of the children of Israel, with the actual administration carried out through leaders such as Moses and Joshua, and through judges such as Eli and Samuel.[10]

The projected vision of Hannah now beholds a new epoch wherein she saw a king to whom Jehovah would give strength and glory as His Anointed. Certainly this was a divine appointment, for the choice was of God. Indeed, it is "His King," "His Anointed." As we have already indicated, Saul was made king after the people's heart rather than after God's heart. His disobedience eventually negated his previous divine selection and appointment.

God, the invisible King of Israel, did not relinquish His authority. He purposed to establish His kingdom on personal eminence. God found this in David and his line. There can be no doubt that Hannah's words are a prediction of God's appointment of David, whose "horn" (symbolic of strength and vigor) the Lord was to exalt, giving him a career of victory over all his enemies.[11]

However, whether or not it was clear to Hannah's mind, certainly the Spirit who inspired her prayer signified not only a King greater than David, but also a more illustrious kingdom than David's. Indeed, as Keil states:

> The anointed of the Lord, of whom Hannah prophesies in the spirit, is not one single king in Israel, either David or Christ, but an ideal king, though not a mere personification of the throne about to be established, but the actual king whom Israel received in David and the race, which culminated in the Messiah.[12]

This, then, was the divine appointment which was directed to David and his kingly line. It is confirmed and manifested by the anointing of God's Spirit. We read: "Then Samuel took the horn of oil, and anointed him in the midst of his brethren: and the Spirit of Jehovah came mightily upon David from that day forward" (1 Sam. 16: 13; cf. 2 Sam. 2:4). This "horn," or vial, of olive oil which was used for the ceremony of anointing, was a narrow-necked jar from which the oil would come in drops, sprinkling oil on the one thus anointed. Priests (Exod. 28: 41, etc.) and prophets (1 Kings 19:16) were also anointed, but the ceremony particularly applied to the installation of kings. The king was often referred to as "the Lord's anointed" (1 Sam. 16:6; 24:6).[13] The anointing with oil was thus an outward act symbolizing a divine inward endowment for a particular purpose.

In this regard, David's anointing was especially meaningful in establishing the royal line of Judah. It also established him and his progeny as the chosen king of Israel. Therefore, David's anointing dramatized the appointment of God, not only of him, but of the Messiah who was to come from his line.

The significance of David's royal authority is intensified by the anointing of God's Spirit, and by the expected coming of the Anointed One sent of God from David's seed. It was this twofold purpose of God in action that lifts the office of king from the level of common man.

His Regal Office

The general purpose of founding the office of king was to unite a divided people. This is indicated by Jacob's vision of Shiloh: "And unto him shall the gathering of the people be" (Gen. 49:10). Certainly, nothing was more desperately needed in the days of the judges.

This was especially true in Hannah's day, during the judicature of Eli, the high priest. Eli himself was a just and righteous leader. But among the priests who shared the responsibility were Eli's two sons, Hophni and Phinehas. They were notorious for their corruption and irreligion. We read: "The sin of the young men was very great before Jehovah; for the men despised the offering of Jehovah" (1 Sam. 2:17; cf. vv. 12-17, 23-25; 3:13). Since the priesthood was hereditary, it passed from father to sons without regard for proper moral character.[14]

After the judgment of the Lord upon Eli's sons, as they were slain in battle against the Philistines, and the sudden death of Eli, Samuel was recognized as prophet and judge. During Samuel's tenure in office, he was faithful unto Jehovah.

As we have already noted, there is an ironic similarity between Samuel's latter years and those of Eli. In each case, trusted sons proved untrue. There does seem to be the difference that the inspired writer nowhere suggests blame for Samuel in the waywardness of his sons. However, such defaming incidents manifested the glaring inconsistencies which seemingly called for the establishment of royalty in the interest of justice and unity.

More specifically, the office of king was founded to save the people from their enemies. As the anointed of God, the king possessed the means of salvation and deliverance. He stands as God's representative among the people. For, from his anointing, he is given a special portion of power and authority to bring about the will of God in the establishment of His kingdom on earth.

It is the regal office of the king to stand as human mediary between God and the people, exerting God-given power, wisdom, and guidance. The king leads them in worship to God, directing them according to God's will, so they may go forth as conquerors to defeat their enemies.

The ultimate purpose of the king was to exercise authority over his people in such a way as to judge them in righteousness, and to establish order, peace, and happiness before God. Thus it can be said: "The regal office of our Saviour consisteth partly in the ruling, protecting, and rewarding of his people; partly in the coercing, condemning, and destroying of his enemies."[14] Whether imperfectly or ideally, this was the proposed function of the kingly office.

However, from the time of the founding of the regal office, it was the frequent mistake of Israel throughout the successive generations to look for an outward, imposing, and worldly accomplishment, rather than an inward, moral, and spiritual fulfillment of this divine purpose. At this point, we cannot help but think of the One who came and said, "My kingdom is not of this world" (John 18:36). Further, the Apostle Paul declares, "For the kingdom of God is . . . righteousness and peace and joy in the Holy Spirit" (Rom. 14:17).

It seems apparent from the implications of the regal office that Hannah envisioned a king greater than even David. As great and good a king as David was, his kingdom was inferior and far from the ideal that is set forth in her inspired prayer. Reaching out, her faith lays hold of God, His salvation, His holiness, His knowledge, His justice, His power, His King, His Anointed (cf. 1 Sam. 2:1-10).

Undoubtedly, the short-range view beheld David as the eminent type of the kingly office. His character and accomplishments measured favorably with the expectations of the people. But the long-range view of faith must look in faith for the actual ideal, the expected Messiah, who would perfectly fulfill every purpose of the office. If we ask, "How can faith achieve such heights?" we must remember that it had been lifted by a divine and glorious answer to prayer.

His Glorious Exaltation

It is interesting to note the development of the personal life of Hannah from humiliation in her childlessness to exaltation in the son Jehovah gave her. Since God had granted her desperate request, she found firm footing to believe that He would also exalt His Anointed in due time.

So, the Expected One became a reality to Hannah, arising out of her own experience of belittling scorn and trouble. With the birth of God-given Samuel, the birth of a heaven-sent King did not seem so preposterous. Moreover, considering the power of God, the state of humiliation made a wonderful beginning for His King (cf. v. 8).

Certainly, this is typified by the lowly origin of David and his course to the throne of Israel. Jehovah's choice of a successor to Saul was to be found among the eight sons of Jesse, the Bethlehemite, of the tribe of Judah. We read that Jesse was the grandson of Boaz and Ruth the Moabitess (Ruth 4:17).

It is also interesting to note that the mother of Boaz was likewise from outside the tribes of Israel. She was Rahab of Jericho, who was saved from the inhabitants for sheltering the spies of Israel. Matthew notes her place in his listing of the genealogy of Jesus (Matt. 1:5).

When Samuel, the servant of God, went to the household of Jesse to anoint God's choice to be king, he went looking for a son with regal bearing. The prophet was soon reminded that "the Lord seeth not as man seeth; for man looketh on the outward appearance, but the Lord looketh on the heart" (1 Sam. 16:7, KJV). After viewing the seven outstanding sons of Jesse without finding God's choice, Samuel learned that the youngest was still out tending the sheep. This was a menial task assigned to the least important son or servant of the household.[15]

However, even from the time Samuel anointed David "in the midst of his brethren" (v. 13), the course to the throne was trying and humiliating. Aside from his occasional personal victories, such as slaying the Philistine giant, Goliath, David had to live in the shadow of King Saul. Saul still ruled for several years after God had rejected him for his disobedience.

In fact, near the end of Saul's reign, David had to live as a hunted outlaw, fleeing from Saul and his armies, to save his life. David actually sought and found sanctuary among the Philistines, a noted enemy of Israel, for a period of one year and four months (1 Sam. 27:7). Then, after Saul's suicide on the battlefield, David was finally crowned king over the tribe of Judah. It was not until seven and a half years later that David was anointed to be king over all Israel.

We must admit that David's rise from humiliation to exaltation was sometimes spectacular and sometimes discouraging. The important thing to remember, as Hannah indicated, was that the king's exaltation would be by the right hand of God, for "he will give strength unto his king" (2:10).

We are reminded of the words of Christ, "All power is given unto me in heaven and in earth" (Matt. 28:18). From our privileged viewpoint, this was exhibited in His resurrection and ascension and His continued possession of supreme honor, authority, and power in the universe.

Finally, as the type of the "King Messiah," David is

100

assured of a universal and everlasting kingdom. Jehovah shall "exalt the horn of his anointed" (v. 10). As the type of the ideal king, as God's chosen and Anointed One for a point in time, David shares the exaltation of the Ideal King, the Anointed One sent from God. Yet David himself is made to realize that One from his line is to come after him to truly establish an everlasting kingdom that would include all peoples.

In this vein, Keil very aptly states:

> The exaltation of the horn of the anointed of Jehovah commenced with the victorious and splendid expansion of the power of David, was repeated with every victory over the enemies of God and his kingdom gained by the successive kings of David's house, goes on in the advancing spread of the kingdom of Christ, and will eventually attain to its eternal consummation in the judgment of the last day, through which all the enemies of Christ will be made his footstool.[16]

Indeed, the exaltation of Jehovah's "anointed" is open-ended. That is to say, there is no suggested point of termination. Rather, as the saying goes: "The future is as bright as the promises of God." So far as Hannah was concerned, the future could not look brighter. She was inspired to expect the ultimate from her God. We cannot say that it was any more strain on her faith to look for the Messiah sent from God than to expect God to answer her prayer and give her a son. Thus, she dared to look for royalty sent of God.

Certainly, Hannah's viewpoint was of no private interpretation. As we shall see, it was shared by none other than King David himself. It seems that at this stage in man's history, the Old Testament expectation of a coming king might very well be duplicated by our faith looking for the coming King of Kings. As their faith became verified, so shall ours be, in the eventual fulfillment of promise.

101

Chapter 6

The Everlasting Kingdom

I have found David my servant; with my holy oil have I anointed him.

But my faithfulness and my loving-kindness shall be with him; and in my name shall his horn be exalted.

I also will make him my firstborn, the highest of the kings of the earth.

His seed also will I make to endure for ever, and his throne as the days of heaven.

(Ps. 89:20, 24, 27, 29)

And thy house and thy kingdom shall be made sure for ever before thee: thy throne shall be established for ever.

(2 Sam. 7:16; cf. vv. 4-17)

At first, it seemed that Jacob's prophecy concerning the rulership of the tribe of Judah was in error. Saul, a Benjamite, was anointed and crowned the first king of Israel. Moreover, it also seemed that Hannah's prediction concerning God's anointed was rather presumptuous.

King Saul became a tragic disappointment. He led the people into disobedience, and then he took his own life on the battlefield to avoid humiliation and defeat by the Philistines. Also, three of his sons—Jonathan, the heir apparent, along with Abinadab and Malchishua—were killed in that conflict at Gilboa. Thus, a series of sad events mark the end of the reign of Saul, which is believed to have lasted 40 years.[1]

Following the catastrophe to the ruling line of Saul at Gilboa, the tribe of Judah gathered at the "fourfold city" of Hebron and "anointed David king over the house of Judah" (2 Sam. 2:4).

The remaining 11 tribes maintained their loyalty to the family of Saul, making his fourth son, Ishbosheth, to be their king. There was a time of armed conflict between Ishbosheth's forces, led by Abner, and David's army, captained by Joab. The men of David were victorious, but there was no move to overthrow Ishbosheth. His reign was abruptly ended within two years by his murder, committed by two of his father's company commanders, Baanah and Rechab. Even so, David apparently did not become king over all Israel for another five and one-half years (cf. 2 Samuel 2—5).

For all practical purposes, the royalty of Saul's house lasted only one generation, ending with his and Jonathan's death. Although Jonathan left a son, Mephibosheth, no one seemed to look upon him as having any title to the throne of Israel. Thus, after David had ruled over the tribe of Judah for seven and one-half years, all the elders of Israel came to David at Hebron, and they anointed him to be king over all the tribes of Israel (cf. 2 Sam. 5:3).

According to the New Testament, 10 generations

passed from Jacob to Jesse, the father of David. Hence, the covenant of redemption proceeded from Jacob, to Judah, to Phares, to Esrom, to Aram, to Aminadab, to Naasson, to Salmon, to Boaz, to Obed, to Jesse, and thence to David (cf. Matt. 1:2-6). Throughout the intervening generations, God had not forgotten His sure word of prophecy to Jacob.

So, in David, the promise of Shiloh is established; the living covenant remains activated; and the prophecy of Jacob, with regard to Judah, is verified. Moreover, Hannah's hope of God's Anointed One was certainly typified. From the first time we hear of David, it is evident that he is approved of Jehovah to carry the divine blessing which King Saul had spurned through disobedience.

Even before Saul's death, Samuel, the prophet of the Lord, is divinely ordered to forget Saul and his household, and to anoint David to be the next king of Israel (cf. 1 Sam. 16:13). Consequently, in spite of Saul's attempts to kill him, David received the divine seal of heir apparent to the throne of Israel some years before he was actually crowned king. There can be no doubt that David's ascension to the throne of God's chosen people was through the movement of divine purpose.

Eventually, every obstacle was overcome, and David became king over all Israel, reuniting a divided people. Their plight required him to lead the people into numerous battles to defeat their enemies, so that Israel might be preserved as a nation. For instance, David's first expedition was to conquer the Philistines and recapture the ark of the covenant lost at Gilboa. Then he struck the Moabites, and thence turned north to the Aramaen kingdom of Zobah. Next came the Ammonites, the Amalekites, and the Syrians (cf. 2 Samuel 8).

Most of the 33 years David reigned as king over all Israel were spent in fighting wars that would broaden and establish the boundaries of the kingdom. At last, the land God had promised to Abraham, Isaac, and Jacob, their forefathers, was being actually taken for their rightful inheritance. The conquest of Canaan had begun under the leadership of Joshua around 400 years before. That which had seemed so impossible was now brought into fruition.

During David's prosperous reign, he also built a city for his servants and a fine palace for himself. His royal dwelling of hewn cedar logs was indeed a marvel to his people who still lived chiefly in tents. When, at last, a time of peace prevailed, David had opportunity to consider the building of a fit house for the Lord. Up to this time, the ark of God was kept within the tentlike structure of the Tabernacle.

David made a proposal to Nathan, the prophet of God, that he would honor God by building a permanent dwelling for the ark of God. Nathan gave immediate approval to David's plan to build a temple of worship because the king's purpose seemed appropriate. However, God did not approve. Soon the clear message of God came that David was not to build Him a house, but that the Lord would build David a royal house of exceptional characteristics (cf. 2 Sam. 7:11).

According to the specifications of this divine promise to David, it not only speaks of a royal house, but of One having royal authority, and of One whose kingdom would be established forever. This personage must be understood to be a man, of the line of David—yet also of Jehovah. The Messiah, coming from David's progeny, to reign forever, must also be God. David was certainly impressed by this far-reaching extent as he contemplated the implications of the divine message through Nathan the prophet (2 Sam. 7:4-17).[2]

Adam Clarke emphatically states that the seventh

chapter of 2 Samuel is one of the most important passages in the Old Testament. As we have previously noted, a comparable promise given to Abraham concerning the divine blessing extended through the coming Messiah is recorded in the account of Abraham's life (Gen. 12:1-3; 22:17-18).

Since David's life is given in more detail than any other person in the Old Testament, a similar promise would be expected, especially if the Anointed One were to descend from David. Thus, Clarke's point is that if there be record of such a promise to David, it must be recorded in this chapter containing God's word given through Nathan to David. But, as Clarke sees it, the promise has largely been missed because of the improper translation of several key verses.[3]

Three reasons have been given by some to indicate that the promise of a Messiah could not be included in Nathan's prophecy: (1) Because, in verse 10, Nathan speaks of the future prosperity of the Jews as being fixed afterwards, which circumstances are totally repugnant to the Jews. (2) Because the son promised here (v. 13) was to "build a house," which house is presumed to mean the temple of Solomon—and that being the case, Solomon must be the son herein promised. (3) Because verse 14 supposes that this son might "commit iniquity," which could not be supposed of the Messiah.[4]

In support of his premise that Christ is promised here, Clarke maintains that the first of the objections is founded on the faulty translation of verse 10, where the words should be expressed as relating to the time, past or present. Certainly, the prophet is declaring what great things God had already done for David and his people; that He had raised David from the sheepfold to the throne; and that He had planted the Israelites in a place of rest and safety from all those enemies who had so often before afflicted them. Thus, the proper translation should be:

> I took thee from the sheepcote; and have made thee a great name; and I HAVE APPOINTED a place for my people Israel; and HAVE PLANTED them, that they may dwell in a place of their own, and move no more. Neither DO the children of wickedness afflict them any more; as before-time, and as since the time that I commanded judges to be over Israel: and I HAVE CAUSED thee to rest from all thine enemies. Moreover, Jehovah telleth thee that Jehovah will make thee a house (2 Sam. 7:8-11).[5]

The second objection is said to be founded on a mistake in the sense. Indeed, David had proposed to build a house for God, which God did not permit. But God was pleased to reward the piety of David's intention by promising that He would make a house for David. This was not to be a material house, but a spiritual house, or family, to be raised up for the honor of God and the salvation of mankind. It was to be built of God by David's seed, and this seed was to be raised up *after* David slept with his fathers. This would seem to exclude Solomon, who was set up and placed on the throne *before* David's death. Thus, this building promised by God was to be erected by one of David's descendants, who was also to be an everlasting King. Both the house and the kingdom were to be established forever (v. 13).[6]

The interpretation that this house or spiritual building was to be set up, together with a kingdom, by the Messiah, seems to be clearly supported by the prophet Zechariah, who writes:

> Behold the man whose name is The Branch; HE SHALL BUILD THE TEMPLE of the Lord: Even HE SHALL BUILD THE TEMPLE of the Lord; and he shall bear the glory, and shall sit and rule upon his THRONE (Zech. 6:12-13).[7]

107

Thus, following Clarke's lead and the apparent direction of the Scriptures, we shall give appropriate consideration to the royal house, the royal authority, and the extended reign which is indicated through Nathan the prophet.

A Royal House

How else could David's house really achieve royal character, if not that its rule was by divine choice and approval? God had raised David from the very low and menial position of the shepherd. As we have already noted, tending the sheep was either given to the servants or as an unwanted responsibility that was passed to the youngest son. Although there was some dignity to this necessary occupation, there certainly was no social standing derived from sheepherding.

Besides elevating him from the shepherd's watch to the throne, God gave David success and victory over all his enemies. We read of the divine partnership with David, as follows:

> And I have been with thee whithersoever thou wentest, and have cut off all thine enemies from before thee; and I will make thee a great name like unto the name of the great ones that are in the earth (2 Sam. 7:9).[8]

Thus, in establishing David on the throne, Jehovah preserved him from the treachery of personal enemies as well as from the opposing forces that stood in the way of the settlement and advancement of Israel as a nation. God not only crowned David with power and dominion in Israel, but He also gave him honor and reputation among all of the other nations. Indeed, as the scripture says, God gave David a great name. He became famous for his courage, his conduct, his prosperity, and his many achievements. David was perhaps the subject of national conversation as much as other men of his day among the nations.

But the promise is beamed beyond David. A blessed establishment is promised to God's chosen people through David. Because of his righteous reign, Israel is given an appointed place, and they are to enjoy peace from their enemies (cf. 7:10-11). It is in this connection that God promises David that He will make him a house.

Not only did God make a great name for David, He further promises him a royal house to support his name across the generations to come. Certainly, to receive the assurance of divine promise that his family would flourish after his death was of great satisfaction to David even while he lived.

Perhaps a portion of promise does apply to Solomon, David's son and immediate successor. However, the emphasis seems to be upon the continuing royal line of Judah through David. The words "I will set up thy seed after thee" (7:12) indicate the continuing favor of God upon David's line. This was much more extensive than Moses, Joshua, any of the judges, or King Saul had received of God. Then the further statement "I will establish his kingdom . . . the throne of his kingdom" declares that the title of David's successive sons to inherit the kingdom would be clear and uncontested. It thus confirms the certain interest and steady administration of his house for all time to come.

In the immediate sense, it appears God would employ Solomon in the important, sacred work of building the Temple, the house of the Lord. David had only the satisfaction of planning and designing it, knowing that God spoke of his successor by the words "He shall build a house for my name" (7:13). In view of Clarke's comments, we are made aware of the distinct possibility that this does not refer to Solomon in the ultimate sense, but rather to "The Branch," as Zechariah identifies him.

We must admit, however, that Solomon did fulfill his father's dream and built the Temple during his reign. It would thus seem that one is faced with a choice of three possibilities of interpretation: (1) That the prophecy refers only to Solomon, (2) That the prophecy refers only to the Anointed One to come, or (3) That the prophecy bears a double meaning, both contemporary and future—to that day when it was delivered to David and the future fulfillment.

It would indeed seem that Solomon is included as an adopted son of God, as a part of the covenant: "I will be his father, and he shall be my son" (7:14). Also, God apparently declares that He would not disinherit him even though he committed iniquity (according to the usual translation): "If he commit iniquity, I will chasten him. . . . But my mercy shall not depart away from him" (7:14-15). One would expect such typical mercy of a loving father when dealing with the inheritance of a wayward son.

If we take the son spoken of here to be Solomon, the record is that he did commit iniquity. He took 700 foreign wives and 300 concubines, who eventually turned his heart to other gods (cf. 1 Kings 11:1-8).

The revolt of 10 of the tribes from the house of David was apparently the correction for his sins. But the continued adherence of the tribes of Benjamin and Judah to the family of David maintained the royal dignity of his house.

It seems evident that the mercy and blessing of God were perpetuated to the descendants of David in such a manner as to uphold the divine promise. Although David's line was cut short because of disobedience, it was never cut off as was the house of Saul. No other family held the ruling sceptre of Judah except the royal house of David.

Certainly, royalty in this sense means not only to rule in power and authority, but it presupposes the God-given right of the house of David to reign over God's chosen people in unbroken succession.

On the other hand, Adam Clarke rejects such an interpretation that would identify the son (in 7:14) as Solomon. In answer to the third objection previously raised with regard to the possibility of Nathan's prophecy being Messianic (that the son in verse 14 could not be the Messiah because he might "commit iniquity"), Clarke suggests what he believes to be a more correct translation of the verse. He believes that the Hebrew words do not necessarily signify what is given in English. He indicates that a verb, which in the active voice signifies "to commit iniquity," may, in the passive, signify "to suffer for iniquity." Hence, nouns from such verbs sometimes signify iniquity, sometimes punishment. Clarke chooses to adopt the latter; for the Messiah, who is possibly spoken of in this passage, will be made more manifest if this verse is translated:

> I will be his father, and he shall be my son: EVEN IN HIS SUFFERING FOR INIQUITY, I shall chasten him with the rod of men, [with the rod due to men], and with the stripes [due to] the children of Adam (2 Sam. 7:14).[9]

This interpretation is supported by Isa. 53:4-5, and an analogy may be constructed as follows:

> He hath carried our sorrows [i.e., the sorrows due to us, and which we must otherwise have suffered], he was wounded for our transgression, he was bruised for our iniquities: the chastisement of our peace was upon him; and with his stripes we are healed.

One could thus say that God declares himself the Father of the Son herein described (cf. Heb. 1:5). He promises that even amidst the sufferings of this Son (for the sins of others, not for his own), His mercy should still attend Him,

111

nor should His favor ever be removed from this king, as it had been from Saul. It therefore follows: "Thine house [O David] and thy kingdom shall, in Messiah, be established for ever before ME [before God]; thy throne shall be established for ever" (cf. 7:16).[10] Obviously, nothing could be established forever in the presence of David, but only in the presence of God.

Whether we agree with Clarke or not, it is evident that the royalty of David's line would, for the most part, be sadly lacking in the necessary character and personality without the promise of God. Moreover, it seems that the promise extended to David and his family should include not only the immediate son of David, but especially the Son of God born through David's line. It is on this basis that the house of David is given genuine royalty, elevating it far above the humanly assumed royalty.

Thus, the unending establishment of David's house, his kingdom, and his throne (cf. 7:16) expressly apply the promise of God to the expected Son that is to be sent within the family of David. Once again it indicates the dependency of humanity upon the intervention of God to resolve man's helpless situation. Any such lesser interpretation of the promise curtails and limits it to the swiftly passing temporal which holds little meaning.

A Royal Authority

From the divine right of David's house to reign, there would flow royal authority as God was obeyed. Because the word of God was obeyed, such royalty was projected on the basis of the eventual divine interjection of the expected Son. It was this projection which intensifies the authority of David's kingdom.

The promises of God to David were not made merely on the grounds of his personal qualifications, but they pointed to One that was to come, of the lineage of David, in whom they would have their full accomplishment. David therefore ascribes all of his blessings to the free grace of God (cf. 7:21), both the great things God had done for him and the wondrous things God had made known unto him. There can be no mistake with regard to the special purpose God had for David.

All of David's multiplied success and authority was "for thy word's sake," that is, for the sake of the expected Christ, the Eternal Word that was to be revealed. The merit of David's ruling power depended heavily upon the divine authority that was made manifest. God's gracious condescension to him, and the honor He bestowed unto him, gave the throne of David majesty and dominion over the people. David wisely recognized the goodness of God, rejoicing in the revelation of His glory throughout the years of his reign.

As far as David was concerned, there was none among the gods of the other nations to be compared with Jehovah. Likewise, there was none among the nations to be compared to Israel (cf. 7:23-24). These truths were expressed because of the mighty works of God in establishing Israel as a prosperous nation, even from their deliverance away from Egyptian enslavement. None had been able to withstand their conquest of the Land of Promise. God had made a covenant with them, that Israel would be a people unto Him, and He would be a God unto them.

Furthermore, God had not only made a covenant with Israel, but He also made a personal covenant with David, His chosen servant. "I have made a covenant with my chosen, I have sworn unto David my servant: Thy seed will I establish for ever, and build up thy throne to all generations" (Ps. 89:3-4). Above all else, this was a covenant of royal authority.

Thus David, as the father of the ruling family, is

recognized as the progenitor of the Christ who was to come in fulfillment of God's covenant of grace. Even though David would not live to see this day, royal authority nevertheless enjoins his reign and his house. Since God had chosen him, He will not ever reject His own chosen servant.

It is therefore David's own relationship to God which elevates his family, and which validates his authority. The "Holy One" to come from David's seed maintains the faltering honor of David's name and of God's selection. This was accomplished in spite of the intervals of iniquity of various other disobedient descendants. It was because of David's personal obedience and submission to God that he was appointed the viceroy of the Messiah. And it is in and through the name of the Lord that the quality of David's reign is exalted above all the kingdoms of the earth (cf. Ps. 89:24).

Just as David was a king of God's own choosing, so is the Christ, and thus both are called God's kings (cf. Ps. 2:6). Although David was chosen out of the common people, and not from among the princes, God exalted him. He laid divine help and wisdom upon David amidst the troubles and trials of his life, preserving him for the appointed position.

God eventually directed Samuel to anoint David for kingship before the throne of Saul was vacant and that ruling family was publicly denied. Thus, David rose to his office as a man of might and courage, discerning in business, to establish Israel, God's chosen people, as a nation among nations.

The attending authority of God's choice and anointing, however, is not significantly applied to David alone. It especially anticipates the Christ, the Anointed One to come. He is the One not only chosen but sent of God. He is the One who is truly mighty, who is perfectly qualified in every way for the unique work of deliverance and salvation He was to undertake. He is mighty in strength, for He is the Son of the Lord God omnipotent. He is mighty in love, for His mercy changes never, and His compassion flows from the experience of His kinship to mankind.

The Christ, the Expected One, is also chosen out of the people, as one of us all, bone of our bone, taking part with us of flesh and blood. He is a Saviour of God's own providing, for the salvation of mankind from sin is only the Lord's doing, from beginning to end. God has therefore laid help upon Him—not merely helped Him, but treasured help *in* Him for every man. It is laid upon Him as a charge to restore the fallen human race, to return them unto the kingdom of God. As Hosea 13:9 infers, God says, "In Me is thy help."

Furthermore, God has exalted the Anointed One by constituting Him as the Prophet, the Priest, and the King of His people. He is clothed with power to establish a holy race of people. In this manner, God has set Him apart and qualified Him for His office, confirming Him in it by His Holy Spirit. This He has done without measure, raising Him infinitely and divinely above His fellowmen. Thus, the Holy One that is to be sent is properly called the Anointed One, the Messiah, the Christ.

In all of this, God purposed the Anointed One to be His own Servant for the accomplishment of His eternal will and for the advancement of the interests of His kingdom among men. Hence, the promises are made to this "chosen one," to David in type, and to the Son of David, the Holy One, in antitype. Because of this close relationship, the royal authority of David's throne is couched in the promises of God, both to David, and to the expected "firstborn" of God (cf. Ps. 89:26-27).

In view of the changeless, enduring covenant of God with David, and with his Son, we are able to trace the continuing royalty of David's house and the extended authority of his reign beyond the bounds of time. Without the timeless nature of the promised kingdom, both the royalty of David's house and the royalty of his authority would have faded into forgotten history long ago. However, the hope attending the kingdom established by David is consummated by the projection of an extended reign. It depends, not upon the long life of David, but rather upon the faithfulness of the promise of God.

An Extended Reign

David's house, his authority, and his kingdom have long since come to an end in human strength and length of years. Actually, there were 18 kings of David's line, but four names were blotted out according to the judgment recorded in the Book of Law (cf. Deut. 29:18-20). The four kings who were unacceptable to God were : Ahaziah, Joash, Amaziah, and Jehoiakim.

However, there are 14 kings who represent David's royal house and the extent of his family reign—except for the Anointed One. They are: Solomon, Rehoboam, Abijam, Asa, Jehoshaphat, Joram, Uzziah, Jotham, Ahaz, Hezekiah, Manasseh, Amon, Josiah, and Jehoiachin (or Jechonias).

During the fourth year of Jehoiakim's reign, Jerusalem was besieged by the Babylonians. But according to the recognition of King Nebuchadnezzar, Jehoiachin, Jehoiakim's son, was Judah's king from the age of eight through his eighteenth year. (This was also according to the recognition of God.) Jehoiachin was taken captive to Babylon along with many of the people of Judah, around 600 B.C.

Then Zedekiah, an uncle of Nebuchadnezzar, was imposed as king of Judah. He ruled for about 10 years, but he was deposed following rebellion against Nebuchadnezzar (cf. 2 Kings 24—25). Thus, Zedekiah and the later period of Herodian kings were imposters. David's line had come to a tragic end with Jehoiachin—until the Christ should come and reestablish the kingdom.

Despite the projected termination of David's family reign, the Psalmist records the timeless nature of the promised kingdom. We note the amazing word of God to David:

> *My mercy will I keep for him for evermore; and my covenant shall stand fast with him. His seed also will I make to endure for ever, and his throne as the days of heaven. . . . It shall be established for ever as the moon, and as a faithful witness in heaven. Selah* (Ps. 89:28-29, 37, KJV).

Certainly, the continuation of David's house, his throne, and his kingdom "for ever" (cf. 2 Sam. 7:13-16), relies upon the One to be sent of God through David's line. It seems apparent that the royalty, the authority, and the duration of the kingdom is not merely of David, but it is of God. It is actually God using and blessing the house of David until men of every point in time shall be blessed.

Except for the expected Son sent of God, the reign of David's house would not only have been interrupted, it would have also suffered the bitter, irrevocable end of displeasing God. In view of the Great Expectation, it is not merely David's kingdom that is extended to everlastingness. Ultimately, it is the Messiah's kingdom, established in direct succession from David's line.

Adam Clarke, considering the reign of David's house "for ever," as prophesied in both Ps. 89:29 and 2 Sam. 7:16, points out an interesting comparison. The angel, delivering his message to the virgin mother (Luke 1:32-33), speaks as if he were quoting from these very prophecies: "The Lord God shall give unto him the throne of his father David, and he shall reign over the house of Jacob FOR EVER: and of his kingdom there shall be no end."[11]

It would seem that if these important verses of scripture, along with numerous others, are to have any cohesive credence, we must assume that they indicate a valid promise made to David. Also, it seems evident that neither the glories of Solomon's reign nor any other individual of David's ruling house can meet the qualifications specified by the promise. The promise and expectation is that from his seed the Messiah should be born and become the everlasting king.

However, according to 2 Sam. 7:14, it would seem that the son might "commit iniquity." But if the Messiah is the Person referred to here, it must indicate His innocent suffering for the sins of others. On the other hand, we are well aware of the sin of Solomon, the son immediately succeeding David to the throne.

In any event, this cannot be a prophecy admitting a double sense, applied to two opposite characters. As the question was put by the Ethiopian treasurer with regard to the writings of Isaiah, we may also ask: "Of whom speaketh the prophet this? of himself, or of some other?" (Acts 8:34). Philip showed him that the person was Jesus only. So it may be asked here, "Of whom speaketh the prophet Nathan this? of Solomon, or of Christ?"

Adam Clarke states that the preceding question must be answered, "Of Christ." He suggests two reasons: (1) Because the description does not agree to the character of Solomon. Therefore, if Solomon is excluded in the single sense, he must also be excluded from a double meaning. (2) Since it would be held absurd to consider the promise of the Messiah made to Abraham as relating to any other person besides the Messiah, it is also equally absurd to give a double sense to the promise here to David.[12]

Furthermore, it may well be noted that from David's

response to God, after receiving the message by Nathan, David plainly understood the Son promised was the Messiah. It was in Him that his house was to be established forever. David sat before Jehovah and said:

> Who am I, O Lord Jehovah, and what is my house, that thou hast brought me thus far? And this was yet a small thing in thine eyes, O Lord Jehovah; but thou hast spoken also of thy servant's house for a great while to come; and this too after the manner of men [or, and is this the law of man?], O Lord Jehovah! (7:18-19).

Clarke says of the latter portion that the Hebrew literally signifies, "And this is [or must be] the law of the man, or of the Adam." That is, this promise thus relates to the law or ordinance made by God to Adam concerning "the seed of the woman." Such an interpretation seems even more evident by a comparison with a parallel passage in 1 Chron. 17:17, where the words of David are translated: "And thou hast regarded me according to the estate of a man of high degree." Again, Clarke says the literal translation should be: "And thou hast regarded me according to the order of the ADAM THAT IS FUTURE, OR THE MAN THAT IS FROM ABOVE."[13]

Whether we agree or disagree with Adam Clarke's translation of these verses of scripture, it still seems we may well conclude that David did indeed follow the faith of the patriarchs of Israel. His conception of the divine promise certainly expected divine intervention to establish his house forever. This could only mean the birth of a heaven-sent king, the King of everlasting reign. Yet, this Son of David was not only to be King; He was also the Son of God, sent to be the Saviour of the world.

David's acceptance of the full counsel of God opened the gates of eternity to the honor and exaltation of his family line, even to the timeless extension of his kingdom. Thus, David recognized that from his line the promised Messiah would come, and He would be the spiritual and triumphant King for ever and ever. That this is indeed David's clear realization is definitely affirmed by Peter in his sermon on the Day of Pentecost:

> Brethren, I may say unto you freely of the patriarch David, that he both died and was buried, and his tomb is with us unto this day. Being therefore a prophet, and knowing that God had sworn with an oath to him, that of the fruit of his loins he would set one upon his throne; he foreseeing this spake of the resurrection of the Christ (Acts 2:29-31).

Therefore, in accordance with the broad testimony of the Scriptures, it seems that we can scarcely be wrong in the conviction that these promises pointed on to the establishment of the kingdom of Christ, rather than to the reign of Solomon and his immediate successors. It is obvious that the promise of an extended reign was not given to David simply because he deserved it. Rather, it was given because of the Anointed One who was to come from his line, sent of God. So, even though we admit no direct reference to the Messiah in David's words here (2 Samuel 7), his writings in the Psalms verify that he did connect the duration of his house with the Messiah's advent.[14]

At this point, we may well consider that the Messiah's coming is still the Great Expectation. He is still the coming King. Although the Christ was born into this world according to prophecy, that which has regard to His everlasting reign is yet to be fulfilled. In many respects it seems as though David's vision was better than our closer viewpoint. He saw the Anointed One coming as the Ideal King, whereas, all too often, we look for no king at all.

Chapter 7

The Ideal King

> The kings of the earth set themselves,
> and the rulers take counsel together,
> against Jehovah, and against his anointed.
> . . .
> Yet I have set my king upon my holy
> hill of Zion.
> I will tell of the decree Jehovah said
> unto me, Thou art my son; this day have I
> begotten thee.
> Jehovah saith unto my Lord, Sit thou
> at my right hand, until I make thine
> enemies thy footstool.
>
> (Ps. 2:2, 6-7; 110:1)

Following the promise of God to David that his throne
should be established forever (2 Sam. 7:16), the questions

arise: To what extent did David and the people recognize the necessity of the coming of God's Anointed One? To what extent did they expect an ideal King, one greater than David or any other man?

We can only surmise with regard to the degree of expectation of the people of Israel in general. However, as we have previously indicated, and as our textual reading confirms, David gives certain testimony in the Psalms concerning his own personal expectation.

In the Book of Psalms there are a number of references which are Messianic in character. A specific group of psalms are classified as definitely prophetic or Messianic in content, namely: 2; 16; 22; 24; 40; 68; 69; 72; 89; 97; 101; 110; 118; and 144.[1] Of these, 16; 22; 24; 40; 68; 69; 101; 110; and 144 are believed to have been written by David. Psalm 2 is listed as anonymous, but it is definitely Davidic. Psalm 45 is ascribed to Korah, and Psalm 72 to Solomon. Psalm 89 is credited to either Moses or Ethan, and Psalms 97 and 118 are anonymous.

Not all scholars attach prophetic or Messianic significance to these and other passages in the Psalms. To them, they do not speak of a future, much less of a Messiah, but only of the contemporary, earthly king of David's line who has just been enthroned. Some of the Psalms could have been used in an enthronement ceremony, so liberal scholars hold that such "royal" psalms, if they may be applied to Christ at all, can be so only by typological interpretation and not because they are directly Christological or Messianic prophecies.[2]

Such scholars generally theorize that the Messianic hope of Israel grew out of their patriotic longing for the establishment of their earthly kingdom (under the rule of God's anointed king). Then, when that kingdom fell, the hope embraced the restoration of an earthly sovereign blessed of God. But such a restoration from captivity and dispersion seemed to be improbable in the foreseeable future, so the coming Messiah's kingdom was projected into a more distant time.

However, it seems that such a theory ignores the concerted Old Testament vision of the nature of God's kingdom. It was not only to be physical, but also ethical and spiritual, established over all the earth, benefiting all nations.

Only in God's kingdom can there be any hope for man, for only God can break the deadly cycle of sin, judgment, redemption, and sin again. So, the expectation of the Anointed One is more than the extension of nationalistic dreams. It is a true grasp of the intended kingdom of God.

It may be further stated that the New Testament persistently relates numerous psalms to Christ, particularly Psalms 2; 16; 22; 40; and 110. Moreover, it is purely hypothetical to suppose that any of these "royal" psalms were actually used in annual enthronement festivals in Israel. No such festival is known from any source other than these psalms, or a supposed parallel with Babylonian customs.[3]

We would readily concede that the royal psalms may have had an immediate occasion in the life of David or some other Israelite king. But as Samuel A. Cartledge points out: "At times a Psalm relating to one of the natural kings shades into a description of the King of kings; at times a description of contemporary blessedness leads to a description of the greater bliss of the times of the Messiah." Also, Harold H. Rowley says of such psalms: "They held before the king the ideal king, both as his inspiration and guide for the present, and as the hope of the future."[4]

Thus, in turning to the Psalms, we see a body of revelation which seems to indicate a second period of Messianic prophecy, including the time of David. (The earlier time of the patriarchs would represent the first period of prophecy, some of which we have considered in the previous chapters.)

This prophetic element in the Psalter cannot be seriously called into question, for, as Wescott says,

> A Divine counsel was wrought out in the course of the life of Israel. We are allowed to see in "the people of God" signs of the purpose of God for humanity. Their whole history is prophetic. It is not enough to recognize that the Old Testament contains prophecies; the Old Testament is one vast prophecy.[5]

As W. G. Scroggie indicates, there are three strands of prophecy which are woven to form the web of Hebrew prophecy. They are the strands which speak of the Messiah, of Israel, and of the Gentiles. All three are found in the Psalms, and it is evident that they are all vitally related to one another. God's Messiah is the hope of the world, and Israel is the medium of the divine revelation and mission, "the instrument for accomplishing the world-wide extension of His Kingdom." Thus, the time is predicted when all nations shall acknowledge the Messiah's sovereignty (Ps. 22:27; 65:2; 66:4; 68:29-33; 86:9; 102:15, 22; 138:4).[6]

Whatever may be one's view of the Messianic kingdom of the future, whether it be regarded as visible, or only as spiritual, there is ample evidence that Israel, through whom Christ came, and from whom we have received the Bible, was chosen of God for its realization. There is every indication in the Scriptures that this race has been preserved of God for the fulfillment of the Abrahamic Covenant (Psalms 68; 88; 96—98; 102:13-16). Such passages certainly imply Israel's own restoration and felicity in the future, of which Psalm 126 especially points beyond any past fulfillment.[7]

But pointing further than the prophecies concerning Israel and the Gentiles are the specific prophecies with regard to the person of the Messiah. The Psalter is full of them. We have Jesus Christ's own warrant for looking for Him in the Psalms. He said, "All things must be fulfilled which were written . . . in the Psalms concerning me" (Luke 24:44). On several occasions our Lord interpreted himself into various passages of the Psalter. For instance, compare Ps. 118:22, "The stone which the builders rejected is become the head of the corner," with Jesus' usage of it in Matt. 21:42 (cf. Ps. 110:1 and Matt. 22:42-45).

Also, the apostles interpreted Christ in the Psalms. Compare Acts 4:11, "He is the stone which was set at nought of you the builders, which was made the head of the corner," again with Ps. 118:22 (cf. 1 Pet. 2:1-7). Compare Matt. 13:35, "That it might be fulfilled which was spoken through the prophet, saying, I will open my mouth in parables; I will utter things hidden from the foundation of the world," with Ps. 78:2 *(et al.)*, "I will open my mouth in a parable; I will utter dark sayings of old." Then compare the zeal spoken of in John 2:17 with that found in Ps. 69:9.[8]

The Messianic reference in some of the Psalms may be rather obvious to all who read and who thus interpret. However, there are numerous other references which are not as evident, but which the New Testament regards as Messianic. They clearly look beyond David and point to One anointed of God that had thus come from David. The inferred characteristics of the promised Messiah are claimed to be fulfilled in Christ.

For instance, the following references tell of: Christ's manhood, Ps. 8:4-5 (Heb. 2:6-8); His sonship, Ps. 2:7 (Heb. 1:8); His holiness, Ps. 45:7; 89:18-19 (Heb. 1:9); His priesthood, Ps. 110:4 (Heb. 5:6); His kingship, Ps. 2:6; 89:18-19, 27 (Acts 5:31; Rev. 19:16); His conquests, Ps. 110:5-6 (Rev. 6:17); His eternity, Ps. 45:17; 61:6-7; 72:17; 102:25-27 (Heb. 1:10); His universal sovereignty, Ps. 72:8;

125

103:19 (Rev. 19:16); His obedience, Ps. 40:6-8 (Heb. 10:5-7), His zeal, Ps. 69:9 (John 2:17); His sufferings, Ps. 69:9 (Rom. 15:3); His betrayal, Ps. 41:9 (Luke 22:48); His death, Ps. 22:1-2 (cf. all the Gospels); His resurrection, Ps. 2:7; 16:10 (Acts 13:33-36); His ascension, Ps. 68:18 (Eph. 4:8); and His coming again to judge, Psalms 96—98 (2 Thess. 1:7-9).

These and other such references may, of course, be classified otherwise. But, in the main, these passages are Messianic prophecies which tell of Christ's person, God and man combined; of His character (righteous and holy altogether); of His work, death, and resurrection; and of His offices (Prophet, Priest, and King).[9]

From these Messianic passages in the Psalms, we now turn to a closer examination of Psalm 110. It is recognized as one of the outstanding Messianic passages of the Old Testament. It has the distinction of being quoted a total of 21 times in the New Testament in relation to Christ and His kingdom, and most notably by Jesus himself. Thus, G. Campbell Morgan states:

> This psalm is purely Messianic, and was always considered to be so. When Jesus quoted it in His conversation with the rulers it is perfectly evident that they looked on it in that light. It is equally certain that He made use of it in that sense.[10]

However, this contention has not gone unchallenged. According to some current criticism, this psalm is the composition of an unknown prophet, addressed to his earthly sovereign. The prophet is considered to be communicating to the king certain divine utterances or oracles (vv. 1, 5) of strange significance, and promising him complete victory over all his enemies. The king is supposed by some to be David; by others, a Davidic monarch or a Maccabean prince or king.[11] Mowinckel expresses this viewpoint as follows:

The descriptions of the kingly ideal which have been handed down are for the most part either idealized descriptions of the great kings of the past (which in effect means David), or wishes and promises for the new king. At the enthronement of the king, the temple prophets promise him all the royal fortune and blessing, power and honor which are proper to a son of Yahweh (Psa. 2; 110). . . .

At the anointing, on the coronation day, he received the promise of a filial relationship to Yahweh, of victory over all his opponents, of world dominion, of "everlasting priesthood," of the seat of honour at Yahweh's right hand. Promises of this kind have been preserved in the oracles of anointing, such as Psalms 2 and 110.[12]

At this point, it should be understood that scholars who assume such a position connect the people of Israel inseparably with all, or at least most, of the historic heathen practices of their neighbors. Such a position ignores not only the possibility of divine revelation, but also the power and influence of that revelation to separate God's chosen people from false beliefs. The basic issue seems to be whether one will approach the Scriptures from the viewpoint of historical criticism, or from faith that anticipates in-breathed divine revelation.

In reality, there does not appear to be sufficient grounds for rejecting the traditional views of authorship and interpretation. According to the title of Psalm 110, it is "a Psalm of David." Also, according to Jesus' comment upon it (Matt. 22:43-45; cf. Mark 12:35-37; Luke 20:41-44), it is an address of David to the Messiah. So, for 15 centuries, Christian commentators have acknowledged this psalm as Davidic and wholly Messianic. It contains the revelation David received concerning the kingdom, the priesthood, and the ultimate victory of the Messiah over the entire forces of evil.[13]

The Divinely Ordained King

> The Lord said unto my Lord, Sit thou at my
> right hand until I make thine enemies thy foot-
> stool.
>
> The Lord will send forth the sceptre of his
> power out of Zion, and he will rule over thine
> enemies.
>
> Thy people shall be glorious in the day of thy
> power; arrayed in the beauty of holiness from the
> womb, I have begotten thee as a child from the
> ages (Ps. 110:1-3, from the *Peshitta* by George
> Lamsa).

This King described here is David's Lord. He sits at
the right hand of God—a Conqueror reigning at Jerusalem.
He is King from all eternity, having also an everlasting
priesthood. He is thus qualified as Judge of all nations,
triumphing over all potentates, persistent in working out
His purpose, and successful in all His enterprises. Obviously, there never was such a king of Israel, nor is it
possible that there could ever be such an ideal ruler, except
that Person be sent and endowed with the Holy Spirit
himself.[14]

As we have already indicated, the Jews contemporary
with Jesus not only believed this psalm to have been
written by David, but that it spoke of the expected Messiah alone. This is particularly demonstrated by the fact
that when Jesus quoted it and drew arguments from it to
support His mission (Matt. 22:41-45), they did not attempt to dispute Him. Nor was there any attempt to
contradict Peter in Acts 2:34 and Paul (in 1 Cor. 15:25;
Heb. 1:13; 5:6, 10; 7:17; 10:12-13) when they used this
psalm to show that Jesus is the Messiah, the King of all
kings.[15]

Since David "in the Spirit" calls him Lord (Matt. 22:

45), he acknowledges his own reign to be by Him. David is thus concerned to be an acceptable servant to his Lord. Moreover, David calls Him his Lord because He was the Lord that was to descend from him—his son, and yet his Lord. In some mysterious way, He was to be David's son according to the flesh, but his Lord as equal to God (cf. Phil. 2:6-7). As made of the flesh and born of a virgin, He might be the son of David; but as Immanuel, the Lord of David (cf. Isa. 7:14). The Jews did not understand this and so could not offer reply to Christ's question (Matt. 22:45).[16]

It is evident that this Person is constituted a sovereign Lord by the counsel and decree of God himself. Clearly the declaration is: "The Lord, Jehovah, said unto him, Sit as a king." He thus receives of God the Father this honor and glory (which Peter ascribes to Christ, 2 Pet. 1:17), for it is God who is the Fountain of honor and power. He is therefore rightful Lord. His title is incontestable. What God has said cannot be changed.

Moreover, He is everlasting Lord, for God has said it from everlasting, that He is predestined to be the Seed of the woman (cf. Gen. 3:15). He will certainly take and retain possession of that kingdom which the Father has committed to Him. None can prevent it. What God has said cannot be unsaid.[17]

In a sense, the King took possession of His kingdom when the Lord said unto Him, "Sit thou on my right hand." He is given the highest honor, and He is entrusted with absolute sovereign power, both in heaven and in earth. All the providence that is given from God to man, and all the service that man offers to God, passes through His hand. Certainly Christ, as the Son of God, is ever at the right hand of God, equal to Him in might and majesty; but, as man, He was exalted to honor, especially at His glorious ascension (cf. Acts 2:34; Eph. 2:20; Phil. 2:9).[18]

129

The King shall thus sit in power and glory as the Mediator between God and men, until His enemies are made His footstool. (It was a common practice of oriental conquerors to place the foot upon the neck or body of defeated enemies.) We may well note that Christ does indeed have enemies that fight against His kingdom, His subjects, His honor, and His purpose in the world.

There are those who will not allow Him to reign over them. They thereby join Satan, the archfoe, who has resisted His reign since the angelic war in heaven. All such enemies will eventually be made His footstool, for He will triumph over them. He will subdue them in such a way as shall be most for His honor and their perpetual disgrace. As the prophet Malachi puts it, "He will tread down the wicked" (Mal. 4:3).

Again, in the light of the New Testament, the King shall sit at God's right hand, until He shall say to all the wicked, "Depart from me, I never knew you" (cf. Matthew 25). Once all His enemies are made His footstool, then He shall visibly rule, sitting at His Father's right hand forevermore. Thus, Christ's place at the right hand of God is a pledge to Him that all His enemies shall at last be defeated and put in their proper place—under His feet.[19]

The beginning of this Kingdom set up in the world is in Zion, at Jerusalem. "The Lord will send forth the sceptre of his power out of Zion" (Ps. 110:2). It is by His word, the gospel, the wisdom of God, that the Kingdom shall be erected, maintained, and administered. The Messiah, when He sits on the right hand of the Majesty in the heavens, will have a Church, a body of followers on earth. He will watch over them and preserve them. For He is King upon the holy hill of Zion (cf. Ps. 2:6).[20]

We should note here that the kingdom of Christ takes rise from Zion, the ruling city of David. Indeed, He was the Son of David, and He is rightful heir to the throne of His father, David. "The sceptre of his power" indicates His everlasting gospel and the power of the Holy Spirit applying it to a needy world. It is, as the prophet Isaiah puts it, the report of the Word and the arm (strength) of the Lord ever accompanying it (cf. Isa. 53:1). Or, as the Apostle Paul describes it, this is the gospel coming to mankind in word, in power, and in the Holy Spirit (cf. 1 Thess. 1:5).[21]

So, by the Word and the Spirit of God, the lives of men were to be first brought into obedience to God. Then they could be ruled and governed according to His purpose. We may well consider that the "sceptre of his power" sent forth also refers to His pouring out of the Holy Spirit, giving both commissions and qualifications to those that preached His Word and ministered the Spirit (cf. Gal. 3:5). Certainly, it was sent out of Zion; for there, in an upper room, was the Spirit given to the believers. It was also at Jerusalem, where the preaching of the gospel to all nations had its miraculous beginning (cf. Acts 2:8-11).[22]

Again, Ps. 110:2 indicates that the King shall reign and His kingdom be established in the world in spite of all opposing forces. His kingdom is of God and it shall stand. His crown sits firmly on His head, and there it shall flourish because none can remove it. The Messiah shall rule, give laws, and govern His subjects justly by them. He shall at last fulfill His own righteous purpose among men. His truth will ultimately prevail, even though it is resisted, and many ignore it.

Then, as the following verse affirms (v. 3), in the full sense of the word, the Messiah can only rule over "willing" hearts. In the day of His power, His people will gladly offer their service and flock to His banner to glorify His name.

Christ's kingdom is destined to be a Kingdom of glory (Phil. 2:5-11), even as it is a Kingdom of grace. Certainly, consecration is always the act of a freely surrendered will. Such an act will characterize His people, for reluctant service cannot satisfy the requirements of divine holiness.

The latter portion of verse 3 characterizes the Lord as "arrayed in the beauty of holiness from the womb." Perowne translates it, "In holy attire; as from the womb of the morning, Thou hast the dew of Thy youth."[23] The Ideal King is born in holiness, rules in perpetual holiness, and He acts to establish a kingdom of holy people. His mission can be no less than this if the original purpose of divine creation is to at last be accomplished.

The Divinely Ordained Priest

> *The Lord has sworn, and will not lie, You are a priest for ever after the order of Melchizadek* (Ps. 110:4, Lamsa).

As the Ideal King, the kingly and priestly functions are combined in the Psalmist's Lord. It is interesting to note that this verse is quoted six times in Hebrews (5:6, 10; 6:20; 7:11, 15, 21). These references give the writer's thought that the priesthood of Christ is of an order different from and superior to that of Aaron, namely a priesthood after the order of Melchizedek.

This priesthood does not depend upon human lineage (Heb. 7:3). It was antecedent to and better than the priesthood of the sons of Levi (7:4-10). It therefore betokens a change of the law (7:11-12). This also explains how the revealed Ideal King, Jesus, of the tribe of Judah rather than of Levi, can properly be a Priest (7:13-14). Furthermore, the order of Melchizedek was a priesthood certified by and grounded in God's oath (7:20-22). And, because it is an eternal priesthood, not subject to a changing human succession of high priests, it becomes the ground of our full and unending salvation (7:23-28).[24]

Obviously, the name Melchizedek is significant, giving particular meaning to the Psalmist's use of it. Melchizedek means "king of righteousness." He was identified in Gen. 14:18-20 as "king of Salem," which means "king of peace." Also, he was spoken of as "the priest of the most high God" 700 years before the Levitical priesthood was ever instituted. Thus, in the kingly priest of righteousness and peace we have a fitting type of Christ, who unites in himself the Old Testament functions of prophet, priest, and king, comprising the Ideal King.[25]

In this manner, then, the Messiah's kingdom is not only foretold, but His priesthood also, under which His prophetical office may be implied. Indeed, the Messiah was to fill the office of priest at His coming. God's word of assurance was given with His oath.

Looking forward to the New Testament revelation, we see that it is in the priesthood of Christ that our redemption lies. God swears that the Messiah shall be a priest to offer himself as a sacrifice for our sin, and to make intercession on our behalf. Without this necessary function, He would be our Prophet and our King in vain.[26] By such divine action we are made aware that God's decree for mercy to sinful man is undeterred.

As Adam Clarke points out, the matter of God's oath is both particular and specific: "You are a priest for ever after the order of Melchizedek." The "You" refers to David's Lord, who is Priest as well as King. Notice that the present tense is reflected by the verb "are." This priest is the "I Am," who inhabits eternity, whose function is not limited in time. As a priest, David's Lord must fill the office as described in Heb. 5:1, "Ordained on behalf of men about things pertaining to God, that he may offer both gifts and sacrifices for sins" (Lamsa).[27]

The priesthood of the Ideal King is also "for ever," and not according to the life-span of service by Aaron and his successors, who were priests. Their function was curtailed by death. "But this one, because he is immortal, has a priesthood which remains for ever" (Heb. 7:24, Lamsa).

It is He who is appointed "after the order of Melchizedek," that is ordained a Priest of God, rather than being born into the priestly line. Certainly, personal divine ordination into the priesthood bears far greater influence.

There is considerable difference between the priestly order of Melchizedek and that of Aaron. We can be sure that the Psalmist had such distinctions in mind when he stressed that his Lord would be both king and priest, after the order of Melchizedek. This implied that the Messiah was not simply to be a king as David, nor a priest consecrated from Aaron's line with limited tenure. Rather, as has already been affirmed, He was ordained Priest by divine declaration, just as Melchizedek (Heb. 7:20-21).

In Aaron's priesthood, the high priest, being mortal, eventually died, and another succeeded him. But this Priest, as Melchizedek, "had neither beginning of days nor end of life" (7:3). As Melchizedek was both priest and king, so is David's Lord. Aaron was just a priest. When we compare the contrasting functions of their respective priestly offices, we see that Aaron's function was national, but this One is a universal Priest. Aaron and his sons had to offer a bullock of the sin offering for themselves (Lev. 16:6). But this priest is inherently holy. He offers no sacrifices for himself—only for the sins of mankind (cf. Isa. 53:9-12).

We further note that whereas Aaron's priestly line were anointed with material oil, the Messiah is anointed with the Holy Spirit. This too is fulfilled in Jesus Christ (Luke 4:18, 21). Such contrasts certainly emphasize the fact that Aaron's priesthood was temporary, but the priesthood of the Ideal King, after the order of Melchizedek, is forever.[28]

We may well ask the question: How is He priest forever? As Adam Clarke indicates, He is "a priest for ever" in respect to His person, office, and effect. David's Lord succeeded no priest, and no other priest succeeded Him. His vocation became immediate at the oath of God. He lives forever, and thus no necessity of replacement will arise to continue His priesthood. He is also Priest forever with respect of the lasting effect of His sacrifice for the sins of the people, "for this he did once when he offered himself" (Heb. 7:27, Lamsa).[29]

Apparently, it is difficult for many to accept a suffering, dying Messiah, even though He were accounted both King and Priest. This has been a great stone of stumbling for the Jews since Jesus' day. But that sacrifice which Christ offered on the Cross is indeed significant. For, by it, He provides the inestimable effects of redemption and regeneration from sin unto eternal salvation. It is in this sense that the priesthood of the ideal King must be forever. The sufficiency of the sacrifice and the continuation of its ability to save both depend on the fact of Christ's everlasting priesthood.

It remains to be shown how He is a Priest forever "after the order" of Melchizedeck—that is, according to the rite, the manner, the word, and the power, given and prescribed to Melchizedek. As we have already noted, Melchizedek was king of Salem, and priest of the most high God (Genesis 14). So was David's Lord to be King and Priest over Jerusalem, God's holy city. Melchizedek is by interpretation "king of righteousness."

Certainly, the prophet Jeremiah had David's King in mind when he wrote:

> Behold the days are coming, says the Lord, when I will raise up for David a righteous Heir, and he shall reign over the kingdom with understanding, and shall execute justice and righteousness in the land.

In his days Judah shall be saved and Israel shall dwell securely; and this is the name whereby he shall be called, THE LORD OUR RIGHTEOUSNESS (Jer. 23:5-6, Lamsa).

Again, Melchizedek, as king of Salem, meant "King of Peace." In this regard, the prophet Isaiah clearly identifies God's Messiah and David's King as the "Prince of Peace":

For unto us a child is born, unto us a son is given; and the government shall be upon his shoulder: and his name shall be called Wonderful, Counsellor, Mighty God, Everlasting Father, Prince of Peace.

Of the increase of his government and of peace there shall be no end, upon the throne of David, and upon his kingdom, to establish it, and to uphold it with justice and with righteousness from henceforth even for ever. The zeal of Jehovah of hosts will perform this (Isa. 9:6-7).

We are further told of Melchizedek that "neither his father nor his mother is recorded in the genealogies; and neither the beginning of his days nor the end of his life" (Heb. 7:3, Lamsa).

The same is true with regard to David's Lord, especially concerning His direct relation to the eternal Godhead. We may also turn to the Gospel of John, who ignores the human genealogy of Jesus Christ, and declares: "In the beginning was the Word, and the Word was with God, and the Word was God" (John 1:1).

Then, we would note the attending blessing of the priesthood of Melchizedek. In Gen. 14:19, we read how he blessed Abram, following Abram's rescue of Lot from the four offending kings. In response to that blessing, Abram gave Melchizedek a tithe (one-tenth) of the spoils. The point implied by the prophecy of Ps. 110:4 is that David's Lord, even Christ, shall bless all those who come unto God by Him for salvation (cf. Heb. 7:25).

Adam Clarke gives an interesting sidelight that as Melchizedek brought forth bread and wine to refresh Abram's army, so Christ instituted the sacrament, setting forth bread and wine at the Last Supper to refresh the hungry and thirsty souls of His true followers.[30]

Thus, the Psalmist certainly prophesies that the Messiah shall be not only King but Priest. His kingdom and His priesthood will abide forever, in spite of all opposition. His power and authority are not derived from earthly might, but they flow directly from God himself. It is this qualification that combines the kingly and the priestly functions to make David's Lord the Ideal King. He is God's Messiah because God has ordained it so. He only awaits the consummation.

The Assurance of Triumph

> *The Lord at your right hand will defeat the kings in the day of his wrath.*
> *He will judge among the nations, he will count the slain; he will cut off the heads of many on earth.*
> *He will drink of the brook in the way; therefore he will lift up his head* (Ps. 110:5-7, Lamsa).

The last stanza of the Messianic Psalm returns to the military tone of verses 1 and 2. It also assumes the character of a hymn addressed directly to the Lord God (Yahweh). "The Lord [Adonai] at your right hand" is certainly Jehovah who stands at Messiah's right hand to protect and defend Him, to give Him victory in every battle (cf. Ps. 16:8; 121:5). Thus, the concluding portion of this psalm, beginning with verse 5, carries on the description of the Messiah's triumph begun in verse 3. The kings to be defeated "in the day of his wrath" must certainly be those rulers who resist the progress of the gospel.[31]

Such a picture of a warrior destroying his foes may seem a very strange representation of the establishment of the Messiah's kingdom on earth. But David described his King's victory over His enemies by images familiar to himself as a warrior. Perhaps we would be too weak in our conceptions of the Messiah if we did not have this and other war-figures to remind us of life and death conflict between righteousness and evil.

On the face of it, there may seem to be a glaring contradiction between the Messiah as the Prince of Peace and the Messiah as triumphant King. However, He may properly be viewed as the mighty Conqueror because sin is indeed an active, hostile force, which righteousness must oppose. Man is helpless in his own strength to overcome it. But it is the Messiah, David's Lord, who takes man's part in delivering him from the destructive dominion of sin.

In the fulfillment of the foregoing victory, the Priest-King shall become the Judge (v. 6). He shall execute His royal office not only over Israel, but over all the nations of the earth (cf. Ps. 7:9; 46:10). However, as Matthew Henry points out, the execution which transpires is not a military slaughter, done in fury. Rather, it is judicial action. Before He condemns and kills, He will judge. The evidence will show that the victims have brought this ruin upon themselves. Certainly, His judgments are true and righteous in every respect.[32]

The effect of this victory shall be the complete and utter ruin of all His enemies. As the King James Version has it, verse 6 says, "He shall wound the heads over many countries." Even kings and rulers, who have had great power and authority, shall be given a fatal blow that will bring an end to their rebellion. Here, Matthew Henry comments that this statement, so translated, seems to refer to the first promise of the Messiah (Gen. 3:15), that He should bruise the serpent's head.[33] Also, Dr. Kay is quoted in the *Pulpit Commentary* as rendering this as follows: "He shall smite him that is head over the wide earth"—either Satan or "the central power of the whole confederacy of evil."[34]

Although it will be the day of evil's terror, it will be the occasion of the Messiah's triumph. Nothing shall prevent His ultimate conquest—neither the duration of the struggle nor the strenuous demands amidst the conflict.

James Moffatt translates verse 7, "He drinks from any stream He has to cross, then charges forward triumphing." The basic action described is that of the Messiah pausing in pursuit of enemies to refresh himself with a drink of water from a brook by the wayside. With such an interpretation, we understand that the refreshing drinks are from the wellspring of truth and righteousness as the Messiah persistently advances on His career of victory.[35]

Bishop Perowne's comment on verses 5 through 7 is:

> The victorious leader, who has made so terrible a slaughter that the field of battle is covered with corpses, is now seen pursuing his enemies. Wearied with the battle and the pursuit, he stops for a moment on his way to refresh himself by drinking of the torrent rushing by, and then "lifts up his head," derives new vigor to continue the pursuit.[36]

David indeed saw the Messiah's advent to subjugate the enemies of righteousness and thus rescue a sin-captured world. From the Christian viewpoint, this psalm plainly tells of the glory of the coming of Jesus Christ. But all that it anticipates has not yet been fulfilled.

Thus, prophetically, the whole psalm speaks of Christ's exaltation. It asserts that He was set at God's right hand of power. By divine oath, He was also made a Priest. Then, in defense of His kingdom and priesthood,

He is seen as subduing, conquering, and judging His enemies.

We cannot help but note, however, that some commentators, such as Clarke and Henry, interpret the last verse of the psalm as telling the means whereby Christ came to this honor. His Cross was the way to the crown. His passion and humiliation were stepping-stones to His exaltation. Henry suggests this, as follows:

> The wrath of God, running in the channel of the curse of the law, was "the brook in the way," in the way of his undertaking, which he must go through, or which ran in the way of our salvation and obstructed it, which lay between us and heaven. Christ drank of this brook when he was made a curse for us.[37]

Nevertheless, *"claritas humilitatus praemium"* ("glory is the reward of humility"). Because Christ thus humbled himself and willingly endured death for the salvation of man and for the glory of His Father, God shall "lift up his head." David's Lord shall rise from the dead and have all power committed to Him in heaven and earth. He shall ascend into heaven, sit on the right hand of the Father, and be constituted the triumphant Judge of the quick and the dead.[38] So He forever bears the worthy credentials of Prophet, Priest, and King.

Despite the clarity of David's prophecy in characterizing the Ideal King, the Psalmist seemed only to be aware of His certain coming. Indeed, the Messiah would be of David's family line. He could easily be identified by His kingly and priestly authority. Yet, in the darkness of despair that hovered over God's chosen people, it soon became evident that they needed a further sign. It was the specific sign of a virgin-born Son.

Chapter 8

The Immanuel Child

> *Therefore the Lord himself will give you a sign; behold a virgin shall conceive, and bear a son, and shall call his name Immanuel.*
>
> (Isa. 7:14)
>
> *For unto us a child is born, unto us a son is given; and the government shall be upon his shoulder: and his name shall be called Wonderful, Counsellor, Mighty God, Everlasting Father, Prince of Peace.*
>
> (Isa. 9:6)

As other men of God before him, the prophet Isaiah ministered to a confused, waiting world that vaguely wondered when and how God's Messiah should come. At the time of this prophecy, Jerusalem, the capital of the southern kingdom of Judah, ruled by King Ahaz, was threatened by a combined attack of the armies of Rezin and Pekah, the kings of Syria and Israel.

Since the unwise rule of Rehoboam, the son of Solomon, God's chosen people had been divided into southern and northern kingdoms. King Ahaz and his people were desperate, for they had already suffered defeat in battle. Now, against the united strength of Israel and Syria, all hope for salvation and survival seemed to be gone.

Isaiah was commissioned to encourage and reassure Ahaz and the people with promise of deliverance and victory. He went with his son, Shear-jashub, as commanded by the Lord, with the message of God's miraculous salvation. But Ahaz would not believe. He was depending on help from the king of Assyria.

In reality, Ahaz was faced with the decision of choosing a "God-with-us" defense for Judah, or ending up with a "God-against-us" blunder in unbelief. When Ahaz refused to listen, rejecting the word of God, the prophet then addressed the house of David, declaring: "Therefore the Lord himself will give you a sign: behold a virgin shall conceive, and bear a son, and shall call his name Immanuel."

Judah could put her faith in the salvation of God, or she could trust in alien military might and know the meaning of the name that Isaiah had given his son, Shear-jashub ("only a remnant shall escape"). If the Assyrian army was to be their chosen deliverer, then they would miss the possibility of divine deliverance. So, the immediate message of Isaiah's prophecy was that God would deliver His people from the invasion threatened by the Syro-Ephraimitic coalition, and bring to naught the designs of Rezin and Pekah. However, the following verses of the prophecy indicate the responsibility of King Ahaz and the people of Judah if they are to receive the benefits of the promise.[1]

God revealed to Isaiah that any calling in of Assyrian forces to aid Judah in her crisis with Rezin and Pekah would mean an indefinite postponement of any hopes for the realization of a Messianic Deliverer. Certainly, the promise of Gen. 3:15 must have been in his mind as he prophesied. It was the substance of the divine covenant with the patriarchs. God's message pertinently revealed the glorious miracle of the Anointed One's birth. Indeed, it was a further revelation of the promise made to Abraham (Gen. 12:1-3), to Jacob (Gen. 49:10), to Moses (Deut. 18:15), and to David (2 Sam. 7:4-17).

As mysterious and startling as the intimations of Immanuel's birth may seem to us, remember that Isaiah's words fell upon hearts whose fondest hope was for the appearance of a glorious Descendant of David. At this time they were all the more sensitive to that hope now that both David's city and David's dynasty were in peril. It seems unlikely that the hearers could possibly understand Immanuel to be any other child than that Prince whose coming was the inalienable hope of Judah.

Those who will hear the inspired words of the prophet receive an enlightening message from the Lord. Certainly, doubt has ever hovered as a fog, proceeding from wondering if Christ would come, to wondering if the account of His birth were actually true. Such haze would dim the brightness of His coming both in promise and in fulfillment.

They no longer stand in darkness, for the light of truth has dawned. The doubts concerning the promised Seed and the long expected fulfillment are driven back. As Isaiah put it: "The people that walked in darkness have seen a great light: they that dwell in the land of the shadow of death, upon them hath the light shined" (Isa. 9:2).

The coming of the Anointed One can no longer be looked upon as an old man's dream or an old wives' tale. How the world needs to know the hope of the coming Saviour! At last the ancient expectation acquires more discernible form, displaying the unchanging character of eternal truth. The Voice that promised hope to the sinful parents of the human race, that called Abraham to father a people of faith, that promised Shiloh to the lineage of Judah, and that promised everlasting extension to David's throne, now gives further word to a lost, worried world.

The truth remains unaltered, and it becomes even more explicit. A child is to be born, and a son is to be divinely given. But there is a twofold difficulty of belief. To the people of Isaiah's day, it was: How can such a thing happen? When is it to take place? To the people of our present day, it is: How could such a thing happen? Did it actually take place?

There is indeed a very basic problem of interpretation with regard to the validity of Isaiah's prophecy for his own time as well as the future. The interpreters may be divided into three classes: (1) Those who refer the prophecy wholly to the immediate situation of Ahaz and Judah; (2) Those who hold that it is specifically a prophecy of the Messiah; and (3) Those who consider it as having a double application, first to an event in the prophet's own time, and also to the birth of Christ.[2]

These views may well be questioned, as follows: (1) If the mother and son belonged to the time of Isaiah, what persons were they? (2) If the virgin and son Isaiah beheld were the Virgin Mary and her Son Jesus, to be fulfilled centuries later, what did that have to do with the immediate problem? (3) If the prophecy is said to have a double application and fulfillment, first in certain persons who lived in the prophet's time, and secondly in Jesus and His mother, does not this weaken the force of the message?[3]

Conservative Christian thought on the proper inter-pretation of the message and the translation of the Hebrew term, often rendered "virgin," moves between two poles. One is the recognition that the Septuagint (the Greek translation of the Old Testament made some 150 years before Christ) understood the meaning to be "virgin," and Matthew so applied it in reference to the birth of Jesus (Matt. 1:22-23). This reinforces the long-range Messianic view. Then, the other extreme is the apparent necessity of protecting the historical fulfillment of Isa. 7:1-20 in the prophet's time, as well as preserving the uniqueness of the virgin birth of Jesus. Perhaps a child of symbol was born in Isaiah's time, but that child was not virgin-born as was our Lord.[4]

In this regard, Dr. Ross Price notes that it is possible to see in Isaiah's use of the term *"almah"* (a young woman of marriageable age) in 7:14 an evidence of divine wisdom, since the Hebrew language also has the word *bethulah,* which means simply a virgin. Of course, the Bible only affirms one Virgin Birth, not two, as would be the case if we both accept the historical accuracy of Isaiah 7 and at the same time insist that *"almah"* here must be trans-lated "virgin."[5]

On the surface, it would seem that any valid under-standing of such a sign to Judah must have been in rela-tion to some maiden (virgin) known at least to Isaiah and Ahaz. Some have concluded that "the young woman of marriageable age" immediately involved here is a young, childless wife of the king himself, or perhaps Abi, the mother of Hezekiah (2 Kings 18:2). For it was Hezekiah who later delivered Judah from the Assyrian domination. However, such a conclusion is seriously weakened by show-ing that, according to the numbers of kings (2 Kings 16:2; 17:2), Hezekiah was at least nine years old in the first year of his father's reign, before which this prophecy could not have been delivered (Isa. 7:1).[6]

Also, there is serious difficulty if we identify the "virgin" mother with Isaiah's wife, the "prophetess" of Isa. 8:3, and make the son to be a child of his, called Immanuel, but in reality his son Maher-shalal-hash-baz (8:1) under symbolic designation. But there is no indication that Isaiah's son gave any typical fulfillment to such a symbolic designation. Moreover, for Isaiah to have given his wife a title such as *"ha-almah,"* "the virgin," would have been strange indeed, for she had apparently already given birth to Shear-jashub.[7]

Viewing the best possible answer to the first question: Who were the mother and son of Isaiah's time? it would seem that they must remain unknown. If we hold that the prophecy had to have application in Isaiah's time, *"almah"* can only refer to some young woman actually present (name, rank, and position unidentified) and her son, called Immanuel. But even this interpretation is faulty, for it does not uphold the body of prophecy, "The Lord himself will give you a sign. . . . Behold!" Also, the attested individual rank of Immanuel (8:8; 9:6) indicates the necessity of at least a recognizable type. He is never identified in the fulfillment of the situation at the time of the prophecy.[8]

A not unreasonable way out of the dilemma is to assume that there is here in Isaiah's prophecy the dual reference that some conservative Bible scholars find in many Old Testament prophecies. Temporarily we will bypass the second question and consider a plausible answer to the third: If the prophecy is said to have a double application and fulfillment, first in certain persons who lived in the prophet's time, and secondly in Jesus and His mother, does not this weaken the force of the message? The answer to this question may or may not serve as a

146

bridge to the polar situation which responsible Christian scholarship endeavors to span.

In a sense, this dual interpretation of the prophecy regards truth as swinging like a pendulum from the immediate situation to the future. The words of the prophet had reference to events about to happen. But, in sweeping fashion, those words had an added meaning for the future that has been seen more clearly since the light of the New Testament revelation.

For instance, Bishop Lowth believed that the prophecy has a double bearing and a double fulfillment. Concerning the immediate application, he said:

> The obvious and literal meaning of the prophecy is this, that within the time that a young woman, now a virgin, should conceive and bring forth a child, and that child should arrive at such an age as to distinguish between good and evil, that is within a few years, the enemies of Judah should be destroyed.[9]

Lowth goes on to say that the prophecy was so worded to have a further meaning, the Messianic aspect, which was the original design and principal intention of the prophet. All the expressions of the prophecy (7:14) do not suit both its intentions. Some are selected with reference to the first, others with reference to the future fulfillment —but all suit one or the other, and some suit both.

The first child may have received the name Immanuel from a faithful Jewish mother, who believed that God was with His people, no matter what dangers threatened. The child may have reached his years of discretion about the time that Samaria (Israel) was carried away captive. The second child is the true Immanuel, "God with us," the king of Isa. 8:8. It is His mother who is spoken of in the expression "the virgin," and on His account is the grand preamble, "Therefore the Lord himself will give you a sign." For through Him, the people of God, the true Israel, are delivered from its spiritual enemies, the allied kingdoms of sin and Satan.[10]

This representative view of the dual interpretation of Isaiah's prophecy has not altogether avoided the horns of the dilemma. It requires a tedious sifting of the integrate parts, a division of truth purportedly to be contemporary from that which is dependent on future fulfillment.

A portion of this interpretation, moreover, is suspended on the uncertain hinge as to the identity of the immediate virgin and son. It would seem that to proceed from an unidentified type to the fulfilled actuality is a compromise position. Certainly, it is easy to see why this prophecy has been the subject of so much controversy.

We now turn to the second question: If the virgin and son that Isaiah beheld were the Virgin Mary and her Son Jesus, to be fulfilled centuries later, what did that have to do with the immediate situation?

It has been objected that a prophecy of a Messiah who was to be born some 700 years later, could not be a sign to Ahaz and Judah of a present deliverance from threatening foes. On the other hand, it might be retorted that it is equally hard to see how the birth of an ordinary child could be a sign or pledge of deliverance. And, in direct answer to the question, it may be pointed out that the assurance of a coming Messiah of the royal line of David, would be a pledge to Judah that they were not to be destroyed by their enemies.[11]

In many respects, a basic Messianic interpretation to the prophecy seems to be the most tenable. In his *Prophecies of Isaiah,* Delitzsch says:

> It is the Messiah whom the prophet here beholds as about to be born; then in chapter 9 as born, and in chapter 11 as reigning—three stages of a triad which are not to be wrenched asunder, a threefold constellation of consoling forms, illuminating the three stadia into

which the future history of His people divides itself in the view of the prophet.[12]

One thing is certain, the circumstances are too solemn, and the evident importance of the event foretold are too great, to find a satisfactory fulfillment in any local event of that time. As has been indicated, the further and fuller reference to this child of promise in chapters 9 and 11 clearly shows that 7:14 is indeed a prediction of the Messiah. The name "Immanuel," "God with us," by which the child was to be called, is too sacred and significant to mean nothing but what is implied by the non-Messianic interpretations.[13]

In all fairness, however, we must admit that there is one outstanding difficulty in committing ourselves to an exclusively Messianic interpretation of 7:14. The scope of the context does seem to indicate a definite reference to existing or near events in which the prophet's words would find fulfillment. This is especially true of the declaration in verse 16, that "before the child shall know to refuse the evil and choose the good, the land whose two kings thou abhorrest shall be forsaken." That is, in a short period, indicated by the increased intelligence of the child, the kingdoms of Syria and Israel would be squelched.[14]

Therefore, some Bible scholars, who firmly believe that this is indeed a Messianic prophecy, feel compelled to interpret it as having reference both to events of the prophet's own time and to the future Messiah. Taking this view, Dr. Pye Smith says, in his *Scripture Testimony to the Messiah:*

> This passage, therefore, comes under the class of testimonies which had a primary, but inferior and partial, reference to some proximate person or event; but had another and a designed reference to some remoter circumstance, which when it occurred would be the real fulfillment, answering every feature and filling up the entire extent of the original delineation.[15]

So far as the eternal quality of God's Word is concerned, it would seem that the Messianic aspect of the prophecy must take precedence over whatever contemporary interpretation is placed upon it. Otherwise, the passage has no vital truth for us.

Whether there was the sign of a son born at that time or not, it is apparent that the hope of the redeeming covenant of God with man remains fastened to a mighty personality. It was a realized hope that awaited even further fulfillment. Indeed, a Saviour is identified with recognizable characteristics that will lead men of faith to worship Him at His coming. Let us take a closer look at this Child.

The Child

There can be no doubt as to the manner of the Anointed One's coming. He shall enter this world as all men do—born of a woman. The Messiah cannot immediately invade this domain of Satan on shining wings of power. He is to come as a tiny, helpless babe, under the watchful care of God-fearing parents. These earthly parents, of the tribe of Judah, of David's line, will be of divine selection.

It is intimated that there is something mysterious, even supernatural, about His birth. He is to be born of a virgin (at least, so reads a number of English translations). As we have already seen, there is some question as to whether the word translated "virgin" *(almah)* necessarily has that meaning as we understand it today. However, it seems apparent that this meaning is borne out by every other place in which the word occurs in the Old Testament (cf. Gen. 24:43; Exod. 2:8; Ps. 68:25; Prov. 30:19; Song of Sol. 1:3; 6:8). We should also note that unless *almah* is translated "virgin," there is no announcement made

150

worthy of the grand prelude: "The Lord himself will give you a sign. . . . Behold!"[16]

Knowingly, men of the world scoff at the mere possibility of a Virgin Birth—other than by artificial insemination. But time and again, God turns the wisdom of this world into ignorance. The promised Seed of the woman, Shiloh, the promised royalty of Judah, the Son "sent," is born thus so that all might know by this sign that the Saviour is come, that God is with us.

God indeed inspired Isaiah to be concerned with the birth of one particular, expected Child. As George Adam Smith indicates, the general significance of the prophecy, apart from Immanuel, is of a certain child. It says that before a certain child, whose birth is vaguely but solemnly intimated in the near future, shall have come to years of discretion, the results of the choice of Ahaz shall be manifest. Judah shall be devastated and her people sunk to the most rudimentary means of living (Isa. 8:21-22).[17]

It thus seems impossible to disassociate so solemn an announcement by Jehovah to Judah, the house of David, of the birth of a Child so highly named. Since the days of its founder there was the expectation of the coming of a Glorious Prince from the midst of the royal family. No matter how mysterious and abrupt the intimations of the Child's birth may seem to us at this juncture, we must remember that the message was given to those who cherished the hope of the appearance of a matchless descendant of David. One may well wonder if Ahaz could possibly avoid the ultimate understanding of the Child, Immanuel, as that Prince whose coming was the inalienable hope of his house.[18]

Certainly, every interpretation of this prophecy that does not see the prophet speaking of the Messiah to be born, the Child given, is false. Oehler, in his *Old Testament Theology,* goes further and suggests that the later

151

prophecy of Micah 5:2-3 is parallel with Isa. 7:14, with respect to the birth of Immanuel from the *"almah."* Reference to the Messiah is also demanded by its connection with Isa. 9:6.[19]

It was from Micah's prophecy that people knew to look for the Child to be born in Bethlehem, the city of David. But notice the further connection to Isaiah's prophecy, as Micah declares:

> *But thou, Bethlehem Ephrathah, which art little to be among the thousands of Judah, out of thee shall one come forth unto me that is to be ruler in Israel; whose goings forth are from of old, from everlasting.*

> *Therefore will he give them up, until the time that she who travaileth hath brought forth: then the residue of his brethren shall return unto the children of Israel* (Mic. 5:2-3).

Judah is still looking for a Child to be born, to be their Ruler, who is from everlasting, yet born from a woman. And when we include Isa. 9:6, we clearly see that the Child is prophetically identified as both human and divine. The words "a child is born," and "a son is given" declare the paradoxical humanity and deity of the promised Messiah.

To be human, the Child must be born of a woman; but to be divine, He must be given, sent of God. As the Son of God, He was given; for as God, He was from everlasting. But, as Son of Man, He is to be born of a virgin—God with us in human flesh. Thus, although the long-awaited Deliverer is to be born as a child, His birth is of utmost importance.

The stone of stumbling for many occurs when the Messiah is declared to be a virgin's child. This means that He is to have no part of the seed of man, but only the woman's seed, quickened by the Holy Spirit of God. Such an interpretation is in direct agreement with the ancient divine edict, "The seed of the woman shall bruise the head of the serpent" (Gen. 3:15).

This holy person who comes to destroy the works of Satan is to be the progeny of the woman, without any concurrence of man. Rather, the Child is to be the union of the divine nature with human nature, in seeming impossible blend. It is termed a sign, a miracle of God, by the prophet. The manner in which this mysterious union is to be thus accomplished is simply explained: "Behold, a virgin shall conceive."

This prophetic event is often falsely classed with the mythical marriages of pagan gods, with one another, or with human beings. For instance, possible parallels of the concept of the Virgin Birth are sought in Egyptian, Babylonian, and Arabian beliefs. The Egyptian doctrine of virgin births is connected with the advent of kings, and is especially marked in the case of the Pharaoh Amenhotep III. Amon-Ra, the sun-god, supposedly descended from heaven and became his father. Amenhotep's mother was also said to be a virgin when the god thus "incarnated himself" so that she might "behold him in his divine form."[20]

However, this Pharaonic cult seems to be a politico-religious combination in which the political element greatly overshadowed the religious. It was apparently forced upon the Egyptians by conquerors who brought their religion with them. So, the purported divineness of the Pharaohs as the offspring of the sun-god was the necessary justification of their right to rule. Its rise in Egypt was coincident with the advance of the conquering usurpers from the south, and it became the embodiment of the political principle known as "the divine right of kings." But this was often in conflict with the native religion, which was a worship of nature as embodied in sacred animals such as the bull Apis, cats, and crocodiles.[21]

Again, the cycle of connection between Jewish Messianic belief and the Babylonian myth of Marduk is attempted with Dan. 7:13, which describes a manlike being. Canon Cheyne holds such a view. Professor Gunkel also points out a supposed point of contact by associating the myth with Revelation 12, in which the woman mentioned under such glowing imagery is purported to be a transformation of the myth of Marduk. The seven-headed dragon (Rev. 12:3), also called the "ancient serpent," is suggested to be Tiamat, whom the god of the springtide sun—Marduk—encountered and overcame.[22]

Another parallel, particularly with the gospel story, is also noted by Dr. Cheyne with regard to the Tammuz cult in North Arabia. In some localities, such as Petra and Elusa, Tammuz (Dusares) was worshipped as "the only begotten of the Lord," and his mother as the virgin. At this point, it should be noted just what the necessary interpretation of the word *virgin* must be. The following definition of Dr. Cheyne reveals the difficulty involved in connecting Israel's concept of *virgin* with that of her neighbors.

> And what was the original meaning of the term "virgin"? As has long since been shown, it expressed the fact that the great mythic mother-goddess was independent of the marriage-tie. In those remote times to which the cult of that goddess properly belonged, the mother held the chief place in the clan, and all women shared a measure of free love. The goddess-mother, in fact, preceded the goddess wife.[23]

Obviously, the myths in which such alleged virgin births occur reflect the ideas of people who had reached the polyandrous stage of social development, in which the woman rules the tribe and has many husbands.

If the miraculous birth promised in the Scriptures is

indeed the advancement of a heathen notion, faith in God is hopelessly debased. Such an association involves the degrading conception of Deity having intimate physical relations with human beings. This is the very essence of heathen idolatry, the prime object of warning and scorn by the Hebrew prophets. So, if the Virgin Birth is a borrowed heathen notion, it involves nothing less than absolute apostasy on the part of those who formulated, promoted, and accepted it.[24]

For various reasons, unbelieving and skeptical men hastily turn aside from the mystery of the virgin-born Child. Because they cannot comprehend such a birth, they confuse the truth with myths or half-truths. Thus, by his unbelief, sinful man would remove God from the helpless human scene, or he would involve God as partaking in the evil debacle. Men of faith must early learn the basic lesson that mystery is not necessarily identified with myth.

The Messiah's birth can never happen for our individual benefit except we become willing to receive the fact that He must be born of a virgin mother. Although there are a number of difficulties to human thinking which attend such a belief, unless we accept the virgin-born Saviour, we stand without a Saviour. In the virgin's Child lies the great mystery of divine incarnation. He is the Son of God coming to take the form and consequences of mankind, while at the same time bringing salvation to lost humanity through the victory of His life.

Whether he realized it or not, Isaiah's prophecy of the Child laid the foundation of the Incarnation, which is declared consummated in the New Testament Gospels. This is the only basis upon which we may worship Christ. His incarnation is so distinct from the ordinary working of human nature, and it is so manifestly the operation of divine nature in the human realm, only a God-inspired faith can receive it. Thus, those who accept Christ as the promised Child of the virgin mother, and as the Son given by the divine Father, will find a glad response to the salvation miracle that stems from His birth.

Born in accordance with human times, the Child comes into the world as every member of Adam's race must come, nourished for months with a mother's own life. At once, He is born as the Son of Man, born of a woman. But He is given of God, sent from heaven—the Son of God, the Only Begotten of the Father.

The Christ child comes as Deity fashioned in the mold of human flesh. Although the Creator, He comes as a creature. Once the Lord of all creation, He comes to be the Servant of all. Once the abiding Subject of prophecy, He comes to be the Fulfiller of prophecy.

Looking from our point in time, the Child comes as Infinity pressed into the swiftly passing moments of a mortal life, as Immortality submitting to die a human death. He comes as a babe, and yet He is a King, heir to the kingdoms of the world. He comes as an infant, and yet He is very God.

This divine Son who was from everlasting was promised because He consented to enter and live in the confines of time to bear the sins of men. Let there be no mistake—never before and never since has there been a child born with such qualifications to be the Saviour of the World.

Certainly, the announcement of the coming birth of the Child meant one thing to Isaiah's day—that God would eventually be with them in the flesh. He would come to the people by means of His incarnation. He would come to be with mankind because of His willingness to be sent of the Father for the redemption of believing men.

He would thus unite himself to human nature that He might become our Saviour. There can be no other purpose for such divine condescension. The very message of His name expresses the mission for which He is sent. What is

His name? The prophet Isaiah declares, "Call his name Immanuel!"—God with us.

Immanuel

This name of the Child is evidently given as a part of the progressive revelation of God concerning the promised Seed of the woman. Mankind may more clearly behold the truth step by step—from the promised Son, to the establishment of a chosen people; from the prophecy of Jacob pointing to Shiloh, to the selection of Judah, the royal tribe; from the choice of the family of King David, now to the prophecy of Isaiah about the virgin's Son, Immanuel, who is God with us.

By the inspiration of divine revelation, the prophet seems to envision the total picture of the covenant of redemption. Indeed, he sees the Deliverer as the Seed of the woman. Further, he sees Him sent of God from the tribe of Judah, of David, the "stock of Jesse" (cf. Isa. 9:7; 11:1-5). And, most explicitly, he sees Him as Immanuel, born to be God with us.

Since God is to be with humanity in such a human, personal manner, it must certainly be to deliver them from the evil works of the devil and to save them from the curse of their sins. The Child's name, Immanuel, signifies that He comes to restore Adam's race back into divine fellowship, drawing believing men into unity with His life. He thereby establishes a foundation for righteous acceptance by the Father.

Furthermore, Immanuel is with mankind to reveal divine love and grace unto their sin-deadened, rebellious situation. He comes to deliver them, not so much from their physical enemies, as from the consequences of their transgressions against God, to redeem them from the degradation of their iniquity. Thus, life-giving light and

157

hope radiate for humanity from the matchless name, Immanuel. It is a name above all others.

Besides the name Immanuel, He is known by His holy characteristics. He is also called Wonderful, Counsellor, the mighty God, the everlasting Father, the Prince of Peace. Obviously, He personifies all of the attributes of God, which implies that He shall not only be known by title, but likewise by His divine character and activity. Such identification should leave little room for doubt and confusion in recognizing Him when He comes. His qualities are such as cannot be duplicated by any other person.

First, the Child, Immanuel, is properly called Wonderful because He is both God and man. In a very accurate sense, the word translated "Wonderful" in Isa. 9:6 can also be translated "Wonder," signifying a miracle.

Professor Delitzsch, the noted German scholar, in his *Commentary of Isaiah,* concerning this word, says:

> As the angel of Jahve (Judges 13:18) answers Manoah's inquiry as to his name (Wonder) and therewith indicates his divine nature, incomprehensible to mortals, so is the God-given ruler (Wonder) a phenomenon beyond human comprehension, not coming to pass in the order of nature. There is not merely this or that in him wonderful: He is Himself wholly and entirely wonder.[25]

Certainly, "Wonderful" or "Wonder" describes every aspect of His existence, His character, His ability, and His activity. Neither word can be rightfully regarded simply as a descriptive adjective. Rather, He is the personification of all that is wonderful, miraculous, so that His name shall be called "Wonderful."

Perhaps the facet of His wonderfulness which challenges men the most is the miracle of His wonderful, condescending love, to enter the destructive history of mankind. Indeed, it is the divine motivation of Immanuel to humble himself so that fallen man might know the joy of

God's salvation, instead of the misery of Satan's damnation.

Immanuel is called Counsellor because He is intimately acquainted with the plan and purpose of God the Father from eternity. As He is clothed in humanity, He personally knows the limitations and needs of His fellowmen. Moreover, Immanuel is the holy Wisdom of the Father, and He is sent that we may become wise from His wisdom.

In this regard, Dr. Ross Price feels that "Wonderful, Counsellor" should be hyphenated, indicating the personification of extraordinary prudence. There can be no doubt that Isaiah is expressing the divine attribute of omniscience—"all knowledge and wisdom."[26] This abundantly qualifies Him to give wise counsel to sin-blinded men, revealing God's gracious deliverance from sin and death.

Also, divine power emanates from the infinite wisdom of Immanuel. He is the Almighty God. Again, as Dr. Price indicates, Immanuel has superhuman powers, not simply because the Spirit of Almighty God rests on Him in anointing, but because the nature of essential Deity resides within Him.[27] Because He is all-wise, so then is He strong, possessing the ability to succeed whatever His undertaking.

Since Immanuel is the Mighty God, He is able to save lost mankind from the uttermost to the uttermost. As Mediator between holy God and sinful man, He is powerful to save all who will receive Him. Here, the divine attribute of omnipotence is revealed. For Immanuel shares the abundant power of the Father that is all-sufficient to achieve the divine purpose in the lives of confessing and repentant men.

Notice that this almighty power is not time instilled—it flows from the fathomless well of eternity. Immanuel is also identified as the everlasting Father, or "the Father of

Eternity." He is thus God, one with the Father, who inhabits eternity, from everlasting to everlasting. He is not only a Father forever, but an ever-present Father existing everywhere at one and the same time, and for all time.[28]

We see a third divine attribute, that of omnipresence, ascribed to the nature of Immanuel. There is no limitation of beginning or ending of time or events with regard to His knowledge or to His presence. His concern for the children of men has been from everlasting, throughout time and eternity.

So Immanuel is the Author of everlasting life and happiness. He is indeed the Father of the blessed world to come. From eternity, He is the Provider of man's redemption, and it is the product of His wisdom and power. Because of Immanuel, that deceitful serpent, the devil, the father of lies, becomes a defeated foe before the prevailing Truth of God.

In spite of His conflict with sin and Satan, Immanuel is nevertheless to be recognized as the Prince of Peace. Why? Because He comes in peace—with healing in His hands. The Hebrew term *shalom* indicates not only an absence of war, but a condition of harmonious and positive well-being.[29] He comes to peaceably restore the lives of men back into a harmonious relationship with God the Father. No one is forced to return unto God against his own will. However, Immanuel comes not only to make peace between God and man, but also to put men at peace with themselves.

Thus, the reign of Immanuel is peaceable in the hearts and lives of those who will receive Him. When He is thus crowned King, He creates peace and He preserves peace. As the Prince of Peace, Immanuel is the Author and Giver of all good in life, of every blessing of peace, both now and forever. This suggests a fourth great divine attribute, that of omnificence—unlimited in creative bounty.[30] There will never be a point in time or eternity when His peace will not prevail. The characteristics of Immanuel abide forever.

Immanuel Forever

The peaceful grace of Immanuel particularly distills the conflict of right against wrong into a glorious Kingdom. Isaiah declares, "Of the increase of his government and peace there shall be no end." Further, His kingdom is said to be established "with judgment and with justice from henceforth even for ever" (Isa. 9:7, KJV). Immanuel in no case should be regarded as a mere transient, bearing only a temporary injunction against sin and Satan. By faith we see the decisive victory of righteousness despite the humble entrance of the Anointed One into the world conflict.

The powerful purpose of the Lord God sent His Son to earth as one of us. But with the personal presence of Immanuel—God with us—all the divine promises are placed in process of fulfillment, and the gracious plan of salvation is made real unto us. God with us becomes our only hope for deliverance from our enemies (including our own selfishness) and the only cure for the deadly disease of sin. Since Immanuel means God with us, He is ever on our side to help us in our struggles. And if God be for us, who can prevail against us?

Certainly, no evil power can triumph over Immanuel. Only a rebellious will, refusing to accept and believe, can enduringly resist God's gift of salvation. Even so, no unbeliever can alter the eternal purpose of God's redemption in this world.

The Child is born, the Son is given, and He is forever called Immanuel—God with us. Yet, the total meaning of the promise of divine salvation for humanity is not embraced unless the full name of the Child is pronounced.

161

The signature of the promised Child is Immanuel Jehoshua—"God with us, saving us from our sins." All divine power and purpose would become void and without meaning if He were not Immanuel forever.

According to the zealous performance of the Lord of hosts, the salvation of God is not limited by time or circumstance, but it shall endure in effect throughout endless ages. The divine covenant of redemption was not, nor is not, a temporary arrangement to deter the reign of sin over man. Rather, it is the glorious and everlasting provision of God to bring salvation to mankind by Immanuel. His birth signals the unshakable testimony of divine purpose and the timely manifestation of divine power. His government is established with judgment and justice forever.

The prophet looked for the dawning of a new day of righteousness. Isaiah saw that sin and evil could not endure unjudged or unpunished. By the birth of Immanuel, a new race in righteousness is born—not to flourish for a time and then wither and die, but to remain related to the Son in life. Thus, the destiny of the redeemed is joined to His eternal destiny.

There will never be a time when Immanuel will forsake the human creation. He is forever committed to the believer. As God, He abides with us forever, ruling and reigning, supplying our needs, forgiving our sins, and cleansing from all unrighteousness. Immanuel becomes the only begotten of the Father to be with us in every human circumstance.

We cannot fathom the great condescension of the divine Son to also become the Son of Man forever. No greater Presence could be given; no mightier Person could enter the stream of human life; no more powerful Ruler could sit upon David's throne. Why? Immanuel is God with us forever.

To consider the endless relationship of Immanuel with

162

mankind is certainly more than we can fully comprehend. However, one thing is sure: it extends the realm of redeeming love throughout eternity, instead of limiting it to the common notion that the divine covenant was completed with the birth of the Child. Even the Psalmist was more observant than many today, for he wrote: "The counsel of Jehovah standeth fast for ever, the thoughts of his heart to all generations" (Ps. 33:11).

All of the wonderful and hopeful words of the prophet concerning Immanuel would have become mockery except that He was to come and be the Saviour of mankind forever. Otherwise, any gain of righteousness, or the partial salvation of the lives of men, would be curtailed whenever His powerful presence ceased. But the accomplishments of Immanuel are not only for this world, but the world to come; they are not for time alone, they are for eternity. This is the abundant joy of having God with us in salvation.

Even though life may be threatened and wrecked by sin and strife, the coming of Immanuel transforms the despair of the world into hope. As the prophet indicates, salvation's door is opened, and the light of Truth shines forth. The gloom of ignorance is swept away.

If man is lost, one reason is because he has not accepted God's eternal redemption. The fact that God is with us makes a transforming difference in our present lives, as well as molding our destiny eternally. The glory of Immanuel will remain undimmed on this earth despite the passing of time and space. Thus, the strength of Isaiah's message of salvation lies in the truth that the Child to be born is indeed Immanuel forever.

In a particular manner, Isaiah has set the stage for the coming of the Messiah. He has identified the event as one of unprecedented character, a clear sign from God. He has also characterized the ensuing reign of the Messiah in such a way as to extend it throughout all eternity. The prophet has, more than ever before, assigned personality and presence to the Anointed One. However, despite the seeming connection with the immediate threat confronting Judah, the prophecy points to a future time of fulfillment.

The even more troublesome question: "When shall He come?" is the burden of another prophecy. With magnificent detail, Isaiah has faithfully relayed the divine word as to how the Messiah will come. It is left to Daniel and other succeeding prophets to tell when He will come and put His mission in action. Therefore, we next consider the time Daniel associates with the ministry of the Messiah.

Chapter 9

The Anointed One

Seventy weeks are determined upon thy people and upon thy holy city, to finish the transgression, and to make an end of sins, and to make reconciliation for iniquity, and to bring in everlasting righteousness, and to seal up the vision and prophecy, and to anoint the most Holy.

Know therefore and understand, that from the going forth of the commandment to restore and to build Jerusalem unto the Messiah the Prince shall be seven weeks, and threescore and two weeks: the street shall be built again, and the wall, even in troublous times.

And after threescore and two weeks

shall Messiah be cut off, but not for him-
self: and the people of the prince that shall
come shall destroy the city and the sanc-
tuary; and the end thereof shall be with a
flood, and unto the end of the war desola-
tions are determined.

And he shall confirm the covenant
with many for one week; and in the midst
of the week he shall cause the sacrifice and
the oblation to cease, and for the over-
spreading of the abominations he shall
make it desolate, even until the consum-
mation, and that determined shall be
poured upon the desolate.

(Dan. 9:24-27, KJV)

The Book of Daniel has perhaps given rise to more numerous and diverse interpretations than any other prophecy.
However, this passage about the 70 weeks has long been
the center of controversy. Even so, it may well be the back-
bone of the entire prophetic system of the Bible. Here, in
the ninth chapter, we find a significant instance in the Old
Testament which refers directly to the Messiah, the
Anointed One, and foretells the time of His coming.

The question is whether or not such predictions and
miracles contained in the Book of Daniel are genuine and
divine. Certainly, if they are, Bible critics have little place
to stand. Many have attacked the authorship and the date
of writing with numerous speculations—all denying that
the book was written by Daniel at the time of Judah's
exile. The earliest critic was probably Porphyry, and his
objections have been repeated by most modern assailants.
So, as Dr. Pusey said, "There was no choice left, except
to acknowledge prophecy, or to deny the genuineness of the
book."[1]

Perhaps one of the most popular theories of the critics is that this book was written in the time of the Maccabees, by some patriotic Jew, to encourage his countrymen against their enemies. In reply to such a theory, we may note two serious objections: (1) There is comparatively little expression of Messianic faith in the Apocryphal books, or in any literature of the time of the Maccabees. It is therefore unlikely that the glowing pictures of the Messiah and His kingdom depicted in Daniel should be a product of that time. (2) A linguistic study of the literature of the Maccabean period indicates that the books were written in Rabbinical Hebrew, which was in use among the Jews from about 200 B.C. till the Christian era. However, the Book of Daniel, like the Book of Ezra, is not written in this later Rabbinical Hebrew, with Greek idioms, but in the Hebrew of an earlier period—the period of old Hebrew corrupted by Chaldeanisms. This is conclusive evidence that the Book of Daniel cannot be discredited by alleging it was written at a later time.[2]

Thus, C. F. Keil, in his *Commentary of Daniel,* states with an unshakable conviction:

> If the book of Daniel were thus the production of a Maccabean Jew who would bring 'certain wholesome truths,' which he thought he possessed, before his contemporaries as prophecies of a divinely enlightened seer of the time of the exile, then it contains neither prophecy given by God, nor in general wholesome divine truth, but mere human invention, which because it was clothed in falsehood could not have its origin in truth. Such a production Christ, the eternal personal truth, never could have regarded as the prophecy of Daniel the prophet, and commanded to the observation of His disciples, as He has done. (Cf. Matt. 24:15; Mark 13:14.)[3]

Furthermore, as Professor A. McCaul has noted in the broader sense, such Messianic predictions which the critics plausibly explain as expressing hopes of earthly grandeur and prosperity, which they pronounce as genuine, are obviously incompatible with the teachings of Jesus. For instance, in his book *Prophecy,* McCaul states:

> The prophecies which represent the Son of Man as a heavenly judge, coming in the clouds of heaven (Dan. 7); Zion's King as meek and lowly, riding upon an ass (Zech. 9); the good Shepherd, sold for thirty pieces of silver (Zech. 11); pierced by the inhabitants of Jerusalem (Zech. 12); despised and rejected of men, cut off out of the land of the living, one upon whom the Lord hath laid the iniquities of us all (Isa. 53)—are the predictions which (they) prove (or declare) to be ungenuine.[4]

However, before we consider the time indicated by the 70 weeks, it is also well for us to consider the evidence that this passage is strictly Messianic. First, Daniel apparently wrote with a full knowledge of what Jeremiah, Isaiah, and some of the earlier prophets had written on this subject (cf. Jer. 29:10-14; 2 Chron. 36:21). Undoubtedly, Daniel was aware of the hopes their prophecies had inspired, adding to the meaning of his prophecy.[5]

In the second place, Daniel's Messianic statements in previous chapters show this discussion in the ninth chapter to be a continuance and a development of the same idea. It was apparent to Daniel that the Kingdom awaited the coming King.

As we have already seen, the Hebrew term *Messiah* and the Greek term *Christ* are the same in meaning, and they signify "the Anointed One." In using the term, Daniel knew that this exalted title had previously been used with reference to priests, prophets, and kings (1 Sam. 12:3, 5; 24:6, 10; 1 Chron. 16:22, etc.). He also knew that it came to be used of Him who should come to deliver and redeem His people (cf. Zech. 9:9; Mal. 3:1-4, etc.).

As was previously noted, there was a very early usage of the Messianic terminology found in the prayer of Hannah, Samuel's mother, some years before there was ever a king in Israel. Her prophetic prayer makes declarations concerning God's Messiah which are definitely paralleled in Daniel: "The adversaries of the Lord shall be broken to pieces; out of heaven shall be thunder upon them: the Lord shall judge the ends of the earth; and he shall give strength unto his king, and exalt the horn of his anointed [Heb., Messiah]" (1 Sam. 2:10).

Daniel beholds the Messiah as the climax and destiny of all history. When interpreting Nebuchadnezzar's prophetic dream (Dan. 2:31-45), Daniel spoke thus of the kings of the last days in relation to the kingdom of God:

And in the days of these kings shall the God of heaven set up a kingdom, which shall never be destroyed: and the kingdom shall not be left to other people, but it shall break in pieces and consume all these kingdoms, and it shall stand for ever. Forasmuch as thou sawest that the stone was cut out of the mountain without hands, and that it brake in pieces the iron, the brass, the clay, the silver, and the gold; the great God hath made known to the king what shall come to pass hereafter: and the dream is certain, and the interpretation thereof sure (Dan. 2:44-45).

Again, in Dan. 7:3-14, we read of Daniel's own vision of the four beasts coming up out of the sea, depicting the great empires of the world. From this passage, in verses 13 and 14, we read of divine judgment upon them, and of the ultimate establishment of God's Messianic kingdom:

I saw in the night visions, and behold, there came with the clouds of heaven one like unto a son of man, and he came even to the ancient of days, and they brought him near before him.
And there was given him dominion, and glory, and a kingdom, that all the peoples, nations, and

169

*languages should serve him; his dominion is an
everlasting dominion, which shall not pass away,
and his kingdom that which shall not be destroyed.*

Because of its significant terms, this prophecy has
been generally accepted by both Jews and Christians as
referring to the Messiah. For instance, Fred Rosenmuller
is quoted by Dr. Pye Smith as saying: "The Jewish interpreters are unanimous in the opinion that the Son of Man,
the person in human form, borne upon the clouds of
heaven, is the Messiah."[6] For Christians, there is an
evident application of the above prophecy by Jesus to himself when He declares: "Henceforth ye shall see the Son of
man sitting at the right hand of Power, and coming on the
clouds of heaven" (Matt. 26:64).

It should be noted that at this point in Daniel's prophecy the character of the Messianic kingdom is specified.
The Son of Man, God's Anointed One, shall one day have a
universal Kingdom, and all peoples shall serve Him. Moreover, His kingdom shall be everlasting. His dominion and
power shall not pass away to any successor. The infernal
powers of earth and hell shall not prevail against Him. His
kingdom shall not be destroyed.

Our third reason for asserting Dan. 9:24-27 to be
strictly Messianic is that the blessings mentioned in verse
24 ("to finish the transgression, and to make an end of
sins, and to make reconciliation for iniquity, and to bring
in everlasting righteousness") are the specific blessings
which Isaiah and other prophets ascribe to the Messiah's
reign. Indeed, Daniel here designates the coming Deliverer
as "Messiah the Prince" (9:25). It should also be noted
that the phrase "cut off" (v. 26), applied to the Messiah
by Daniel, is identical with the language of Isa. 53:8, "cut
off out of the land of the living." Thus, we may well conclude that Daniel refers to the same Person and the same
event, only with greater definiteness with regard to time.[7]

As Dewart suggests, there are at least two things that stand out clearly regardless of all differences and disputations: This passage from Daniel (1) is a direct prophecy of the Messiah, and (2) specifically refers to the time of His coming and death. Neither the obscurity of some aspects of the prophecy nor the difficulty of reaching positive conclusions can discredit what the language, the repeated references, and the whole analogy of Messianic prophecy clearly indicate.[8]

Daniel, in our textual reading, records the message which the angel Gabriel personally delivered to him. It opens a door of prophetic insight which reveals a larger dimension of God's purpose, not only for Israel but for the entire world. This expanded dimension of revelation specifically concerns the personal work and reign of the Messiah.

As we have noted, the subject had been introduced previously to Daniel through dreams and visions, as to Nebuchadnezzar in the great image (2:44-45), and as in Daniels own vision of the four beasts (7:3-14). But here (9:24-27) the divine message is given in the dimension of time, placed in a setting of "seventy weeks," reiterating the paradox of salvation by sacrifice. Again, as in Isaiah 53, Daniel couples the suffering, dying Messiah with eventual victory.

Our consideration of this prophecy of God's Messiah shall include: (1) The ministry and times of the Messiah; (2) The significant period of 70 weeks; and (3) The end of the age.

The Ministry and Times of the Messiah

The message of understanding which Gabriel brought to Daniel does not seem to have any immediate bearing upon the subject of Daniel's prayer. He had apparently been thinking of Jeremiah's prophecy of the 70 years (Jer. 29:10-14) and of the fact that the completion of this time was at hand. Indeed, the fulfillment did soon occur by the edict of Cyrus and the release of the Jews to return to Jerusalem (Ezra 1:1-4) around 536 B.C.

Daniel learned from the angel that the 70 years of captivity would not end Israel's dispersion, and neither would they usher in the Messianic kingdom. These events were revealed to be still some time in the future. Several great events, revealed to Daniel at this time, were to happen first. Daniel had been right in supposing that the kingdom of the Anointed One would be set up. But he was mistaken as to the time. So, it was with regard to the matter of time that the angel came to inform Daniel, specifying the intervening ministry of the Messiah.[9]

Some interpreters would limit the scope of the 70 weeks indicated, and the Messiah's work therein included, to the people of Israel, the land of Palestine, and the holy city of Jerusalem. It does seem that there is special pertinence in the message to this people and to this land, for the first clause states: "Seventy weeks are determined upon thy people and upon thy holy city" (v. 24).

But as the message develops, it becomes apparent that this clause may also have an inclusive connotation rather than an entirely exclusive note. God's plan in the Messiah is indeed for Israel, and certainly the main redemption events of the New Testament transpire at Jerusalem in Palestine. However, in God's provision for Israel is also salvation for all mankind (cf. Rom. 11:1, 11-12, 25-26). The culmination of the gospel is that salvation is through Christ and Him alone, whether for Jew or for Gentile.[10]

Within the total span of the symbolic "seventy weeks," a complete and final work of man's redemption is to be accomplished. Apparently, in the span of time this

172

would extend even beyond the desolations of humanity "until the consummation" (v. 27), until the end of this world. Moreover, since the key personage in this passage is the Messiah, it is evident that this is His work.

We immediately see six aspects of the Messiah's redemptive ministry in verse 24. They are: (1) "To finish the transgression"; (2) "To make an end of sins"; (3) "To make reconciliation for iniquity"; (4) "To bring in everlasting righteousness"; (5) "To seal up the vision and prophecy"; and (6) "To anoint the most Holy." A survey will indicate that the Messiah's work is divided. The first three of these aspects have to do with the complete conquest of sin. The remaining three have to do with the positive aspects of the accomplishment of redemption.[11]

It should be noted that despite the revelation to the contrary, the Jews were expecting a Messiah that would deliver them from foreign rule and give them temporal power and wealth. Even though they were clearly told that the Anointed One was coming to perform a more important work, the spiritual work of regeneration and reconciliation to God, they still primarily looked for a conquering king to be raised up. The fact is, Christ came to take away sin, to abolish it. It was sin that alienated man from God, that put dishonor upon God and brought misery upon mankind. The great undertaking of God's Messiah is to destroy the works of the devil, to finish transgression and sin in the world.[12]

So the first aspect of the Messiah's redemptive ministry set forth in verse 24 is "to finish the transgression." This apparently refers back to what Daniel had been praying with regard to his people: "We have sinned and have committed iniquity, and have done wickedly, and have rebelled, even by departing from thy precepts and from thy judgments" (Dan. 9:5). It may thus be interpreted that

173

within 70 weeks all this transgression was to be brought to an end.[13]

Daniel further indicates that the full meaning of the passage may be found in the books of Moses. In verse 11, Daniel declares: "Yea, all Israel have transgressed . . . therefore the curse is poured upon us, and the oath that is written in the law of Moses the servant of God, because we have sinned against him" (cf. v. 13).

Both the blessing and the curse are proclaimed in Deut. 28:15: "It shall come to pass, if thou wilt not hearken unto the voice of the Lord thy God to observe to do all his commandments and his statutes which I command thee." Then, in vivid detail, Moses proceeds to list all the things that would happen (and have happened) to the Jews in the long years of their dispersion.[14]

Even so, we must say that the transgression goes back to the first transgression in the Garden. To finish the transgression, the Messiah must break the power of it, bruising the head of the serpent. He must take away the usurped dominion of that deceptive tyrant, and establish a Kingdom of holiness and love in the hearts of men. For where sin and death had reigned, righteousness and life must reign through the grace of God. Thus, to finish the transgression ultimately means the destruction of Satan's kingdom here, and the founding of the Messiah's kingdom upon its ruins.[15]

The second aspect of the Messiah's redemptive ministry given to Daniel by Gabriel is "to make an end of sins." Some couple the first two aspects together. However, "to finish the transgression" is not the same as "to make an end of sins." To make an end of sin means to abolish it so that it may not rise up in judgment against men of faith in God. Furthermore, it means to obtain the pardon of it, that it may not be man's ruin. This points

174

to verse 26 where the message declares the Messiah shall be cut off, "but not for himself."

Thirdly, the Messiah is come to make reconciliation for iniquity. Here, the word "reconciliation" means atonement—"the offering of an atoning sacrifice." The Messiah comes to satisfy the justice of God, to make peace and bring God and man back together. He is not only the Peacemaker, but the Peace. He is himself the "At-one-ment" that reunites the life of man with the life of God.[16]

The fourth aspect—"to bring in everlasting righteousness"—is closely associated with the offering of an atoning sacrifice. It is significant that the other time "everlasting righteousness" occurs in the Bible, it is directly attributed to God. The Psalmist declares: "Thy righteousness is an everlasting righteousness" (Ps. 119:142). Viewing the revelation from the New Testament perspective, we see that only in Christ is such a righteousness found, for "it is not possible that the blood of bulls and of goats should take away sins" (Heb. 10:4).[17]

God might justly have made an end of sin by making an end of the sinner without hope of salvation. However, by the Anointed One sent, another way was provided. By Him, an end was made of sin, so as to save the sinner who looked to the Saviour. The merit of His sacrifice is our plea, and it becomes our righteousness. This, then, is everlasting righteousness; for Christ, who is our Righteousness and the Prince of our peace, is One with the everlasting Father.[18]

Concerning this passage in Daniel, the *Pulpit Commentary* makes the following observation:

> These two, "atonement for sin" and "everlasting righteousness"—His atoning death, and the righteousness which He brings into the world—are found in Christ. It is true that when Daniel heard these words spoken by Gabriel, he might not have put any very

distinct meaning on them. In that, Daniel was just like other prophets, for the prophets did not know the meaning of their own prophecies.[19]

Although Gabriel was sent to Daniel to give him understanding, it is unlikely that Daniel fully comprehended the extent of the truths that Gabriel declared. Indeed, Daniel knew about the righteousness which Christ was to bring forth. It was a new righteousness which was not through human attempts at compliance with the law, but through reliance on the Anointed One.

Several centuries later, after the ministry of Jesus Christ, the Apostle Paul wrote: "But now the righteousness of God without the law is manifested, being witnessed by the law and the prophets; even the righteousness of God which is by faith of Jesus Christ unto all and upon all them that believe" (Rom. 3:21-22). This is certainly the righteousness Gabriel was talking about.[20]

The fifth aspect of the Messiah's ministry is "to seal up the vision and prophecy." That is, with His coming, He will fulfill all the prophetic visions of the Old Testament. By so doing, the Messiah will confirm their truth as well as verify His own identity. There is a sense in which His coming also completes this manner of divine revelation, by He himself becoming the "more sure word of prophecy" (2 Pet. 1:19).

In no case can the meaning of sealing the vision and prophecy be limited to the fulfillment of Jeremiah's prophecy. The *Pulpit Commentary* definitely supports the necessity of a futuristic interpretation, by stating:

> This does not refer to Jeremiah's prophecy, because his prophecy referred merely to the return from Babylon, and Daniel's words refer to a period which is to continue long after that. Though Jeremiah's prophecy was about to be verified, this new prophecy required 490 years ere it received its verification. It seems that some event, to happen nearly half a millennium (500 yrs.) after Daniel,

176

is to prove the prophecy which God has given him to be true.[21]

The sixth and last aspect of the Messiah's redemptive ministry mentioned here is that He came "to anoint the most Holy." That is, the Messiah himself was anointed by the Holy Spirit, appointed and qualified for the holy work of redeeming lost humanity. As we have previously noted, the Hebrew word *Messiah* means "anointed." Although anointing was used on rare occasions with reference to things, its usual application was the anointing of persons such as priests, prophets, and especially kings. Thus, the reference in the phrase, "to anoint the most Holy," is primarily to the Messiah. It points forward to verse 25, where "the Messiah the Prince" is set in time.

On the other hand, this reference to anointing the most Holy has troubled some Christian commentators because Jesus Christ was not officially anointed King, but He was instead rejected and crucified. However, we must recognize that the fulfillment of this prophetic message given to Daniel was not completed by the first advent of Christ, but that it looks forward to the Second Advent, when He shall indeed be recognized as "the Anointed" by Israel.[22]

In surveying the culminating work of the Messiah, we see that He specifically comes to bring all things for all time under the righteous rule of God. Furthermore, He comes to seal up the vision and prophecy by bringing their projections to fulfillment. And, by coming "to anoint the most Holy," the Anointed One sanctifies the communion of man with God. Some view this as taking place in "the heavenly sanctuary" which is the eternal antitype of the earthly holy of holies in the Temple.[23]

At this point, Keil holds that:

> We must refer this sixth statement (to anoint the most Holy) also to that time of the consummation, and

177

understand it of the establishment of the new holy of holies which was shown to the holy seer on Patmos as "the tabernacle of God with men," in which God will dwell with them, and they shall become His people, and He shall be their God with them (Rev. 21:1-3). In this holy city there will be no temple, for the Lord, the Almighty God, and the Lamb is its temple, and the glory of God will lighten it (vv. 22-23). Into it nothing shall enter that defileth or worketh abomination (v. 27), for sin shall then be closed and sealed up; there shall righteousness dwell (II Pe. 3:13), and prophecy shall cease (I Cor. 13:8) by its fulfillment.[24]

Thus, the prophetic expectation of the Messiah's advent is symbolically indicated further in verse 25, "from the going forth of the commitment . . . unto the Messiah the Prince shall be seven weeks and threescore and two weeks." These words have been variously interpreted and understood, but it seems well established that at the time of Christ's first advent there was an unprecedented surge of expectancy of the Messiah. The documents of the Qumran community from the Dead Sea caves with their heightened tone of apocalyptic fervor confirm this.[25]

It is interesting to note that the Covenanters of the Qumran community, who produced the oldest existing biblical manuscripts now known, had a special regard for the Book of Daniel. According to the fragments recovered from their caves, it is evident that they possessed numerous copies of the book. Certainly, living as they did in turbulent times following Antiochus Epiphanes (168 B.C.) and until the destruction of Jerusalem in A.D. 71, they had a deep interest in the apocalyptic hope of God's Messiah.[26]

Moreover, the Apocryphal books of the intertestamental writers had somewhat to say about the Anointed One to be sent of God. For instance, we read:

And as for the lion which thou didst see, roused from the wood and roaring, and speaking to the eagle and reproving him for his unrighteousness and all his

178

deeds, as thou hast heard: This is the Messiah whom the Most High hath kept unto the end of days, who shall spring from the seed of David, and shall come and speak unto them;
For at the first he shall set them alive for judgment; and when he hath rebuked them he shall destroy them. (2 Esdras 12:30-32).

Indeed, there were signs from various quarters speaking of the soon coming of the Messiah. John the Baptist was not the first of his day to cry out for preparation for God's Anointed One. And where, do we suppose, did the wise men from the East gather evidence that a King was to be born in Judah at that particular time? It seems unlikely that the star alone would have been sufficient notice without some previous teaching or tradition that would give a basis for an approximate time of expectancy. At least one of those men came from Babylonia, the country where Daniel was captive, where the revealed weeks of years were undoubtedly known and discussed.[27]

Looking back to the time of Daniel's prophecy, we may be sure that Gabriel's mysterious message, couched in terms of times and numbers, caused eager hearts to look with hope and expectation long after Daniel's death. The Messiah-Prince, the Anointed Priest, and the Prophet of prophecy, was clearly revealed as the Hope of Israel and of the whole world. We therefore pass from a discussion of the ministry and times of the Messiah to a specific consideration of the meaning of the 70-week time span.

The Period of Seventy Weeks

The 70 weeks of Daniel (9:24-27) have been as a rock upon which numerous systems of interpretation have broken themselves. There is perhaps no subject of the Scriptures that has occasioned a greater variety of opinions. The main questions that have divided commentators

179

are: What is the nature of the designated weeks? What does their division into three segments signify? Are the 7 weeks an independent period apart from the 62? What is the commandment "to restore and build Jerusalem" from which the time is to be calculated? Who is the prince that shall come to destroy Jerusalem?[28]

E. J. Young outlines four principal classes of interpretation which show the divergent views:

1. *The Traditional Messianic Interpretation.* This view holds that the 70-weeks prophecy points to the first advent of Christ, especially to the event of His death, and culminates in the destruction of Jerusalem. Following Augustine, who first set forth this interpretation, its proponents have included Pusey, Wright, and Wilson. Young also supports this view.

2. *The Liberal Interpretation.* This view regards the 70 weeks not so much as prophecy, but as a description of the days of Antiochus Epiphanes and his ultimate overthrow by Judah under the leadership of the Maccabees. The Messiah who was cut off is identified as the high priest Onias, who was slain for his defiance of Antiochus.

3. *The Christian Church Interpretation.* In this the sevens are understood not as exact weeks of years, but rather as symbolical numbers covering the time between the edict of Cyrus to repatriate the Jews, through Messiah's first advent and death, to the rise of Antichrist and his eventual destruction at the end of the age.

4. *The Parenthesis Interpretation.* Here the 70 weeks of years are divided into periods of 7 sevens, 62 sevens, and a final seven detached from the rest by an indefinite parenthesis or hiatus. The 69 sevens cover the period to Messiah's first coming and death, followed by the destruction of Jerusalem. The final seven represents the period of Antichrist to the end of the age.[29]

Most interpreters since the days of Jerome, with the exception of those of the liberal school, have understood the 70 sevens as weeks of years, totaling 490 years. Thus, Jerome wrote:

> Now the angel himself specified seventy weeks of years, that is to say, four hundred and ninety years from the issuing of the word that the petition be granted that Jerusalem be rebuilt. The specified interval began in the twentieth year of Artaxerxes, king of the Persians, for it was his cupbearer Nehemiah who . . . petitioned the king and obtained his permission that Jerusalem be rebuilt.[30]

The ultimate question is: What do the words spoken by Gabriel to Daniel actually tell us? (1) That 70 weeks (a period amounting to 490 years) are to pass before the spiritual blessings and the fulfillment of the prophecy shall be revealed; (2) That from the going forth of the commandment to build, unto the Messiah the Prince, shall be 7 weeks and 62 weeks (483 years); (3) That the holy city of Jerusalem shall be built again in troublous times; (4) That after 62 weeks (434 years) the Messiah shall be cut off; (5) That the people of the prince shall come and destroy the city and the sanctuary; (6) This evil prince shall confirm the covenant for one week, and in the midst of the week he shall cause the sacrifice and oblation to cease.[31]

The first time period mentioned is 70 weeks. Then reference is made of 7 weeks, 62 weeks, and 1 week, which evidently make up the same 70 weeks. Something of importance takes place at the end of each period. The coming in of the Messianic kingdom takes place in 70 weeks of years; the appearance of the Messiah after 69 weeks of years; 62 weeks after the building of Jerusalem the cutting off of the Messiah; and, in the midst of the last week, the ceasing of the sacrifice.[32]

There has been some uncertainty expressed in determining the date of the order to build Jerusalem. And it is even more difficult to fix the time of the completion of the Restoration, which is assumed to occupy the seven weeks mentioned. Four different decrees are mentioned in Ezra and Nehemiah. Passing over that of Cyrus and that of Darius, the edict given to Ezra in the seventh year of Artaxerxes seems to be the most formal and important. But it does not refer directly to the building of Jerusalem. The royal authority given to Nehemiah in the twentieth year of Artaxerxes referred expressly to the building of the walls of Jerusalem.[33] Thus, many of the differences in interpretation of the 70 weeks prophecy occur because of variations in the choice of the beginning point of the time period.

For instance, Calvin insisted that the reckoning of time must begin with the edict of Cyrus for the return of the exiles to Jerusalem, thereby connecting Jeremiah's prophecy of 70 years to Daniel's 70 weeks. By this means, Calvin identifies Christ's baptism as the time of His official manifestation. However, the total of the years would not coincide. More than 530 years intervene between the edict of Cyrus in 536 and the birth of Jesus in 4 B.C., plus 30 additional years to His baptism. Thus the time would need to be extended to at least 565 years to cover the death of Jesus, here set at A.D. 29. But Calvin does not consider this to be an important discrepancy.[34]

Young agrees with Calvin at this point, for he holds that the exact number of years is not significant, since they are symbolical rather than chronological. In *The Messianic Prophecies of Daniel,* he writes:

> "Seventy heptads"—7x7x10—is the period in which the divine work of greatest moment is brought to perfection. Consequently since these numbers represent periods of time, the length of which is not stated, and since they are symbolical, it is not warrantable, to seek to discover the precise length of the sevens. This cannot

be done, nor for that matter, can the length of any of the individual sevens be discovered or determined. . . .

One thing, however, should be clear. It is that, according to Daniel, the important matters are not the beginning and ending of this period but the remarkable events which took place within it. . . . We believe . . . that when the seventy sevens were completed, so also the six purposes of verse 24 were accomplished. And that is the important matter. When Jesus Christ ascended into heaven, the mighty salvation which He came to accomplish, was actually accomplished.[35]

Keil likewise supports the symbolical view of measuring the stated span of 70 weeks. He says:

By the definition of these periods according to a symbolical measure of time, the reckoning of the actual duration of the periods named is withdrawn beyond the reach of our human research, and the definition of the days and hours of the development of the kingdom of God down to its consummation is reserved for God, the Governor of the world and the Ruler of human destiny.[36]

Where as Keil holds that the 70 weeks cover the history of the kingdom of God to the consummation in the end of time, Young believes that the time when the Messiah is cut off (v. 26) culminates not only the 69 weeks but the seventieth as well. Thus, the covenant that is confirmed with many (v. 27) is the gospel which Christ proclaimed, and His crucifixion in the midst of the week put an end to the validity of all other sacrifices and oblation. Furthermore, it rendered the Temple, which was dedicated to such sacrifice, an abomination. So the desolation which came upon the Temple and the holy city of Jerusalem under the hand of Titus in A.D. 70, was but an outward enactment of the inner desolation that had already occurred.[37]

Other scholars feel that such a symbolic interpretation does not satisfy the apparent timeliness of the message. They insist that the years of the 70 weeks be taken much more literally. Dr. Pusey, for example, counts the 70 weeks from the decree to Ezra. He takes the year 457 B.C. to be the time of the first authorization of Artaxerxes Longimanus given to Ezra to return to Jerusalem. Calculating and interpreting 7 and 62 weeks, amounting to 483 years from this base date, Pusey suggests that the prophecy points to A.D. 27, the time of Jesus' baptism and the occasion of His anointing by the Holy Spirit. The first half of the seventieth week is taken to be occupied with the public ministry of Jesus. His "cutting off" comes in the middle of this crucial week, after 3½ years. Then, for 3½ years more the gospel is preached exclusively to the Jews until the door of opportunity is opened to the Gentiles at the house of Cornelius. This signals the end to Israel's special privilege. The destruction of the Temple and the devastation of Jerusalem thus follow in due course.[38]

Hengstenberg also takes the 70 weeks as a literal time period, but he begins his calculations from the decree given to Nehemiah (which we previously noted was the time base for Jerome). A strong point in favor of taking the decree given to Nehemiah as the starting point is not only that it is the only specific decree to build the city, but Nehemiah is quoted as saying to Artaxerxes: "The city, the place of my fathers' sepulchres, lieth waste, and the gates thereof are consumed with fire. . . . Send me unto Judah, unto the city of my fathers' sepulchres, that I may build it" (Neh. 2:3, 5).[39]

Therefore, if we take the twentieth year of Artaxerxes as the year 454 B.C., and calculate the 7 plus 62 sevens, or 483 years, we come to A.D. 29. This was indeed the climactic year of the ministry of Jesus Christ. For in the spring of that year He appeared in Jerusalem as both Messiah and Prince, riding in triumph, attended by a rejoicing multitude (Zech. 9:9; Matt. 21:5). It was also at this time that

He was cut off, crucified (Isa. 53:8; Matt. 27:35). And this was not for himself, but "for the transgression of my people was he stricken." So, in the midst of the seventieth week, God's one great Sacrifice for sin was offered.

Scholars such as J. A. Seiss, Gaebelein, and others of the dispensational school, who also take an exact view of the 70 weeks, hold that the seventieth week also embraces the end time. The particular characteristic of this interpretation is the parenthetical time between the close of the sixty-ninth week, when the Messiah is cut off, and the opening of the seventieth week, which is reserved for the reign of the Antichrist and the end of the age.

This interpretation holds that the "prince that shall come" (v. 26) is not "Messiah the Prince" (v. 25), but the "little horn" of chapter 7. The covenant which he confirms (v. 27) is a perfidious treaty by which he wins the confidence of the Jewish people. But after three and a half years, "in the midst of the week," he breaks the covenant, outlaws religion, and opens the way to the torrent of unrestrained evil which constitutes the "time of trouble" (12:1).[40]

If, indeed, this prophecy given to Daniel refers not only to the first advent, but also includes the second advent of Christ, then the 70 weeks must run until His second coming. It is obvious, when we consider the nearly 2,000 years since the birth of Christ, that this prophecy must refer to far more than an unbroken period of 490 years. The prophecy is hardly explainable if 490 years are to run consecutively without a break. For in the midst of its fulfillment the Messiah is cut off, and His kingdom does not materialize, other than in the hearts of men.

Moreover, it seems belittling to the prophecy to suppose that such an establishment of a spiritual Kingdom was all that was divinely intended. In fact, one could very well say that the Messianic kingdom was in force in the hearts of believing men even before He came.

Neither is our understanding of this prophecy enhanced if we hold that the Messiah had to come before His kingdom could be established, and maintain that the prophecy envisions nothing concerning the Messiah beyond His "cutting off." If it ends there, it ends in futility.

On the other hand, if we recognize that the period of grace flows from Calvary, from the Messiah's "cutting off," that serves as an important intermission before the final act. Such a view clarifies that the 70 weeks are directly related to the Jewish nation. When they rejected God's Messiah, they also postponed His kingdom. Meanwhile, the salvation of God was preached to the Gentiles.

For centuries, until 1948, Israel remained under Gentile domination, and, until the summer of 1967, the holy city of Jerusalem was withheld from their control. At this time it would seem that the intermission is terminating, and the final act of the seventieth week is on stage.

So, one more week remains to be fulfilled. It will usher in the end of the age. Before Daniel seemingly refers to this remaining week, he speaks of "the people of the prince" (v. 26) that shall come and destroy the city and the sanctuary, and of resultant wars and desolations. Indeed, the destruction of Jerusalem and the Temple was etched into history by the Roman armies under Titus in A.D. 70. But this apparently took place after the sixty-ninth week had been fulfilled and before the seventieth week commenced.

Ever since that destruction, there have been wars and rumors of wars and desolations without end. We, therefore, still look for the end of the days when the destruction and desolation inspired by the allies of the prince shall at last be brought to an end, when the Messiah shall ascend His throne.

The End of the Age

Let us further explore this opinion of some scholars, that between the sixty-ninth and seventieth weeks there is a parenthesis which has lasted for more than 1,900 years. The seventieth week has apparently been timed by God himself, who orders the times and the seasons according to the response of people to the truth. It would seem that when the Messiah was slain on the Cross, the prophetic clock stopped, and there has scarcely been any movement of that clock for over 19 centuries. Thus, it is felt that only as Israel returns to God will this present age come to an end.

We have already noted that Daniel designates the last division of the 70 weeks as 1 week (or seven years). Evidently, this last week is yet to take place, for the events of this week did not occur immediately after the Crucifixion. It therefore seems that a so-called Dispensation of Grace intervenes between Daniel's sixty-ninth and seventieth weeks.

As history indicates, the Jewish nation was rendered inoperable, and a new era was begun, dominated by the Gentile Church, for "blindness in part is happened to Israel until the fulness of the Gentiles be come in" (Rom. 11:25, KJV).

Perhaps we should again note what is specifically predicted in Dan. 9:26-27:

> And after threescore and two weeks shall Messiah be cut off, but not for himself: and the people of the prince that shall come shall destroy the city and the sanctuary; and the end thereof shall be with a flood, and unto the end of the war desolations are determined.
> And he shall confirm the covenant with many for one week: and in the midst of the week he shall

*cause the sacrifice and the oblation to cease, and
for the overspreading of abominations he shall
make it desolate, even until the consummation,
and that determined shall be poured upon the
desolate* (KJV).

As Arthur Bloomfield suggests, these two verses are
difficult to interpret because of the condition of the text
and the difficulty of obtaining a good translation. The
versions all differ. However, it seems that the general
meaning is clear. In verse 26 there are three outstanding
subjects of prediction: (1) Messiah "shall . . . be cut off,
but not for himself"; (2) "The prince that shall come," and
(3) "The end thereof shall be with a flood."[41]

1. *Messiah "shall . . . be cut off, but not for himself."*
As has been previously indicated, from the Christian viewpoint, when Jesus was crucified, the Messiah was cut off.
It is true that crucifixion was a Roman form of execution
perhaps unknown to the Jews of Daniel's time, for it is
unspecified in the Old Testament. However, crucifixion is
definitely inferred in Old Testament passages such as
Psalm 22 and Isaiah 53. Certainly His death was not for
himself but for the sins of the people. Again, so far as the
Kingdom was concerned, long promised and expected,
Christ's death terminated that possibility at that time. His
humiliation and death left Him with nothing kingly to
offer. As Hengstenberg points out, the portion of verse 26
"but not for himself" may be rendered, "there shall be
nothing to Him." In either event, it is not that the real
object of His first coming (establishing His kingdom,
physical or spiritual) should be frustrated, but that the
earthly kingdom anticipated by the Jews should, for the
present, come to naught, and not then be realized.[42] So
the rejection and "cutting off" of Messiah brings us to the
conclusion of 69 weeks (483 years), to approximately A.D.
25 to 38, depending on the date of initial computation.

2. *"The prince that shall come."* Shortly after Jesus' crucifixion, the Roman armies came and destroyed the Temple and Jerusalem. The time is not indicated in Daniel, but it was actually some 40 years following, in A.D. 70. Perhaps we should observe that no mention is made that the prince himself would come and destroy the city, but rather the "people of the prince." There is in prophetic view a prince who is yet to play a part in the completion of man's day. This prince has not yet appeared, but his people (the Romans) were used as the scourge of God to punish Israel for their sin and unbelief. This prince that shall come must certainly be the Antichrist. Jesus referred to this passage and applied it to the end of the age. He said, "When therefore ye see the abomination of desolation, which was spoken of through Daniel the prophet, standing in the holy place (let him that readeth understand), then let them that are in Judea flee unto the mountains" (Matt. 24:15-16). These events are surely the necessary prelude to the return of Christ in glory.[43]

3. *"The end thereof shall be with a flood."* This is not necessarily a literal deluge of water, but rather an overrunning of armies. Bloomfield suggests that there will also be a flood, following a great earthquake which will divide the Mount of Olives and cause a deep valley to appear. This will open up an underground river which will flow out of Jerusalem in two directions, flooding much of the surrounding land (cf. Zech. 14:8; Ezek. 47:1-5).[44] On the other hand, some scholars take this to be the apt description of the desolation wrought by the overrunning army of Titus. But there is cause to suspect that this tragic war was not the only catastrophe in Daniel's prophetic view. The further statement connected to the figure of the flood is "and even unto the end shall be war." Apparently the war and desolation of the actual end time can be expected to surpass all previous history.

189

Thus, a plausible interpretation of this segment of the Scriptures may be directed to the end of the age, because of the unfulfilled events ascribed to the seventieth week. As by a turbulent flood, the people of Israel are to be destroyed by their enemies, scattered throughout the world. And, until the end of time, there shall be wars and desolations.

This is exactly what Christ said with regard to the time approaching the end. In Matt. 24:6, we read: "Ye shall hear of wars and rumors of wars; see that ye be not troubled: for these things must needs come to pass; but the end is not yet." In relation to Daniel's prophecy, the end must be at the fulfillment of the seventieth week.

Over and over in the Book of Daniel we find the expression "the time of the end." It is also found in other prophetic scriptures. This time period is clearly allotted to God's chosen people, Israel, and it at least seems to be on the brink of commencement.

Currently, we are particularly involved with the extension of God's saving grace, an intervening period which some have called "The Great Parenthesis." However, as God draws man's probationary period to a close, the prince, whose armies have already worked havoc on the earth, will make himself known. Daniel seems to speak of him in 9:27, "And he shall confirm the covenant with many for one week: and in the midst of the week he shall cause the sacrifice and oblation to cease."

Certainly, the time of the end must include the confirmation of God's covenant with His people. The question is: Who is confirming (or appearing to confirm) this covenant? The answer scholars give, varies. To some, the confirmation of the covenant can only be assigned to Christ, following the prophecy of Isaiah, "I will give thee for a covenant of the people" (i.e., He in whom the covenant between Israel and God is personally expressed).

Also, Mal. 3:1 speaks of "the angel of the covenant," and Jeremiah describes the Messianic covenant in full (31:31-34). The covenant (God's covenant with Israel) "prevails with many during one week." That is, God's covenant to send a Messiah—a part of the eternal covenant with Israel—would prevail with the acceptance of Him by many Israelites during one week. If we would reckon Jesus' ministry to have begun in A.D. 30, and the conversion of Saul (Paul) to have taken place in A.D. 37, it is suggested that the proper interval is accounted for.[45]

On the other hand, although the covenant is undoubtedly God's covenant with Israel, it is also this very covenant that Antichrist endeavors to confirm. He thus deceitfully assumes God's position as the protector of Israel.

At this point, Bloomfield indicates that the confirmation of this covenant is not necessarily with all Jews or Israel as a nation, but with "many." Apparently the "many" include the leaders and those who are in power. Because of their disloyalty to God, the entire nation will suffer. Whatever benefits are negotiated with the Antichrist are short-lived, for in the middle of the "week," Israel will experience terrible desolation under his rule.[46]

Jeremiah apparently speaks of this as "the time of Jacob's trouble." His prophecy is as follows:

And these are the words that Jehovah spake concerning Israel and concerning Judah.

For thus saith Jehovah: We have heard a voice of trembling, of fear, and not of peace.

Ask ye now, and see whether a man doth travail with child: wherefore do I see every man with his hands on his loins, as a woman in travail, and all faces are turned into paleness?

Alas! for that day is great, so that none is like

191

*it: it is even the time of Jacob's trouble; but he
shall be saved out of it* (Jer. 30:4-7).

Also, Daniel seems to refer to this same time in chapter 12, verse 1, in very distinct language:

> *And at that time shall Michael stand up, the
> great prince who standeth for the children of thy
> people; and there shall be a time of trouble, such
> as never was since there was a nation even to that
> same time: and at that time thy people shall be
> delivered, every one that shall be found written in
> the book.*

Daniel may well have seen a break between the sixty-ninth and the seventieth weeks without visualizing a time gap. The 69 weeks, which began with the commandment to restore and build Jerusalem (9:25), was terminated by the "cutting off" of Messiah (v. 26). Here, the meaning was not revealed to Daniel, but it is later revealed in the New Testament by the crucifixion of Jesus Christ and by the unfolding of the mystery of His Church (cf. Ephesians 3). Jesus offered the Kingdom to Israel when He made His triumphal entry into Jerusalem, but their answer was death on a Roman cross.

One might say that the Kingdom was again offered through the gift of the Holy Spirit after Jesus' resurrection (Acts 3:17-21). This offer was rejected by Israel by the imprisonment of the apostles and the stoning of Stephen. Some seven years thereafter, the gospel was given to the Gentiles.

Thus, because of the rejection of Christ and His crucifixion, Israel's prophetic fulfillment was sidetracked for a time, and the Church of Jesus Christ became the means of divine revelation. In the end, Israel's terrible sufferings will prepare her to receive the Messiah when He returns to establish His kingdom.

Along this same line of thought, we read in Zech. 12: 10:

> *And I will pour upon the house of David, and upon the inhabitants of Jerusalem, the spirit of grace and of supplication; and they shall look unto me whom they have pierced; and they shall mourn for him, as one mourneth for his only son, and shall be in bitterness for him, as one that is in bitterness for his firstborn.*

Then, in the following chapter, Zechariah prophesies that two parts (or two-thirds) of Israel will be slaughtered. During World War II, under the extermination practices of Hitler's Nazi regime, approximately one-third of the world's Jewish population perished—a total of more than 6 million men, women, and children. As horrendous as that memorable, blood-stained history seems, the Antichrist will purge Israel to the terrifying extent that the body count will at least double the previous affliction. Zechariah assesses this grim occasion as follows:

> *And it shall come to pass, that in all the land, saith Jehovah, two parts therein shall be cut off and die; but the third part shall be left therein.*
> *And I will bring the third part into the fire, and will refine them as silver is refined, and will try them as gold is tried. They shall call on my name, and I will hear them: I will say, It is my people; and they shall say, Jehovah is my God* (Zech. 13:8-9).

These prophecies of Zechariah apparently verify the interpretation of Dan. 9:26-27 that the "prince that shall come" is indeed the Antichrist. In view of the fact that everlasting righteousness was not ushered in around A.D. 37, the seventh year following Christ's crucifixion, and since during that time there is no record of any "prince

193

that shall come" (v. 26), we may conclude that the completion of the seventieth week of Daniel is yet future to our present Church age. Indeed, it is the time commonly designated as the tribulation period.[47]

It is during this tribulation period, the seventieth week of Daniel, that "the prince," the Antichrist, appears on the scene. He is the world dictator, the beast of Rev. 13:1-10. He apparently emerges from the same people who destroy Israel's city and sanctuary (Dan. 9:26). History records that this destruction was accomplished by a Roman army. There is good reason to conclude that the world empire during the tribulation period, prior to the establishment of the Messianic kingdom, is the revived Roman Empire.[48]

As profitable and as politically expedient as it seems, the emerging European Common Market could at least symbolize the sea from which the beast arises.

In summary, we see that the prophet Daniel, while in captivity in Babylon, was given a precise timetable and sequence relating to the future events of the people of Israel that would also involve all the peoples of the earth. Daniel was told that there would be a certain number of years from the time a proclamation was given allowing the Jewish people to return from Babylonian captivity and restore their homeland, to the time of the coming of Messiah. As we have already indicated, the time of the proclamation can be established by scriptural history in Ezra 1:1-4 or Neh. 2:1-10. Also, archeologists have uncovered evidence of this same proclamation in the ancient Persian archives.[49]

From the time permission was given to return and rebuild the city of Jerusalem and the Temple, until the Messiah would come as the Prince and heir apparent to the throne of David, would be 69 weeks of years, or 483 years. But Daniel was given more than specific years. He was also given the sequence of major historical events which cannot be denied: (1) The proclamation given to the Jews to return from captivity and rebuild Jerusalem and the Temple; (2) After this, the Messiah would come as the Prince; (3) Then the Messiah would be "cut off" (an idiom for being killed); (4) After the Messiah was killed, an army would invade and destroy the Holy City and the Temple which had been previously rebuilt by the returned exiles.[50]

Even if we stop here with our interpretation of Daniel's 70 weeks, as a number of scholars do, Daniel's prophecy confirms that whoever the Messiah was, He had to appear before Jerusalem was destroyed in A.D. 70 by Titus of Rome. By such a process of elimination, we may very well declare that there was only one person who was taken seriously as the Messiah before A.D. 70, and that was Jesus of Nazareth.[51]

We cannot tell how far into the future Daniel really saw. It seems, however, that no violence is done to the Scriptures if we conceive that Daniel was also cognizant of the end time. In fact, the prophecy is enhanced by such a view. It seems that if this prophecy speaks to us, it not only applies to the past, but also to our present and future.

One thing is certain: Even though the Messiah is rejected, He will not be denied His kingdom forever. Through tribulation God's own chosen people shall at last recognize His sovereignty. And not until Christ returns will the tribulation cease.

Just as the world of Daniel's day was being told to expect the coming of the Anointed One, we in turn are being notified of His imminent return. The focus of prophecy never envisions the Messiah in hopeless defeat—not even when He is seen as being "cut off." The constant word concerning Him is that He is the coming King.

Chapter 10

The Messenger of the Covenant

The voice of one that crieth, Prepare ye in the wilderness the way of Jehovah; make level in the desert a highway for our God.

Every valley shall be exalted, and every mountain and hill shall be made low; and the uneven shall be made level, and the rough places a plain;

And the glory of Jehovah shall be revealed, and all flesh shall see it together; for the mouth of Jehovah hath spoken it.

(Isa. 40:3-5)

Behold, I send my messenger, and he shall prepare the way before me: and the Lord, whom ye seek, will suddenly come to

196

*his temple; and the messenger of the cove-
nant, whom ye desire, behold he cometh,
saith Jehovah of hosts.*

*But who can abide the day of his com-
ing? and who shall stand when he appeareth? for he is like a refiner's fire, and like
fuller's soap:*

*And he will sit as a refiner and purifier
of silver, and he will purify the sons of Levi,
and refine them as gold and silver; and
they shall offer unto Jehovah offerings in
righteousness.*

(Mal. 3:1-3)

Both Isaiah and Malachi allude to the ancient custom of
sending pioneer "trailblazers" to clear the way for the
journey of an Eastern monarch when they described the
mission of the forerunner preparing the way for the coming
of Christ. The messenger will be an advance agent, opening the way by preaching righteousness, thereby removing
the obstacle of sin which stood between God and His people.

In a sense, the prophet is Jehovah's messenger, answering questions voiced by a doubting people, such as,
"Where is the God of judgment?" (Mal. 2:17). The divine
answer is that God is coming to show himself the God of
judgment and justice.

The prophetic word is: "Here He is; He is just at the
door; the long-expected Messiah is ready to appear, and
He says, 'For judgment have I come into this world, the
judgment you have so impudently defied.'"

According to Matthew Henry, one of the rabbin says
the meaning of this is that God will raise up a righteous
King to set things in order, even the King Messiah.[1] From
the Christian viewpoint, the beginning of the gospel of

Christ is expressly said to fulfill the prophecy of Isaiah and Malachi. In Mark 1:1-3, we read the New Testament response to the Old Testament promise:

> *The beginning of the gospel of Jesus Christ, the Son of God.*
> *Even as it is written in Isaiah the prophet, Behold, I send my messenger before thy face, who shall prepare thy way;*
> *The voice of one crying in the wilderness, Make ye ready the way of the Lord, make his paths straight.*

It may be asked: "How can the prophecy of Malachi be related to Isaiah?" Because of their apparent relationship, the two prophetic messages were coupled at the beginning of this chapter. The passage in Malachi seems to rest on that of Isaiah, his predecessor. Since this is taken to be the case, the New Testament writer refers to the original source of the prophecy in order to mark its dependency and connection.[2]

There is another important relationship which Mark directly infers, and that is the divine sonship of the Christ. This was certainly previously inferred by both Isaiah and Malachi. The prophets speak the part of the Messiah when the announcement is given: "I, the Messiah, the messenger of the covenant, the seed of God, will send my messenger, and he shall prepare the way before me: and the Lord, whom ye seek, will suddenly come to his temple." Indeed, as Adam Clarke suggests, and as we noted in the previous chapter, the Messiah they are expecting is also from the account of Daniel in his prophecy of the 70 weeks in Dan. 9:24.[3]

We may readily observe that the prophecies of Isaiah and Malachi predict two significant events: (1) the coming of the Lord's messenger to prepare the way for God; (2) the coming of the Lord, the Messiah himself, identified as "the messenger [angel] of the covenant." As J. M. Powis Smith notes, "the messenger of the covenant" can hardly be identical with the forerunner, called "my messenger" in Mal. 3:1. Indeed, his coming is made simultaneous with that of "the Lord," who cannot be other than Jehovah himself, and the coming of "my messenger" is explicitly announced as preceding the coming of the Lord.[4]

In order to present a more detailed discussion of this area of Messianic prophecy, we shall consider the development of the following: (1) The Forerunner, (2) The Messenger of the Covenant, and (3) The Goal of Messiah's Coming. For all practical purposes, this represents the closing word of Old Testament prophecy with regard to the Anointed One sent of God. Although God's word was repeatedly given and reiterated by the prophets, every message has its place, its point to inscribe upon the minds of men.

The Forerunner

The scriptural term "my messenger" indicates a privileged person entrusted with the truth of God. At least in a general sense, it seems that Hengstenberg is justified in thinking that "messenger" includes the long line of prophets headed by Elijah (whose name is representatively used in Mal. 4:5), and terminating in John the Baptist as the last and greatest of the prophets (Matt. 11:9-11).[5]

However, in a more particular sense, the prophet Malachi was "my messenger," for this is the meaning of his name. He was the last of the prophets to the restored remnant of God's chosen people after Judah's 70 years of captivity. So he probably prophesied as a messenger of God in the time of confusion during Nehemiah's absence from Babylon to rebuild Jerusalem (cf. Neh. 13:6).

Although Malachi has a distinct place as a prophetic messenger of God, he cannot seriously be considered as being "my messenger" who is the forerunner of the Messiah. Malachi's message was delivered nearly 400 years before the coming of Christ. Thus Malachi, and Isaiah before him, point to a prophet that will be especially commissioned of God to prepare the way for the Anointed One.

As we have already indicated, the New Testament response to this Old Testament prediction of the coming of the Lord's messenger to prepare the way, identifies that man as John the Baptist in Mark 1:4. It reads, "John came, who baptized in the wilderness and preached the baptism of repentance unto remission of sins."

Consider also the verifying words of Jesus which we previously cited in Matt. 11:9-11:

> But wherefore went ye out? to see a prophet? Yea, I say unto you, and much more than a prophet.
>
> This is he, of whom it is written, Behold, I send my messenger before thy face, who shall prepare thy way before thee.
>
> Verily I say unto you, Among them that are born of women there hath not arisen a greater than John the Baptist.

The ease with which the New Testament interlocks itself with the Old Testament and corroborates the prophetic truth certainly contributes to the establishment of the Christian viewpoint. Douglas Rawlinson Jones very aptly gives the Christian interpretation of this prophecy, as follows:

> The point here is that, though the contemporary priests are men-pleasers, the Lord will send a true messenger to prepare for his coming in judgment. Very soon this figure was understood to be a prophet, a veritable Elijah (4:5). Once the visitation of the Temple was seen

200

to have been made by Jesus, then in all respects John the Baptist could be recognized as the one who fulfilled the promise of the herald.[6]

Thus, from such a standpoint, Mal. 3:1 may be paraphrased to say as Adam Clarke suggests: "I, the Messiah, the seed of God, will send my messenger, John the Baptist."[7] Certainly, John, as the representative prophet, assuming the role of the forerunner of the Messiah, gathered in himself all the scattered features of previous prophecy. Hence, Jesus termed him "much more than a prophet" (Matt. 11:9), and indicated that he was indeed the greatest of the prophets (11:11). John vividly reproduced all of the awful and inspiring utterances of prophecy. His coarse garb was like that of the old prophets, confronting his audience with a visible dramatic exhortation to repentance.

The wilderness in which John preached symbolized the lifeless, barren state of the Jews at that time, both politically and spiritually. His sermon topics were always on sin, repentance, and salvation in the kingdom of God at hand. John thus presented for the last time, before the coming of Christ, the condensed epitome of all the previous teachings of God through the prophets. Both because of his message and because of the immediacy of its fulfillment, John the Baptist is preeminently God's "messenger."[8]

It was also the testimony of Josephus, the Jewish historian of the first century, that John "was a good man, and commanded the Jews to exercise virtue, both as to righteousness towards one another, and piety towards God."[9] So, he must indeed be acknowledged as a special messenger for a special time, with a commission direct from heaven, and not of men.

The people of John's day did recognize him to be a prophet, God's messenger, because he was not a man-pleaser. His message condemning sin and calling to repentance was a familiar hallmark to the Jews. But along with a number of the other prophets, it eventually cost John his life. The time allotted him to prepare the way for Christ was brief. It was apparently a span of no more than two years, from around A.D. 26 to A.D. 28, when he was imprisoned by Herod Antipas.

But who was this John the Baptist, and from whence did he come? He was a descendant of the priestly class by both parents. His father, Zacharias, was himself a priest of the course of Abia or Abijah (1 Chron. 24:10), and his mother, Elisabeth, was one of the descendant daughters of Aaron (Luke 1:5). His birth was not according to the ordinary laws of nature, but it was accomplished through the interposition of divine power. The event was foretold by an angel sent from God, which is related at length in Luke 1.

Moreover, from his birth, John was ordained to be a Nazarite (Luke 1:15). Then, just a single verse contains the whole scriptural record of John's history for the period of around 30 years, the whole time which elapsed between his birth and the commencement of his public ministry. "The child grew and waxed strong in spirit, and was in the deserts till the day of his showing unto Israel" (Luke 1:80). Thus John lived alone in the wild and thinly populated region west of the Dead Sea. There he prepared himself by self-discipline and by constant communion with God for the wonderful office of "messenger" to which he had been divinely called.[10]

Many scholars think John the Baptist was an Essene who might have had some association with the Qumran community, who produced and preserved the Dead Sea Scrolls. F. F. Bruce concurs with this idea. He notes John's residence in the wilderness of Judea, his asceticism, and his baptismal teaching and practice. With regard to the latter, Bruce indicates that Josephus' account of John's baptismal teaching accords more closely with the Qumran doctrine than does the New Testament account. Thus, he concludes: "John may have had some contact with the Qumran community; he may even have belonged to it for a time."[11]

In any event, it seems the very appearance of John presented a lesson to his countrymen. His clothing was that of the old prophets—a garment woven of camel's hair (2 Kings 1:8), attached to the body with a leather girdle. His food was that which was readily available in the desert—locusts (Lev. 11:22) and wild honey (Ps. 81:16).

Once John came forth to perform his calling, the people's knowledge of his extraordinary birth; his rigid, ascetic life; his reputation for holy character; along with the general prevailing expectation that some great One was about to appear, attracted multitudes of people "from all the region round about the Jordan" (Matt. 3:5). The crowds came without the attraction of any display of miraculous power, for "John did no miracle" (John 10:41, KJV).

John's startling exhortation to the people was: "Repent ye; for the kingdom of heaven is at hand" (Matt. 3:2). Thus preaching repentance, John was echoing the cries of the Old Testament prophets. Indeed, he was the last of this succession. But even though he belonged to the old regime, he also stood on the threshold of the new.

When John cried, "Repent ye!" he may well have had the words of Isa. 1:16-17 in mind: "Wash you, make you clean; put away the evil of your doings from before mine eyes; cease to do evil; learn to do well." Or he may have been thinking of Isa. 55:7: "Let the wicked forsake his way, and the unrighteous man his thoughts: and let him return unto Jehovah, and he will have mercy upon him: and to our God, for he will abundantly pardon." Or again, the background of John's message may be found in Jer. 7:3-7, where the prophet said: "Amend your ways and your doings. . . . For if ye thoroughly amend your ways and doings . . . then will I cause you to dwell in this place, in the land that I gave to your fathers, from of old even for evermore."

But to emphasize his call to repentance, John also quoted from Isa. 40:3. He identified himself as "the voice of one crying in the wilderness"—the wilderness of man's sin and spiritual need. Certainly, John's description of himself as a "voice" is in keeping with his role as a herald. He was not speaking for himself but, rather, for another.[12]

Thus, as the forerunner of the Messiah, the task of John the Baptist was to warn men: "Prepare ye the way of the Lord." They were, in a sense, to build a royal road on which their King might come. John's hearers were thus to repent because "the kingdom of heaven is at hand." This added a strong note of urgency in his call to repentance. It was almost as if he said: "It's now or never!"

The climactic events of the next few years—the rejection and crucifixion of the Messiah, and the destruction of Jerusalem in A.D. 70—were sufficient to justify the look of his eyes and the tone of his voice. Those indeed proved to be the "last days," or "the days of the Messiah."[13]

In Matt. 3:11, John refers further to his role as the forerunner of the Messiah. He declares: "I indeed baptize you in water unto repentance: but he that cometh after me is mightier than I, whose shoes I am not worthy to bear: he shall baptize you in the Holy Spirit and in fire." Mark records this even more vividly, with John saying of the Messiah, "the latchet of whose shoes I am not worthy to stoop down and unloose" (1:7). Tying and untying the "thongs" of the master's "sandals," and carrying the latter for him, were the menial tasks of the humblest slave. Yet John did not consider himself worthy to do even these things for the Messiah.

Nevertheless, it became John's privilege to baptize Jesus. John tried to avoid this, for he felt that he needed to be baptized by Jesus. But Jesus said: "Suffer it now: for thus it becometh us to fulfill all righteousness" (Matt. 3:15).

With the baptism of Jesus, John's special office ceased. However, he still continued to present himself to his countrymen in the capacity of witness to Christ. He bore witness that Jesus, upon whom he had seen the Spirit descend as a dove, was the Son of God (John 1:33-34). Again, the next day, he looked on Jesus and said, "Behold the Lamb of God, that taketh away the sin of the world!" (John 1:29, 36).

Shortly after John had thus given testimony to the Messiah, his public ministry was brought to a close. Now that the "messenger of the covenant" himself was here, the forerunner's task was complete. Because John had reproved Herod Antipas of the sin of taking his brother Philip's wife for his own, he was imprisoned. Eventually, at the request of Salome and Herodias, her mother, John was beheaded. This supposedly occurred just before the third Passover of Jesus' ministry (March, A.D. 29).

The Messenger of the Covenant

Besides predicting the coming of the forerunner, Malachi prophesies of the appearing of the Messiah, the coming of the Lord himself. He says: "The Lord whom you seek, will suddenly come to his temple, even the God of judgment, who, you think, has forsaken the earth, and you wonder what has become of Him" (cf. Mal. 3:1). Furthermore, although the Messiah has long been called "He that should come," Malachi now assures the people that He will come shortly.[14]

Malachi's prophecy also teaches that judgment indeed

begins at the house of the Lord, as did Ezekiel (9:6). "The Lord," as Malachi uses the term, is not the sacred name of Yahweh, nor is it "Adonai," the form which is usually substituted for it in reading. Rather, the word is "ha-Adon," the literal equivalent of "the Lord," which is occasionally prefixed to Yahweh as in Exod. 23:17 and Isa. 1:24. Whose coming, then, is Malachi foretelling?[15]

It is interesting to note that the earliest Christian confession was the words "Jesus is Lord" (cf. 1 Cor. 12:3; Phil. 2:11). On the Day of Pentecost, Peter declared, "God hath made that same Jesus, whom ye have crucified, both Lord and Christ" (Acts 2:36, KJV). Following the distinction indicated by Malachi, the Christian conviction is that Jesus is God, not God the Father, but God the Son: "God was in Christ" (2 Cor. 5:19).

In retrospect, Jesus Christ was not accounted a mere man among men, no angel clothed as a man, no secondary divinity created in eternity, but God the Almighty, the only true and living God, come down to us as Jesus of Nazareth. Again, the New Testament word was: "No man hath seen God at any time; the only begotten Son, who is in the bosom of the Father, he hath declared him" (John 1:18). Undoubtedly, the prophetic focus of Malachi is upon this same Jesus.[16]

This person is indeed the Messenger of the covenant, that blessed One sent from heaven to reconcile man unto God. He is the One commissioned by the Father to return sinful man back to His kingdom by a covenant of grace. We recall that at the dawn of history, man violated and fell from the divine covenant of innocency under which he was created. Now the Messenger comes to fulfill the great purpose of God initiated by the covenant with Abram, that in his Seed all the families of the earth would be blessed (cf. Gen. 12:1-3).

Lest some may fail to differentiate between Malachi's

terms "my messenger" and "messenger of the covenant," the following distinctions should be noted. "The messenger of the covenant" can hardly be identical with the forerunner, "my messenger," for his coming is prepared for and made simultaneous with the coming of "the Lord." According to J. M. Powis Smith, the "messenger of the covenant" can hardly be anyone but Yahweh himself, and the coming of "my messenger" is explicitly announced as preceding that of Yahweh.[17]

T. T. Perowne has given a definitive treatment of this title which Malachi assigns to our Lord. The summary is as follows:

> The idea of the messenger, which pervades this prophecy, culminates (as do the Old Testament ideas of the prophet, the priest, and the king) in the Messiah, who is in the highest sense the Messenger of God to man. The Angel, or Messenger, whose presence in the Church was recognized from the beginning (Acts 7:38; Exod. 23: 20-21; Isa. 63:9. et al.), follows up these "preludings of the incarnation" by being "made flesh and dwelling among us." The covenant, which was before the Law (Gal. 3:17) and yet by virtue of its later introduction "a new covenant" (Jer. 31:31-34; Heb. 8:7-13), He comes, in fulfillment of promise and prophecy (Isa. 42:6; 55: 3), as its Messenger and Mediator (Heb. 12:24), to inaugurate and ratify with His blood (Matt. 26:28; Heb. 13:20); while He vindicates His claim to be "the God of Judgment" whom they desired, by the work of discriminating justice which He performs (vv. 2-5).[18]

The Messiah is thus the Fulfiller of prophecy as well as the Subject of the prophets. He is the Messenger or "angel" of the covenant, by whose mediation it is brought about and established, even as God's covenant with Israel was made by the disposition of heavenly messengers.

The Lord comes not only as the Messenger and Mediator of the covenant; He is given for a covenant (Isa. 49:8). Though He is the Prince of the covenant, yet He condescended to be the Messenger of it, that mankind might have full assurance of God's goodwill, and experience His own word and presence.

The divinity of the Messiah is thus unequivocally asserted. As the Messenger of the covenant, He is identified with the Lord. He is also the covenant Angel who guided the Israelites to the Promised Land, and He is seen in the various theophanies of the Old Testament. Now in Him are fulfilled all the promises made under the old covenant, so in the New Testament He is called the Mediator of the new covenant (Heb. 9:15).[19]

All the manifestations of God in the Old Testament, the Shekinah (glory) and human appearances, were made in the person of the divine Son (Exod. 23:20-21; Heb. 11: 26; 12:26). But it is evident that with the coming of the Messenger of the covenant, the old covenant must give way to the new by reason of His very presence. The Messiah would come, not as Israel expected, to flatter the theocratic nation's prejudices, but to subject their principles to the fiery test of His heart-searching truth (Matt. 3:10-12).[20]

Nevertheless, pious Jews had long been seeking and anticipating the coming of the Messiah. In looking and waiting for Him, they looked for redemption in Jerusalem and waited for the consolation of Israel as a nation (Luke 2:25, 38). Indeed, according to the prophet Haggai, the coming One is the Desire of all nations (2:7, KJV). But He was specifically the Desire of the Jewish nation because the promise of His coming was actually made to them, as children of Abraham.

Certainly, if the Messiah is really one's Desire, He should also be the heart's Delight. Israel, as well as the whole world, had every reason to delight in Him who is the Messenger of the covenant. He comes to gloriously fulfill the divine purpose of man on this blighted planet. Despite their anticipation of His coming, very few were ready to receive Him when Christ finally came.

As we have already noted, Malachi viewed His coming as suddenly, to His Temple. His coming was no longer in the dim distance as the patriarchs had beheld it. The prophet now views His coming as immediately after the forerunner appears. "When the morning star appears, believe that the Sun of righteousness is not far off."[21] Even so, the Messiah will come suddenly in that He will come when many do not look for Him. It is a tradition among the Jews that the Messiah is among the things that come unawares.

The place to look for Him is at His Temple, the Temple in Jerusalem, which, in Malachi's time, had been recently rebuilt. By giving this specific location of His appearing, the Messiah must come at least while the Temple is standing. For a time, this would present a stable proposition to the Jews, until the Temple was again destroyed in A.D. 70. But, for the most part, the Jews missed His coming.

According to the New Testament revelation, Jesus Christ, when 40 days old, was presented in the Temple. At that time, a just man, Simeon, who was guided by the Spirit, visited the Temple by the direction of Malachi's prophecy, and saw Him (Luke 2:27). Again, at 12 years of age, Jesus was in the Temple about His Father's business (Luke 2:49). Then, when He rode into Jerusalem in triumph on that final Passover Feast, it would seem that He went directly to the Temple to cleanse it (Matt. 21:1-13), and the blind and the lame came to be healed (v. 14).

The certainty of the coming of the Messenger of the covenant, the Messiah, is verified by the Lord of hosts himself. "Behold, he shall come, saith the Lord of hosts." Surely, one can depend upon the Word of God himself. Malachi would say, "You may depend upon His word, who cannot lie; He shall come, He will come, He will not tarry." So the coming of the Messenger of the covenant is not only prophesied, it is promised by God's own unchanging Word.

Undoubtedly, the prophet here regards the mission of the Messiah as a whole, from the First to the Second Advent. The Messenger of the covenant, by His very coming, began the process of refining and separating the godly from the ungodly. It continued during Christ's short ministry on earth, and it has been going on ever since. It will thus be carried out until the final separation of judgment described in Matt. 25:31-46. This indicates that the ultimate mission of the Messiah has not yet been achieved. The goal of His coming is not totally fulfilled.

The Goal of Messiah's Coming

Obviously, according to Mal. 3:2-5, the prophet clearly recognizes a twofold goal in the coming of the Lord: (1) To purify the priesthood, and (2) to execute judgment upon sinners. As has already been suggested, in his presentation of the full scope of the mission of the Messenger of the covenant, Malachi seems to blend the first and second comings of Christ into one event. From our vantage point, we are aware that His first coming was a time of sifting and severance, according as those to whom He came did or did not receive Him.[22]

In verse 2, we read the word of God through Malachi: "But who can abide the day of his coming? and who shall stand when he appeareth? for he is like a refiner's fire, and like fuller's soap." Malachi's countrymen expected the Messiah to come and judge the heathen idol worshipers, but the prophet warns that they themselves shall be judged first (cf. Amos 5:18). Thus, Malachi saw the future Judge in the coming Saviour.

210

John the Baptist was evidently echoing the message of Malachi when he proclaimed the separating judgment of Christ. "He shall baptize you in the Holy Spirit and in fire: whose fan is in his hand, and he will thoroughly cleanse his threshing floor; and he will gather his wheat into the garner, but the chaff he will burn up with unquenchable fire" (Matt. 3:11-12).

We cannot help but note the words of Jesus himself in this regard. "For judgment I am come into this world, that they which see not might see; and that they which see might be made blind" (John 9:39, KJV). Also, Jesus declared, "He that believeth on him is not condemned: but he that believeth not is condemned already" (John 3:18, KJV).

These words indicate that every soul of man is related to God in some manner, either in God's favor or under His wrath, and "every one shall be salted with fire" (Mark 9:49). The ultimate choice is either the fire of the Holy Spirit baptism in purification or the unquenchable fire of Gehenna in everlasting destruction.[23]

This intensifies the questions of Malachi: "Who can abide the day of his coming? and who shall stand when he appeareth?" Since "God is a consuming fire" (Heb. 12:29), who must by His very nature burn out the dross, He must either destroy the sin within man by His grace, or He must consume us with it, in hell. It is left to the choice of humanity collectively and individually, the manner in which the fire of God will be applied. John Calvin comments: "That power of fire, we know, is two-fold for it burns and it purifies; it burns what is corrupt but it purifies gold and silver from their dross. The prophet no doubt meant to include both."[24]

Considering the awesomeness of the Messiah's appearance, it may well be wondered: "Who can stand up under the burden of this severe judgment?" The Vulgate

Version, *"Quis stabit ad videndum eum?"* points to the brightness of His presence, which the eye of man cannot endure.[25] Nevertheless, in spite of the manner of judgment which attends His coming, the Messiah comes primarily, not to condemn the world, but that the world through Him might be saved.

Thus, as the prophet indicates, He shall be like a refiner's fire which separates the impurities from the precious metal by melting the ore. So the Lord at His coming shall separate the good among men from the evil (cf. Isa. 1:25; Jer. 6:29; Zech. 13:9). And, to continue the analogy, He is also "like fuller's soap." A "fuller" was a bleacher of cloth, who by the strength and formula of his soap was able to remove the dirt and grime from soiled clothing. This idea is parallel to the concept of Refiner.

Isaiah also combines the two: "When the Lord shall have washed away the filth of the daughters of Zion, and shall have purged the blood of Jerusalem from the midst thereof, by the spirit of justice, and by the spirit of burning" (Isa. 4:4).

When Christ comes, He discovers men, that the thoughts of their hearts might be revealed (cf. Luke 2:35). He thereby distinguishes men to separate the righteous from the vile, for His "fan is in his hand" (Matt. 3:11). Hence, there is inevitably a dual effect on men as they are tried by the truth of the gospel of God. The gospel shall thus work good upon those that are disposed to be good, for to them it shall be the impact of life unto life (cf. Mal. 3:3).[26] As in history, the Angel of the covenant, in leading His chosen people out of the bondage of Egypt by the pillar of cloud and fire, had an aspect of terror to His foes, but of love to His friends.[27]

In this manner, the Messiah comes to sit as a Refiner. As such a purifier of metals, He sits before the crucible, watching the metal, taking care that the fire is

212

not too hot. And He keeps the metal in the flame until He knows the dross to be completely removed by seeing His own image reflected in the purity of the molten mass (cf. Rom. 8:29). Certainly, He sits down to this work, not in a perfunctory manner, but with patient love and unflinching justice. This same separating process goes on in the world as in each individual believer. Finally, when the godly are completely separated from the ungodly, the world, as people now know it, will end.[28]

Who are those, then, that the Messiah shall purify? "He will purify the sons of Levi," says the prophet, "and refine them as gold and silver; and they shall offer unto Jehovah offerings in righteousness" (Mal. 3:3). Again, we note that divine judgment is to begin at the house of God (cf. Ezek. 9:6). It is especially initiated with the sons of Levi, the priests, who ought to set the example of righteousness. They must be purified so they might properly teach the people holiness and obedience.[29]

This purifying consists not only in exterminating the evil from God's chosen representatives, but also from those who will not allow the correction of God. When we recall Christ's purging of the Temple, and His denunciations of the teaching body among His contemporaries, we may see that the doctrine of God tries His ministers in all ages. Indeed, it is that "they shall offer unto Jehovah offerings in righteousness." A pure offering can only be offered by a purified heart.[30]

Looking beyond the manger and the Cross, to an Upper Room, Malachi's prophecy finds a greater measure of fulfillment after the outpouring of the Holy Spirit at Pentecost. In Acts 6:7, we read that "a great company of the priests were obedient to the faith." So in an even fuller extent, we recognize that Christ's gospel was also to purify His Church through the regeneration and cleansing of His Holy Spirit. It was to this end that He gave himself for the

Church, "that he might sanctify it, having cleansed it by the washing of water with the word" (Eph. 5:26), "and purify unto himself a people for his own possession, zealous of good works" (Titus 2:14).

Thus, as the great Refiner, Christ will purify the sons of Levi, or all of those that are devoted to His praise and employed in His service, as the tribe of Levi was. He now purposes to make spiritual priests unto God (Rev. 1:6), establishing "a holy priesthood, to offer up spiritual sacrifices, acceptable to God through Jesus Christ" (1 Pet. 2:5). According to the New Testament sense, all true Christians are "sons of Levi," set apart for God, to render obedient service in His kingdom. This, then, is the primary goal of Messiah's coming—to purify the priesthood, and make them acceptable to God.

How will Messiah purify them? Again, as the prophet graphically illustrates, He will purge them, refine them as gold and silver. In the spiritual sense, He will not only wash away the soiled spots from their external lives, but He will make them holy inwardly, taking away the dross that is found. He will separate them from their indwelling corruptions which had rendered their faculties worthless and useless, making them like refined gold, both valuable and serviceable.

Why does Messiah come to purify His people? The answer is obvious. It is that His purified ones may survive the coming judgment. In Mal. 3:5, the prophet answers the initial question: "Where is the God of judgment and justice?" (2:17). God speaks through Malachi, saying:

> And I will come near to you to judgment; and I will be a swift witness against the sorcerers, and against the adulterers, and against the false swearers, and against those that oppress the hireling in his wages, the widow, and the fatherless, and that

214

*turn aside the sojourner from his right, and fear
not me, saith Jehovah of hosts.*

So, after the Temple, the house of God, has been
cleansed and prepared for the divine Messenger of the covenant, His very presence will judge the impenitent people.
The gospel of Christ is not only a message of salvation, but
it also stands as a body of evidence against all evildoers.

Despite the seeming silence of God and the tarrying of
His messenger, Malachi declares that both salvation and
judgment are certain. This was soon to be announced by
the messenger ("my messenger"), or forerunner, of the
"messenger of the covenant" ("the Lord") himself.

We may well observe that this prophecy was fulfilled
by the coming of John the Baptist, the forerunner, and by
the coming of Jesus Christ as the Messenger of the covenant. However, this extent of fulfillment does not satisfy
the evident ramifications of the scope of this prophecy.

From the New Testament view, we recognize that the
promised salvation of God has come. Also, looking back on
the subsequent events in history, the fate of God's chosen
people may rightfully be interpreted as at least the partial
result of the judgment of God upon their rebellion.

However, in spite of these workings toward the purpose of God, we cannot yet say that the goal of Messiah's
coming has been accomplished. Although it is doubtful
that the prophet had any inkling whatsoever that the
Messenger of the covenant would necessarily become the
Suffering Servant, so that the justice of God now awaits
His return, the fact remains that God's purpose is declared
to be unchanging (cf. v. 6). We see, then, that the prophecy of Malachi anticipates the time when God shall forever
silence the doubters and put an end to sin.

For a time, the purifying process is carried on. There
is a sense in which Messiah's salvation is here, and there is
a sense in which His kingdom is at hand. There is a sense

in which judgment has already been meted out, but there is also a sense in which terrible judgment is still coming. The fruition of this prophecy awaits the triumphant shout: "Behold, the King is here!"

Chapter 11

The Messiah as Word and Wisdom

Eventually the voices of prophecy became silent. But through all the dark hours of Israel's history, the promised and expected Messianic redemption was the "one hope and stay" of the Jews. The continuing expectation of the One who was to come was, especially in times of crisis, the only stable factor in Israel's changing world.

We have noted that during the prophetic ministries of Isaiah and Malachi, the Davidic monarch, who had stood as the anointed one, the representative of Jehovah, had become threatened with extinction. Perhaps more than ever before, the Messianic hopes and conceptions in Israel thus became connected with "the end time," the anticipated period of Israel's perfection, of ultimate peace and divine blessing.

As such, the Messianic hope of the One who is coming

became intimately associated with the eschatology, the new age of the nation or people. So, entering what may be called the intertestamental period, whether the Messiah was considered to be a person or a corporate personality, it is always Jehovah in him that is Saviour.

With the ultimate collapse of the monarchy, the Messianic hopes apparently became centered in the people of Israel as the servant of the Lord, which the prophet seems to indicate. For instance, in Isa. 49:3, we read_ "And he said unto me, Thou art my servant; Israel, in whom I will be glorified" (cf. Isa. 41:8-10; 44:21; 48:20). To a great extent, the personal Messiah, as Davidic king, receded into the background for a time. The divine presence thus became the revelation of God incarnated in Israel.

However, following the Babylonian captivity, Israel's restoration once again elevated the priesthood to prominence. Then, eventually, a union of the priestly and kingly offices occurred, as in Zerubbabel. This was because a renewed realization of iniquity was focused upon the significant concept of atonement. We particularly find this thought expressed in Zechariah, Haggai, and Malachi, the prophets of the restoration.

Such developments, along with God's providential treatment of Israel, altered her concepts of the future and varied her ideas of God's presence and operation in the world. The more reflective thought of Israel's religious leaders departed from the view that the operations of God in creation and in providence, in history and in revelation, were mediated by anthropomorphic agents such as angels or divinely anointed men. Rather, these divine operations were viewed as mediated by qualities of God himself, His Word, His Wisdom, His power, to which objective existence was given. Their activity could only be represented as that of intelligent agents, and the effort to represent

218

them vividly eventually attached distinct personality to them.[1]

In considering the ideas which continued to project the hope of the coming of the Anointed One of God, we would especially emphasize the significant concept of Word *(Logos)* and Wisdom *(Sophia)*. Indeed, as we shall see, this idea has its roots in the Old Testament and in postcanonical Jewish literature. This does not necessarily mean that such a concept completely supplanted all previous ones, but it does indicate that the divine qualities of Word and Wisdom became incorporated into the composite Messianic portrait.

We may recall the important features of the characteristics of the anointed prophet, of the anointed priest, and ultimately, of the anointed king. They all classically represented God before His own people, and the people before their God. Now are added the creative power of the Messiah as the divine Word, and the penetrating knowledge of the Messiah as the personification of divine Wisdom.

Although Word and Wisdom may have been unconsciously used as the accepted means of divine mediation for a time, their recognized acts gradually took on further meaning. They were given character to become the identifiable traits of the Anointed One. This is particularly evident in the concept of the New Testament, in John's characterization of Christ as the Word.

Thus, it became an integral part of the expectation that whoever the Messiah might be, He must possess creative power and penetrating knowledge. In outlining this development, we shall consider: (1) Word and Wisdom in retrospect; (2) Logos (Word) in Greek context; and (3) Word (Logos) in the Gospel of John. However we view the coming Messiah, we cannot escape the impact of the eventual personification of the divine qualities of Word

219

and Wisdom. Perhaps more than some would care to admit, this development clarifies the relation of God to this world.

Word and Wisdom in Retrospect

The development of the meaning of Word *(Logos)* and Wisdom *(Sophia)* proceeded throughout the Old Testament into the postcanonical Jewish literature. The basis of the Logos idea, so far as the Jew was concerned, was the thought that to the Jew a word was not simply a sound in the air. Rather, a word was a unit of energy and of effective power. A word not only *said* things, a word also *did* things.[2]

This concept of a word may be better understood in considering how effective towards action the words of some great orator can be. His words can move men to laughter or to tears; he can set them out on some political campaign or some military action. An orator's words are indeed dynamic units of power, not only producing an effect in the minds of men, but moving them to action.

Then, when we relate the prevailing concept of God from the patriarchal age on, as that of almightiness, the power of a word spoken by God is infinitely intensified. This is seen as God spoke to Moses and said, "I am Jehovah: and I appeared unto Abraham, unto Isaac, and unto Jacob, by the name of God Almighty *[El Shaddai]"* (Exod. 6:2-3).

With this basic consideration, the word of Jehovah is regarded as the fiat of His almighty will. The outstanding example is the spoken, creative word of God. Every act in the drama of creation begins with the words: "And God said" (cf. Gen. 1:2, 6, 9, 11, 14, 20, 24, 26). Thus, in Ps. 33:6, we read, "By the word of Jehovah were the heavens made, and all the host of them by the breath of his mouth."

Thus, Word also became poetically personified, as when it is said that God's Word shall accomplish that which He pleases, as in Isa. 55:10-11:

For as the rain cometh down and the snow from heaven, and returneth not thither, but watereth the earth, and maketh it bring forth and bud, and giveth seed to the sower and bread to the eater; so shall my word be that goeth forth out of my mouth: it shall not return unto me void, but it shall accomplish that which I please, and it shall prosper in the thing whereto I sent it.

By a natural extension of the meaning of the term, the Word of God becomes recognized as a name for the revelation or message of Deity to mankind. In this sense the prophets are said to see the word of the Lord. For example, in Isa. 2:1, we read: "The word that Isaiah the son of Amoz saw concerning Judah and Jerusalem."

The Word of God is even more distinctly personified in passages where divine attributes, such as rectitude and power, are ascribed to it. In Ps. 33:4, it is written: "For the word of Jehovah is right; and all his work is done in faithfulness." Then, in Jer. 23:29, "Is not my word like fire? saith Jehovah; and like a hammer that breaketh the rock in pieces?"

In the Wisdom books of the Old Testament this personification proceeds a step further. Here, Jewish thought began to give Wisdom a very high place in the order of the world. Indeed, Wisdom became recognized as an agent of God in the accomplishment of His will and purpose amidst the affairs of men.

For example, in Job, Wisdom is the secret of life, hidden from the common observation of men. It is "that path no bird of prey knoweth, neither hath the falcon's eye seen it" (28:7). But God knows where it dwells. He has searched

Wisdom out and declared it unto men: "Behold the fear of the Lord, that is wisdom; and to depart from evil is understanding" (v. 28). Again, "Wisdom," says the Sage, as it may be translated, "is the principal thing" (Prov. 4:7).

Such a concept of wisdom is affirmed most explicitly in Proverbs chapter 8. Here, Wisdom is God's messenger who lifts up her voice in the street and at the city gates and bids men to walk in her pure and pleasant ways. We read: "Unto you, O men, I call; and my voice is to the sons of men" (8:4). Then, Wisdom speaks noble things (v. 6); her treasures are greater than gold or silver or jewels (vv. 10-11); by her, kings reign and rulers decree what is just (v. 15); hers are the only enduring wealth and prosperity (v. 18). Still, the concept of Wisdom is even more comprehensive. Wisdom is regarded as the companion of God before the world began, and as His agent and helper in creation (vv. 22-30). This promotes the idea of Wisdom as existing as a person before time with God, and as the co-adjutor of God in the world of creation.[3]

These poetic forms of thought in the Old Testament certainly set forth the idea of Jehovah's almighty and active energy, emphasizing His self-revealing nature through His Word and His Wisdom. Indeed, they were used as means of describing the transcendent, living God who does not remain shut up within himself, apart from the world. They also help close "the gap" of God's seeming separateness from the world by visualizing and expressing His nature in acts of power and providence, with the mighty energy of His Word through the agency of His infinite Wisdom.

It is from this background of ideas that the enlarged concepts of Word *(Logos)* and Wisdom *(Sophia)* may properly be considered in connection with the development of the Jewish Messianic hope. Even when it seemed that there was no great prophet as spokesman for God, no sincerely consecrated priest to intercede with God, and no Davidic king who righteously stood as representative before God, there was the underlying awareness of the personal potency of God's Word and Wisdom. The power of the divine Word and the agency of Wisdom could not be disregarded as having a definite place in the establishment of God's kingdom on earth.

During the intertestamental period of Jewish history, it is apparent that the concept of Wisdom continued to develop, and this similarly contributed to the idea of the Word. The personification of Wisdom found in Proverbs is elaborated further in the apocryphal wisdom literature.

In Ecclesiasticus (The Wisdom of Sirach), Wisdom is noted as the first creation of God, and she becomes the friend of all who fear and love Him (cf. 1:4, 10). We read: "Wisdom was created before them all, and sound intelligence from eternity. . . . But he bestowed her liberally to those who loved him."

Wisdom indeed issues from the mouth of God, characterizing the word, and she inhabits even the remote places of earth and heaven. However, Wisdom dwells in Israel in a special manner, for she has established her throne in Zion. Thus, Ecclesiasticus 24:10-12 declares:

> *I ministered before him in the holy tent, and so I was established in Zion. He made me rest likewise in the beloved city, and I had authority over Jerusalem. I took root in the glorified people, in the portion of the Lord, and of his inheritance.*

Wisdom thereby makes her instruction to shine as the morning, and she sends forth her light afar. She pours out her doctrine for the benefits of even the most distant generations (cf. 24:32-33).

Again, we find the same idea in the Book of Wisdom (The Wisdom of Solomon). The origin and nature of Wisdom are vividly described in these writings. She is one to be loved above health and beauty; she is to be chosen in preference to light (7:10). Further, Wisdom is "the fashioner of all things," a holy and subtile spirit, "more mobile than any motion," and penetrating all things by reason of her pureness (cf. 7:22, 24). The description continues:

> For she is the breath of the power of God, and a pure emanation of his almighty glory; therefore nothing defiled can enter into her. For she is a reflection of the everlasting light, and a spotless mirror of the activity of God, and a likeness of his goodness. Though she is one, she can do all things, and while remaining in herself, she makes everything new. And passing into holy souls, generation after generation, she makes them friends of God, and prophets. For God loves nothing but the man who lives with wisdom (7:25-28).

In essence, then, Wisdom is the breath of God and the effulgence of the glory of the Almighty (7:25). She is also the unifier of all things (7:27). And, since she was present at the creation, she is God's creating agent (cf. 9:1-2, 9).

At this point, it should be noted that the Greek word *"logos"* not only means "word," but it also means "mind" or "reason." This close relation of meaning no doubt contributed to the association of the idea of the word with the idea of wisdom. The identification of truth and wisdom with the spoken word of God, and their connection to the creative power of His Word, add to their significance.

Although the concept of Logos may be best known as a Greek philosophical feature, Jewish thought and literature provide ample background for their own development of the Logos idea. This is particularly the case with regard to the Jewish view of the closeness of the Word to God and the action of the Word in the creation of the world.[4]

A further development in Judaism assisted in promoting the idea of the Word. In later Judaism the concept of God became even more transcendent. God, as it were, became elevated higher above the depraved scene of man, and thus ever more distant from the affairs of the world.

The Old Testament period had a very anthropomorphic view of God. It did not hesitate to speak of God in human terms. It could speak of the hands, the arms, the feet of God. It could speak of God as someone to be met as simply and directly as the meeting of another human being.

However, to the later Jewish thinkers such conceptions seemed all too human for Deity. So, in making the Targums, the Aramaic translations and paraphrases of the Old Testament, they "dehumanized" the concept of God. Where some anthropomorphic idea had been set forth in the Old Testament, in the Targums they substituted the Word, the Memra of God.

For instance, in Exod. 19:7, we read that Moses brought forth the people out of the camp to meet with God. This, for the Targumists, was too human a way to speak of God. So, the statement was changed to say that Moses brought the people before the *Memra,* the Word, of God. Again, Isaiah, in a poetic passage, wrote: "My hand has laid the foundation of the earth; and my right hand has spanned the heavens" (Isa. 48:13). This became: "By my Memra I have founded the earth, and by my strength I have hung up the heavens." Also, Deut. 33:27 speaks of the "everlasting arms" of God. In the Targums this reads: "The eternal God is thy refuge, and by his Memra the earth was created."[5]

Hence, the word "Memra," or Word of God, is scattered hundreds of times throughout the Targums. The Memra of God was thus conceived as a kind of intermediate agent between the transcendent God and the material world. It became an entirely natural way to speak of God, ascribing the anthropomorphic acts of Jehovah to the divine Word. Jehovah is viewed as expressing himself and executing His will through the Memra. Therefore, the expression "the Memra" (the Word), became a substitute for the name and action of God. In popular thought, the Memra took the place of the Almighty himself.[6]

Leading up to what may be called the New Testament period, we can take a panoramic look at the complex development of the Jewish Messianic hope. The Great Expectation is seen to arise from the covenant relationship of the patriarchs with God, from the divinely anointed offices of prophet, priest, and king, as the individuals faithfully represented the will of God for His people.

Now, without any faithful witness, the Word and the Wisdom of God are viewed in personified terms to bring God near. It is left for the Apostle John to answer the ultimate question: Will the Word ever be made flesh?

The point is that the Messianic attributes eventually ascribed to the Word *(Logos)* have foundation, not in the basic impact of Greek philosophy, but from a genuine Jewish development of their own concept of God. Moreover, we need not regard such developments as fallacious, but rather, as a part of the unfolding of the revelation of God to mankind.

As we shall see, the Logos concept in understanding the acts of God, and His place in the world, is divinely utilized in the New Testament. It seems that there can be little doubt that this highlight of the Messianic picture is as much a part of the description as the more specific Old Testament prophecies.

It should also be noted that the Targums, personifying the acts of God, with its concept of the Word *(Memra),* were in current use among the Jews during the apostolic age. Then, this popular personification of the Word is sometimes connected to the later Logos concept of Philo, who was an Alexandrian Jewish philosopher. His thought flourished about the middle of the first century after Christ. We shall deal with this connection in the following section.

Logos in Greek Context

Philo, born in 20 B.C., was an Alexandrian Jew who was accomplished in both Greek and Jewish thought. His system was a composite of diverse elements, for he endeavored to harmonize the Old Testament and Greek philosophy. Philo shared the ideas current in late Judaism respecting the absolute transcendence of God and His total separation from this finite and sensible world.

Judaism had bridged this gulf between God and the world by its doctrine of angels and its personification of Wisdom and the Word. Philo accomplished the same object by resort to the Platonic theory of ideas. Thus, to him, the Word (Memra) of the Old Testament Scriptures became the sum or chief of the ideas or powers through which God mediated His communication with the world.[7]

To Philo, then, the Logos is the image of God, and in a unique sense, the bridge between God and man. Sometimes the Logos denotes the immanent reason of God; sometimes His active, self-revealing energy and wisdom. In this latter sense the Word is the agent through whom God creates and administers the world. Logos is the bond which holds the world together, the high priest through whom God communicates with men. Logos is the highest messenger, the Firstborn Son of God, the second God, but perhaps only in a figurative sense. At times, however, it seems probable that the Logos was conceived of as a person distinct from God.[8]

What the Logos became in the thought of Philo we

shall see by considering the concept in a fourfold relation: (1) to God, (2) to the Powers, (3) to the world, and (4) to man.

In relation to God, Logos is first of all Wisdom. In the Alexandrine Book of Wisdom, written probably under Stoic influences, this character assumes new titles and significance. He is "the loving Spirit of the Lord that filleth the earth," holy, only begotten, "the brightness of the everlasting light, the unspotted mirror of the Power of God, the image of His Goodness."[9]

Philo apparently translates this hymn of praise into scientific terminology when he calls the Word the Intelligible World. (That is, it is viewed as the sum of the thoughts of God, or again, the Idea of ideas, which imparts reality to all lower ideas, as they turn to all sensible kinds.) The Logos (Word) is the whole *nous* (mind) of God, considered as operating outside itself, and expressing itself in act.[10]

Hence, the Word is styled the Impress of the divine mind, its Likeness, its House. This is the Word's abstract Greek side. In the more realistic Hebrew aspect, Logos is the Shekinah or glory of God; or, as that glory falls in our view only veiled and dimmed, Logos is seen as the shadow of God. Conceived in an even more personal and definite sense, Logos is the Son, the Eldest Son, the Firstborn Son of God. As such, many of the divine titles are His by natural right.[11]

Secondly, in the relation of Logos to the other Powers, there is the same graduated ascent from the abstract to the real. If the Powers are Ideas, the Word is their Sun. He is the Book of Creation, in which all the subordinate essences are words. Again, Logos is their Creator, the King's Architect, in whose mind the plan of the royal kingdom is formed. He stands between them dividing, yet uniting, like the fiery sword between the cherubim at the gates of Eden.[12]

Then, as related to the world, Logos is on the one side the Archetypal Seal; He is the Divider, differentiating, making each thing what it is. He is the Bond, insofar as all existence depends upon permanence of form. So, in Logos, both worlds, the intelligible and the sensible, form one great whole.[13]

The figure of this is the vesture of the high priest. On the head is the plate of gold with its legend "Holiness to the Lord"; the blue, the purple, the scarlet of the robe are the rainbow of nature; the bells about the feet, whose sound is heard when Aaron goes into the holy place, signify the joy of the human spirit when it penetrates into the divine mysteries. The robe is woven of one piece of cloth, and may not be rent, because the Word binds all together in life and harmony. Even thus far, the Greek influence is much in evidence.[14]

But then, Logos is the Instrumental Cause, the Organ of Creation. He is the Creator, the Helmsman and Pilot of the universe. Philo says:

> God with justice and law leads His great flock, the four elements and all that is shaped thereof, the circlings of sun and moon, the rhythmic dances of the stars, having set over them His upright Word, His First-born Son, who will receive the charge of this holy flock as a Vicegerent of the Great King.[15]

Here it seems that Philo is not merely thinking of the quality of Wisdom, but of the creative "God said" of the Book of Genesis. The Word is not the Spirit only, or the Mind, but the Will of God. In the ultimate sense, the Word is involved in accomplishing the will of God on earth. Even to this extent, Philo seemingly expects outside help from God with the human dilemma.

So, we turn to the last of the fourfold relations, that

of Logos to man. The question is: What is this so-called Son of God to man? Philo gives the answer by the peculiar position of the Logos, who stands between God and man partaking of both natures. Man, as regards his reason, is the image of the Logos, just as the Logos is the image of God.[16]

In this manner, the Logos is the mediator, the "Heavenly Man," who represents the human family upon earth before God. He is not considered the point of union because we may rise above Him. The knowledge which Logos gives is a lower knowledge, the knowledge of God in nature. Hence our allegiance to Him is only temporary and provisional. However, Logos is necessary as the door through which we must pass to direct communion with the Father.[17]

The Logos is further regarded as the prophet of the Most High, the Man whose name is the Dayspring, the Eternal Law. He is the Giver of the divine Light and is therefore the Saviour. Sin, to Philo, is characterized by darkness. But it is not enough that man's eyes should be opened to the light of truth. The visual ray within us is weakened or quenched by vice, and our rebellions have alienated us from God. Man must find strength and sustenance beyond his own. We therefore need an atonement, a reconciliation with God.

All these requirements are satisfied by the Logos. Philo found a fitting symbol for the atoning function in his type of the high priest. In the abeyance of the throne of David, since the days of the exile, the high priest had risen in Jewish eyes to almost superhuman dignity. His vesture, as we have seen, was the type of the whole world, for which he interceded with its Maker.

The high priest alone might pronounce the ineffable name. He alone might enter into the holy of holies, behold the glory of God, and yet live. He held this rich prerogative, because when he entered into the sanctuary he was, says Philo, with an audacious perversion of the text, "not a man" (cf. Lev. 16:17).[18] The true high priest is sinless. If he needs to make an offering and utter prayer for himself, it is only because he participates in the guilt of the people whom he represents.

The Word is the Supplicator, the Paraclete, the Priest who presents the soul of man "with head uncovered" before God. He is figured by Aaron, who stands with burning censer between the living and the dead. Philo has him say, "I stand between the Lord and you, I who am neither uncreated like God nor created like you, but a mean between the two extremes, a hostage to either side."[19]

And as the Word teaches, as He atones, so He feeds and sustains His people, falling upon every soul as the heavenly manna fell like dew upon the earth (cf. Exod. 16:4). In this sense, He is also typical of the everlasting priesthood. He is as Melchizedek, priest of the Most High God, king of Salem (Peace), who met Abraham returning from his victory over the four kings, and refreshed him with the mystic Bread and Wine (cf. Gen. 14:17-20).

Such a division in the divine nature leads to a corresponding distinction in the moral and spiritual life of man. To know God in His powers is one thing; to know Him in himself is another and a higher accomplishment. The first life is comprised of faith, hope, discipline, effort; the second is that of wisdom, vision, and peace. Those who are still struggling upwards in obedience to the Word are servants, whose proper food is milk. Those who have emerged into the full light are grown men, the "friends of God," "the seeing Israel."[20]

As Jacob cried, awaking from his dream, "How dreadful is this place! this is none other than the house of God" (Gen. 28:17), so the one starting from the sleep of indifference learns with a shock that the world is not a tavern, but a temple.

To Philo, this sensible world is indeed the house of God, the gate of heaven. For the spiritual world of ideas can be comprehended only by climbing upwards from what we see and feel. Philo says, "Those who wish to survey the beauty of a city must enter in at the gate; so those who would contemplate the ideas must be led by the hand of the impressions of the senses."[21]

Thus, we come to know God as He is manifested to us in the experience of life, first by fear of His justice, then by love of His goodness, before we can attain to Jerusalem, the Vision of Peace. But the powers are all summed up in the Word. Hence, the interpreter Word is the God of those who are imperfect; but of the wise and perfect, the First God is King.[22]

With regard to the relation of Philo's Logos concept and the development of the scriptural Messianic expectation, we clearly see that his Logos is not the Messiah of the Old Testament or the Christ of the New Testament. Indeed, it seems that the traces of a Messianic hope in Philo are very indistinct. We would therefore reject his extreme abstractions of Logos as having much bearing upon the development of either the Jewish or the Christian concept of the Messiah.

Granted, Philo does interpose the logoi between God and the material world. But this corresponds to the Platonic ideas supposed immanent in God, and to Stoic forces, the operative ideas immanent in matter. As Plato comprehends all the ideas in the one supreme idea, the Good, so Philo finds the unity of all the logoi in the one Logos. On the one side, his premises demand that the Logos, as reason, should be eternally immanent in God. However, on the other side, the Logos, as implicated in this material world, must be distinct from God.[23]

This dualism of Philo has a further consequence in philosophic alienation from the actual world. The soul of man can find its true happiness only in rising above the world and the body, ascending by reason or soaring in contemplation to the world of ideas, in rapt ecstacy to God. Thus, Philo, despite his attachment to his Jewish heritage and his regard for the Scriptures, seemingly has little definite interest in the national hope or the restoration of independence. Although he may have manifested hope that the dispersed of Israel would return, the rule of a Messianic king could not be the religious end for Philo.[24]

Perhaps the closest Philo comes to regarding the Logos as a Messianic figure is when he compares the Word to the high priest. Indeed, the high priest is the anointed of God. He is the mediator between God and man. He is the instrument whereby man is sustained before God. But the priestly figure apparently has no definite part in any Messianic concept of the last day.

Again, although God is acknowledged as King, there is evidently no consideration given to any perfected earthly Kingdom ruled by a Messiah. It seems apparent, then, that the Logos concept of Philo, as influenced by classical Greek philosophy, has made no definite contribution to the development of Messianism other than possibly being an undefined influence upon the attitudes of men. To follow Philo in search of some enlightenment on the Great Expectation is like going down a dark alley or a dead-end street.

Although much of the above discussion may appear to be extraneous to our subject, it has been included here for good reason. There are some who have attached great importance to the influence of Greek philosophy upon both Judaism and Christianity. Furthermore, a number have thought that the Logos concept offered in the Gospel of

John was an adaptation from Philo. These are both errone-
ous views.

So we now turn to the concept of Logos (Word) in the
Gospel and in the Epistles of John. We shall endeavor to
fairly consider their possible relation to Philo's concept.
However, we shall particularly examine the Gospel Logos
with regard to its apparent role in the revelation of the
Messiah.

Word (Logos) in the Gospel of John

The Logos does have a very important place in Philo's
thought, but the key point is that he probably did not
regard the Logos as actually personal. His language is in-
decisive and inconsistent at this point.

As one writer has put it, Logos to Philo means "Reason" rather than "Word." Certainly, any idea of the
Incarnation would have been foreign to his concept. Furthermore, his Logos has no relation to the Messianic hope
advanced in the Scriptures, for it has no special connection
with Jewish history.[25]

Even if it were conceded that Alexandrian philosophy
influenced Christian theology at an early period, it seems
obvious that a deep gulf separates the Logos of Philo and
the Logos of John. For instance, the conception of God's
relation to the world as given in the Fourth Gospel is certainly not Philonic. Some scholars feel that instead of the
doctrine being borrowed from Philo, it was far more likely
to have proceeded from Palestinian theology. As we have
already considered, there is in the Targums the doctrine
of the Memra or Word.

Then there is another possibility involved in the origi-
nation of John's usage of Logos. It has been pointed out
that the term may have been derived from the writings
of Hermes Trismegistos, known as the Hermetic literature.

234

There are several analogies between the Poimandres and the Fourth Gospel. The combination of Logos, Life, and Light occurs in both in a way not paralleled elsewhere. *Pleroma* (fullness) is a common term in Hermetic literature, and the Door, the Shepherd, and the Vine also have their analogies. But there is variety of opinion as to the date of these writings and as to the extent of their actual influence upon the Gospel doctrine.[26]

The author of the Gospel obviously exhibits his own remarkable knowledge of the Messianic beliefs current in Judaism at that time. As we have considered the development of the Logos doctrine within Judaism, it would indicate that John's employment of the term *"Logos"* or "Word" in application to Christ was a natural sequence. The author thereby took a word which had long been in use among his countrymen as a name for the principle of revelation in God, and to which a wider meaning had been given by its contact with Greek speculation.[27]

Under the inspiration of the Holy Spirit, John purposefully uses Logos, a term of current speech, giving it a new application and filling it with new content. Certainly, the history of "Logos" does not entirely explain its meaning in John's writings. He employed it for a purpose which went beyond its previous uses. Hence, the author put his own stamp on it, and gave it new significance, according to this further divine revelation.

Turning to the prologue of the Fourth Gospel, we find that the apostle uses the term *"Logos"* or "Word" to denote the preexistent Son of God, who became incarnate in Jesus. His first assertion is: "In the beginning was the Word" (1:1; cf. v. 2). The author here presumes the absolute eternity of the Logos. Christ is thus considered premundane. In John 1:3, we read that all things came into existence through His agency, for He was in the beginning.

This testimony to the preexistence of Christ seems to

lead to the author's further affirmation of the absolute eternity of the preexistent Son of God. The statement is that the Logos was in relation to God (1:1), that is, existed in a living, dynamic fellowship with the Father.

We should also note the phrase "who is in the bosom of the Father" (1:18). Here again, a living relation of the Logos to God seems to be implied, in fulfillment of which the life of the Son not only proceeds from the Father, but retains connection with the Father.

Having asserted the eternity of the Logos and his active relation to the Father, the author adds: "And the Word was God" (1:1). Thus far the Logos has received a threefold characterization: (1) He preexisted in eternity; (2) He was distinct from but in living relation to the Father; and (3) He is included within the category of Deity. In this manner, the apostle affirms a distinction of persons, but a community of essence, between the Word and the Father.

The author's next statement is that the creation of the universe was mediated through the agency of the Logos. "All things were made through him; and without him was not anything made that hath been made" (1:3, cf. v. 10). He is also the Giver of life and the Dispenser of light to men (1:4-5). He was the "true light" who came into the world and lighted every man (1:9).

The Logos is a Source of light and life to mankind universally. Throughout the whole course of human history, His light has been shining down into the darkness of the world's sin and ignorance. The Eternal Son is thus viewed as the Agent of God in revelation and salvation from the beginning. Indeed, He has been regarded as the Great Expectation of man since the Fall.

These statements of the nature and functions of the Logos (1:1-5) are followed by a sketch of His historical manifestation in the flesh, in Jesus (vv. 6-8). John the

Baptist, the last Old Testament prophet, announced His advent in human form as the heavenly Bearer of light and life to men (vv. 6-8). The author is careful to exclude the supposition that He first began to be or to work when He was thus born among men (vv. 9-10).

Also, when the Word came in visible form, He offered himself first to His own peculiar possession, the Jewish people. Yet, even though they were His own, they received Him not (v. 11). They were His own because He had especially been operative in their history. This had been the divinely appointed means of preparation for His coming, because He was born and reared as a member of the tribe of Judah, of the nation of Israel.

Repudiated by His own people, Jesus, the Word, extended His saving benefits to all who would receive Him. All who would believe on Him as the true Messiah and Saviour might thereby obtain the privilege of becoming God's children (v. 12). Their acceptance would not turn upon terms of lineage, but solely upon an inward spiritual transformation (v. 13). Thus did the Logos assume human nature and dwell among men (v. 14), manifesting the glory of His nature and the fullness of His grace, revealing and interpreting the truth of the invisible God to men (vv. 15-18).

Again, in comparing the Logos doctrine of John with that of Philo, we admit the two have points of contact. But they are radically different in character, and they rest upon different presuppositions. Both introduce the Logos as a Mediator between God and the world, but with Philo this mediation is part of a metaphysical theory of the universe. With John, the mediation of the Logos is involved in personal, divine revelation and salvation which is grounded in the self-imparting love of God. The Word made flesh is the divine Embodiment of all the hopes of humanity to overcome their separation from God by sin.

From Philo's viewpoint, the world is inherently evil, and God is wholly separate from it. The Logos is thus used as a means of resolving the resultant dualism. Whereas, the apostle takes up the term as a convenient means of emphasizing that Jesus is the true Agent of God's self-revelation, recognizing Him as the true Mediator between God and man. Because the apostle uses this common concept, his doctrine thus seems to be historical rather than speculative, as in Philo's system.

The starting point of John's teaching concerning the "Word of life" is the fact that Christ had been manifested in human flesh: "That which was from the beginning, that which we have heard, that which we have seen with our eyes, that which we beheld, and our hands handled concerning the Word of life" (1 John 1:1). Thus, the usage of the term *"Logos,"* as applied to Christ in the New Testament, was especially adapted to express both His agency in creation and in revelation, which was derived from His personal preexistence and essential unity with the Father.

In John we have what we do not find in Philo—or anywhere else, for that matter—a clear and consistent personification of the Logos. As we have noted, Philo's conception of Logos is wavering and often unclear. He uses the term to denote immanent reason, then the uttered word; at times he seems to be only a poetic figure, and again appears as a distinct hypostasis. Various synonymous titles are also used, such as: the Wisdom of God, the Son of God, the Archangel, and the Man of God.[28]

But in John the title always has one, clear meaning. It is a name for the eternal Son of God, who came into the world in the historical person, Jesus Christ. The apostle's doctrine of the incarnation of the Logos is radically opposed to the dualistic principles of Philo. The Logos of John is the Christ of his own experience and awareness of the eternal existence and activity which he knew his Master had claimed for himself.

Again, John's conception is summarily explained and justified by a principle of extended reach: "No man hath seen God at any time; the only begotten Son who is in the bosom of the Father, he hath declared him" (1:18). This principle may be paraphrased and explained thus:

> Monotheism has failed because men have found the invisible to be an inaccessible God; they feel after Him, and want to handle Him; but one who is simply the negation of all their experience they can neither conceive nor believe. And so He has stooped to their need, and has sent out from His own bosom, clothed in palpable flesh and blood, His only begotten Son, that He might declare Him, make Him actual, visible, tangible to the dwellers in the world of sense.[29]

We come now to the actualization of the Messianic hope of many previous generations. Because of successive unfolding prophecies and divine revelation, mankind has been brought to the point in time when his Great Expectation is to be realized. Many ideas and many hopes had been hollow and fruitless. But this expectation of the coming Messiah had survived in spite of numberless disappointments. Soon the lives of men would coincide with "the fulness of time," and His coming would be a reality.

As we have seen, the Messiah and His history are not presented in the Old Testament as something separate from, or superadded to, Israel. The history, the institutions, and the predictions of Israel all run toward the Messianic Figure. He is specifically of David's royal line, of Aaron's priestly line, of Jeremiah's prophetic class. And, at times the strains become united as in the mysterious Melchizedek, priest-king of Salem, or in Zerubbabel, who performed the priest-king functions in postexilic Israel. The Messiah is the typical Israelite, even typical Israel itself. He is the Crown, the Completion, the Representative of Israel. He is the Word, the Wisdom of God. He is the Son of God and the Servant of the Lord.

It was in this sense that the apostle could apply such Messianic characteristics to Jesus. The desire of many to know God on a personal basis provided the soil for this concept to take root and develop. John's Logos was naturally presented as the operation and presence of God in Israel, which he saw fulfilled in the historical Christ. Although this was not necessarily the kind of Messiah the people were wanting and expecting, it was the kind they needed.

Thus, the great developmental step the apostle initiated was to describe the Memra (Word) of God as incarnate. It is at this critical juncture that we can look back on the progression of Messianic thought and expectation in relation to Israel's concept of Jehovah. We soon discern that as Word and Wisdom (Logos and Sophia) became the express characteristics of God, and the tendency was toward personification, Word and Wisdom provided a vital background for Messianic thought as it developed. This, then, is the necessary place for Logos and Sophia in the development of Messianism—until it is incarnate, the Word made flesh.

The prospects of such an event ever happening seemed preposterous. Mary, the chosen mother, voiced the haunting question of all those who were awaiting His coming, when she asked: "How shall this be?" (Luke 1:34), even as she was informed of her part in the divine plan.

The answer of the angelic messenger was clear and simple: "For with God nothing shall be impossible" (Luke 1:37, KJV). It is this truth that makes the coming of the Messiah a reality. It is this truth that transforms the Word and Wisdom to flesh and blood among us.

Chapter 12

Jesus—
Child of the Holy Spirit

When his mother Mary had been betrothed to Joseph, before they came together, she was found with child of the Holy Spirit. . . . Behold an angel of the Lord appeared . . . saying, Joseph, thou son of David, fear not to take unto thee Mary thy wife: for that which is conceived in her is of the Holy Spirit.

And she shall bring forth a son; and thou shalt call his name JESUS; for it is he that shall save his people from their sins.

Now all this is come to pass, that it might be fulfilled which was spoken by the Lord through the prophet, saying,

*Behold, the virgin shall be with child,
and shall bring forth a son, and they shall
call his name Immanuel; which is being
interpreted, God with us.*

(Matt. 1:18, 20-23)

The prophet Isaiah had said that the virgin would conceive
and bear a Son (7:14), and it was so. Here, in the New
Testament, Matthew narrates the event in full (1:18-25),
as does Luke (1:26—2:40). Matthew sees this miracle as a
definite fulfillment of Isaiah's prophecy.

Luke describes the sequence of events in beautiful
pastoral detail, also viewing the miracle as a basic historical fact in the divine work of redemption. In his account,
a Palestinian maiden is told by an angel that through her
the Saviour is to be born. Awed and humbled by the
announcement, she says: "Behold the handmaid of the
Lord; be it unto me according to thy word" (Luke 1:38).

God's coming to be with His people was not a dor-
mant promise in time. From generation to generation, man
may discern the active and faithful fulfillment of all that
He said would come to pass. Because of God's verity, His
Word should never be taken lightly, no matter how impossible its achievement may seem. The Word of the Lord
will never pass away. Neither can it be changed one jot nor
one tittle by evil powers. Whatever God has spoken, that
will He do. It will actually come to be in His own good
time, for God is not slack concerning His promises.

For instance, without doing violence to the intent and
meaning of God's word unto Moses generations before, we
may very well consider that promise kept in the birth of
Jesus. God had said to Moses: "I have surely seen the
affliction of my people. . . . I am come down to deliver
them. . . . I will be with thee . . ." (Exod. 3:7-8, 12).

It seems that these words state the same basic truths that are found in Matthew: "Thou shalt call his name JESUS; for it is he that shall save his people from their sins . . . and his name shall be called Immanuel, (which means, God with us)."

According to the scriptural record, as we have considered it, the divine message was given with ever increasing clarity throughout the various stages of revelation. From the earliest promise to the last prophecy, there is no shadow of turning aside from the exact fulfillment of God's plan of redemption for mankind. There is never any suggestion of deviation from the sign that was given.

The sign of the virgin, revealed through the prophet Isaiah, as to the manner of the Messiah's birth, was indeed a high point of God's immutable Word. Accordingly, the New Testament account of the Saviour's birth purposefully verifies what had already been divinely revealed. We read: "Now all this is come to pass, that it might be fulfilled which was spoken by the Lord through the prophet" (Matt. 1:22). So, the sign given in Isaiah is enacted in the New Testament Gospel. Matthew reveres Isaiah almost as much as a historian as a prophet of the Saviour's nativity.

It is apparent that the history of God's plan of salvation has run concurrently with the history of man's enslavement by sin. God has ever acted in loving, saving concern. Now, at last, we see this mighty concern culminating in the birth of His Son among men. The New Testament revelation of God's redeeming love for lost humanity is that Mary, descendant of Judah and of David, is the virgin mother of the Christ child. Moreover, it certifies that Jesus, the Son, is Emmanuel, "God with us," the Child sent to save a world of sinners.

From the very first promise, to the established cove-

243

nant, to the prophetic signs, the Great Expectation had developed. The coming Messiah was not promised and named, nor were His character and personality described, merely for indefinite, hopeful thoughts. Rather, it was all given as a dependable body of truth that would be verified and actualized at the right time in man's history.

Here, conclusively, in the fullness of God's appointed time, the generation of Christ is announced, His personal relationship is proclaimed, and His definite parentage is affirmed. Mary, of the royal lineage of David, is identified as His mother. Joseph, also of the house of David, is identified as His earthly father, His foster father. But primarily, Jesus is the Child of the Holy Spirit, the blessed Manifestation of God in human flesh.

Scriptural support is unassailable for the Virgin Birth as the method God chose to send His Son into the world. Bible scholars have long been convinced of the integrity of the narratives of the Virgin Birth. We may note that around the turn of the century, after much research, James Orr of Scotland wrote a book entitled *The Virgin Birth of Christ,* strongly affirming it. Then, a generation later, J. G. Machen, of Princeton University, very ably supported the genuine unity of the Gospel accounts. And even recently, Karl Barth, one of the most influential theologians of our time, has written: "No one can dispute the existence of a biblical testimony to the Virgin Birth."[1]

Notwithstanding the veritable "cloud of witnesses" that affirm the supernatural birth of Jesus, the event is not without question. It is also evident that from the very time when God gave the sign through Isaiah its certitude was open to misunderstanding and doubt. Although every promise of God demanded a response of faith, perhaps this sign, more than all others, required a total reliance upon the workings of the Almighty.

Difficulties of Belief

There have always been those who were unwilling to accept and unable to expect any such miraculous intervention of God. Presently, many are "hung up" on the scientific requirements as a specific charted body of knowledge, which, in this case, refers to the field of biology. Some view the Virgin Birth as a cohabiting of God with mankind, as in pagan mythology. But this was no biological event. It is entirely beside the point to try to explain the phenomenon scientifically, for known laws do not apply.

However, there is nothing unscientific about the matter. It is rather beyond science, in the realm of God's free activity. So, even if nonpaternal human births could take place, they would have nothing to do with the lofty miracle by which Mary conceived through the power of the Holy Spirit. Perhaps more than anything else, it was the humble and obedient reception of God's word on the part of Mary that made such a birth possible.

Across the centuries, Bible-believing Christians have simply been satisfied to know that an honored maiden conceived through the Holy Spirit; and, in the normal time of gestation, the eternal Son of God was born into human life. Thus, to those who will accept it, the whole of Matt. 1:18-25 is an express description of the miraculous character of the Birth.

Along with this is the beautiful passage in Luke 1:5—2:52. It is included in a second-century harmony of the Gospels, in all the Greek manuscripts of Luke, and in all the language versions. So those who assail the supernatural conception must also face up to the fact that all extant manuscripts include the phrase "as was supposed" in Luke 3:23, where we read, "And Jesus himself began to be about thirty years of age, being (as was supposed) the son of Joseph . . ." The true intent cannot be glossed over to explain the phrase as indicating that a man other than Joseph may have been Jesus' father.

Obviously, the basic objection is not simply to this particular event which originates Christ's earthly life, but to the whole idea of any of Christianity's divine and supernatural concepts. But if we begin by saying, "I believe God," the difficulty of accepting the Virgin Birth is eliminated. The first and most natural doubter as to this manner of birth was the virgin mother herself. She asked the angel who announced this astonishing proceeding to her, "How shall this be, seeing I know not a man?" The answer of the angel was: "For with God nothing shall be impossible" (Luke 1:34, 37, KJV).[2]

The eventual fact of the Incarnation must of necessity come to involve certain individuals. Although every Hebrew family may have cherished the hope that the promised Messiah would be born from their line, the genuine expectation based upon prophetic revelation understood that the Deliverer would come from the royal house of David, of the tribe of Judah. Thus, this promise became more than an expected principle of God's coming to men. It becomes transposed into the miraculous reality of human birth, officially recorded in the genealogy of His own people.

In the Gospels of Matthew and Luke are recorded the genealogies of Joseph and Mary, indicating that the Son was a direct descendant of David. It is well known that family trees were preserved with care in almost every Jewish family. The Gospel accounts were evidently compiled from private and public records. Their reliability is confirmed by the fact that the sacred books compiled after the return of the Jews from Babylon—1 and 2 Chronicles, Ezra, and Nehemiah—with their long tables of descent, show that these family records existed then.[3]

We may also note that Josephus, a recognized historian of the second century, gives a personal example of the care of the Jews about their genealogies. He writes: "Thus have I set down the genealogy of my family as I have found it described in the public records."[4]

We are told that Rabbi Hillel, the renowned teacher who lived in the days of Jesus, belonged to the poor among the people. Yet he was able to prove from the existing records that he was one of David's descendants. Some 70 years later, the grandchildren of Jude, the reputed brother of the Lord, were summoned to Rome, and appeared before the Emperor Domitian as descendants of the royal house of David.[5]

However, those who object to the virgin birth of Jesus point to the apparent manner in which the genealogical tables in both the Gospels of Matthew and Luke trace the descent of Jesus through Joseph from David. They say this could have no meaning unless Jesus were the natural son of Joseph. Others emphasize the seeming differences that exist between the two genealogies. Then there are those who view the silence of the Gospels of Mark and John on the subject as an indication that the circumstances related in Matthew and Luke are false.

On the other hand, it should be noted that the Gospels approach the ministry of Christ from divergent points of view. For instance, after the declaration of the fact of the Incarnation—that the Word, which was God, became flesh and dwelt among men—John, like Mark, commences with the public ministry of Jesus and His baptism by John the Baptist. Luke is the only one who goes back and relates the fascinating account of the birth of John the Baptist, the forerunner, to the priest Zacharias and his wife Elisabeth. Just because the Gospels do not all give the same details does not mean that the one which does (or does not) is false. The proper way to consider the account of the

Virgin Birth is to say that the only two Gospels which tell of the birth of Jesus say that He was born of the Virgin Mary.[6]

So far as the genealogies are concerned, we note that the genealogy given by Luke differs from that presented by Matthew. It is because Luke has extricated the line of Mary from family records, while Matthew has elected to chronicle the family of Joseph. This solution of the differences between the two genealogies was apparently first suggested by Annius of Viterbo, at the close of the fifteenth century. It has been accepted by scholars such as Professor Godet and Dean Plumptre.[7]

It is sufficient here to suggest that the two narratives of Matthew and Luke are themselves the key to the existence of two distinct genealogical tables. In both Gospels the events of the birth and infancy of Jesus Christ are told. They were probably based on written or oral memories, evidently proceeding from two distinct focal centers of believers. Many of them were eyewitnesses of the things they related, or of which they preserved a faithful memory in writing.[8]

The one circle of believers, of which Joseph was the center, apparently consisted of Cleopas, and his brothers James and Jude, the sons of Joseph. James was the first bishop of the church in Jerusalem. Also included in this group was Simeon, a son of Cleopas, and the first successor of James. The narratives preserved among these persons could have easily been the source of Matthew's Gospel, who doubtless lived as a part of this circle.[9]

However, another circle of narratives must have formed itself around Mary. Luke undoubtedly preserved those which focused upon the mother of Christ. Thus, the genealogy of Matthew, which has Joseph in view, must have proceeded from his family line. On the other hand, that given by Luke apparently issued from the circle of which Mary was the center.[10] There appears to be sufficient evidence of this view to disregard the attempts to discredit belief in the Virgin Birth because of the seeming contradictions of the two genealogies.

Again, although Mark and John and Paul do not relate the event of the Virgin Birth, none of them even raises a question about it. Rather, all of them make great statements about Jesus which are in harmony with the narratives of Matthew and Luke. In the case of Mark, he commences with this tremendous introduction: "The beginning of the gospel of Jesus Christ, the Son of God." John opens his account by saying: "In the beginning was the Word, and the Word was with God, and the Word was God." The Apostle Paul tells us that "when the fullness of the time came, God sent forth his Son, born of a woman, born under the law" (Gal. 4:4). Such statements certainly do not deny or contradict the Virgin Birth. In fact, they would require us to assume such a miraculous entry into the world, even if Matthew and Luke had not specified how He came.[11]

Despite the harmonious scriptural support for the Virgin Birth, there are those who claim that this was merely the method of Jesus' disciples in accounting for the preeminence of Jesus. They are thus said to have applied to Him a myth of miraculous conception and birth after the manner of the pagans. For example, Thomas Paine, in his *Age of Reason,* said:

> Mythology had prepared the people for the belief of such a story as the Virgin Birth. Almost all the extraordinary men that lived under the heathen mythology were reputed to be sons of some of their gods. It was not a new thing at that time to believe a man to have been celestially begotten.[12]

Writing centuries before, Origen had already answered this charge. In reply to the heretical beliefs of one Celsus, he wrote:

> Since Celsus has introduced the Jew disputing with Jesus and tearing in pieces, as he imagines, the fiction of his birth from a virgin, comparing the Greek fables about Danae and Auge and Antiope and Melanippe, our answer is that such language becomes a buffoon, and not one who is writing in a serious tone.[13]

Anyone who objectively reads the story about the birth of Hercules, or Augustus Caesar, or Zoroaster, will discern at once the gulf which separates such myths from the sublime narratives of the Gospels. Nothing is more preposterous than that the first Christian disciples and writers of the New Testament should have borrowed the myth of the Virgin Birth from the pagans, and thus accounted for the birth of their Saviour and God. This would have been contrary to all their inherited and traditional Jewish prejudice against such pagan thought and custom.[14]

We cannot disregard the foundation of belief laid in the Old Testament by the prophets. The very fulfillment of prophecy and the fact of the Incarnation follows a long line of selected participants in the progressive revelation. The Expectation is now consummated in the miraculous reality of the Saviour's birth. The Virgin Mary and her betrothed husband, Joseph, are quietly chosen for their respective roles of responsibility.

Theirs is the sacred task, even the privilege, of submitting their lives and their wills to the Almighty to be used in this unique way. The miracle of the advent of Christ is necessarily dependent upon such human instrumentality. Mary, the virgin, is to become the only one that ever was, or ever shall be, a mother in this way. Likewise, Joseph, her husband, was entrusted with the special responsibility of being the earthly father to the Son of the Most High God.

Son of God

As Immanuel, Jesus is God with us, the incarnate Son, the Word made flesh. John 1:14 declares: "And the Word was made flesh, and dwelt among us, (and we beheld his glory, the glory as of the only begotten of the Father,) full of grace and truth" (KJV).

This Son was not born after the will of the flesh, according to the desire and the function of men; but He was conceived according to the will of God. Thus, if we believe that God was manifest in the flesh in the person of Jesus Christ, we readily accept the Virgin Birth as the means of accounting for that divine coming into human life.

In the conception of Jesus, a new being was not formed unto life as in all other cases. Rather, He is One who existed from eternity and who thus entered into vital relation with human nature in a miraculous manner. Because Jesus was divinely conceived, and because He inhabited eternity as Deity, the Scriptures also teach that no man can ever claim paternal connection with Him.

Joseph did assume the role as Jesus' foster father. Although Joseph's neighbors regarded Jesus as the carpenter's son, the Scriptures always treat this as an error of thought. Excluding the part of man, the Scriptures put the Holy Spirit in the foreground as the Author of Christ's conception. It is affirmed twice in our textual background, and also in Luke 1:35, which states: "The Holy Spirit shall come upon you, and the power of the Most High will overshadow you; therefore the child to be born will be called holy, the Son of God" (RSV).

There is a chain of meaning with regard to the term "Son of God" as it is used in the Scriptures. This is not a title which Jesus or the New Testament writers invented. It is in fact a title with a long and varied history. Aside

251

from relating the term to Jesus, it is scripturally associated in four other aspects:[15]

1. In the Old Testament *the angels are called the sons of God.* The Genesis account tells how the sons of God saw that the daughters of men were fair and took to wife such as they chose (Gen. 6:2). In the prologue of the drama recorded in the Book of Job, we read that there was a day when the sons of God came to present themselves before the Lord, and Satan also came among them (Job 1:6). Again, we read that on the day of creation the morning stars sang together and all the sons of God shouted for joy (Job 38:7). Although the angels are called the sons of God in the Old Testament, as the writer to the Hebrews asserts (Heb. 1:5), no individual angel is ever called the Son of God.

2. Elsewhere in the Old Testament, *the nation of Israel is at times called the son of God.* It is first recorded in the message and the demand of God to Pharaoh: "Thus saith Jehovah, Israel is my son, my firstborn: and I have said unto thee, Let my son go, that he may serve me" (Exod. 4:22-23). Again, Hosea heard God say: "When Israel was a child, then I loved him, and called my son out of Egypt" (Hos. 11:1). Thus it is proper to speak of God's chosen nation as God's son.

3. Since the nation as a whole was viewed as the son of God, it became natural to speak of *the king of the nation as being God's son* in a special sense. In Ps. 89:27, we read: "I also will make him my firstborn." It was God's promise in regard to Solomon: "I will be his father, and he shall be my son" (2 Sam. 7:14). So, in a special sense God's chosen king from among His chosen people was designated as His son.

4. Then, in the New Testament, in Luke's genealogy of Jesus, the lineage of Jesus is traced back to *Adam, who, as Luke says, was "the son of God"* (Luke 3:38). And in the

Beatitudes, according to Jesus, *"the peacemakers" are "called the sons of God"* (Matt. 5:9).

As we have previously indicated, the heathen world was well acquainted with the practice of calling men the sons of God. Pagan mythology was full of heroes whose birth was ascribed to the union of a god with a mortal maid, or a man with a goddess. For example, Hercules was said to be the son of Alkmene and the god Zeus; Achilles was purported to be the son of Thetis the goddess and Peleus the mortal man.

Moreover, it was commonplace for races and nations to trace their origin back to some divine founder. In the Hellenistic world kings provided themselves with pedigrees extending back to the gods. Thus, the Ptolemies of Egypt traced their origin back to a god, and Alexander the Great claimed a lineage stemming from Zeus. Indeed, the ancient world was very familiar with stories of heroes and demigods who claimed an origin which made them sons of the gods.[16]

Even so, despite such common usage by the pagans, any attempt to explain the account of the birth of Jesus Christ mythologically misses the context of the story and the scriptural usage of the title "Son of God." Such a term is in accord with a very special act of the Spirit in the unique event by which Jesus, who is the Son of the Father, is born as a human child of Mary. This limits any speculation. Consequently, any attempt to draw a parallel between this act of the Spirit and mythological relationships mistakenly tries to give an explanation of that which finds its origin in the power of God.[17]

This act of the Holy Spirit, of which both Matthew and Luke testify, points out the uniqueness of Christ's birth which can be known only by divine revelation. Revelation alone can shed the light of truth on this story, not biological theories or historical speculations. It bears no marks of human construction; it speaks only to the fulfillment of that which had been prophesied.[18]

So it was according to the power of God that the Eternal Son adopted the form of a human servant by becoming partaker of bodily flesh and blood. As the Word, the divinity of Jesus was from everlasting, without a mother, and His humanity was begotten without a father. He was conceived by the power of the Holy Spirit, but not by any communication of His essence, as in human paternity. Rather, a miraculous and mysterious operation enabled the virgin to perform the functions of maternity and yet remain a virgin.

Jesus is therefore properly called the "child of the Holy Ghost," not because the Holy Spirit is the father, as we relate the term, but because this "holy thing" is conceived by the Spirit's special operation. Certainly, Jesus must be called the Son of God, as the Scriptures call Him. The Christ child was not born simply through the activity of the Holy Spirit alone, but the Spirit was also cooperating with the Father and the Eternal Son in this divine act. Thus, it was the Triune God that prepared the human body of the mediating God-man.

From the Father, of whom are all things, proceeded the material body of Jesus, the creation of the human soul, and all His gifts and powers, along with the complete plan of the Incarnation. Then, from the Son, who is the Wisdom of the Father (as well as the Word), disposing and arranging all things in creation, there proceeded the holy disposition and arrangement to be God with us, embodied in human nature. As the correlated acts of the Father and Son in creation and providence receive animation and perfection through the brooding of the Holy Spirit, so the Spirit moved in the Incarnation that the acts of the Father and the Son might be made manifest.

Therefore, it is said in Heb. 10:5, of the Triune God:

"A body thou hast prepared me," and it is also implied that the Child which is conceived in Mary is of the Holy Spirit. It is the same body that will be offered as the final Sacrifice for sin (v. 10). This is but a glimpse of the eternal purpose of God in planning for the atonement, through the offering of the body that was prepared for the Son in Mary.

We should keep one thing straight: Jesus was *born* the Son of God. He did not gradually achieve that divine position, nor was it superimposed upon Him at baptism or any other significant event. This seems evident because the key to the peculiar self-consciousness possessed by Jesus as a lad, when He indicated to Mary and Joseph, "I must be about my Father's business" (Luke 2:49, KJV), was existent in an already dawning sense of special relationship with His Heavenly Father. Such a relationship may well have dated into His early childhood. There is no satisfactory explanation for such a self-consciousness unless we admit the birth of Jesus as the Son of God.[19]

The Christ child was thus born the Son of God for two supreme reasons. First, the divine personality that was made flesh is only that of the Son, the Second Person in the Trinity. As a distinct Person in the Godhead, He brings His total divine nature into humanity. He is the coequal, coeternal Son manifested in human flesh and nature. So, although Christ is clothed in humanity, He is no less divine.

Then, the second reason Jesus was born the Son of God is that His birth was only brought about by the cooperative activity of the Trinity, energized by the Holy Spirit. We have already considered the fact that as the Son of God, Jesus is seen to be more than the Child of the Holy Spirit. However, since He was conceived by the Holy Spirit, and then fully prepared by the Trinity, the Child cannot be properly called anything but the Son of God, the Son of the Highest.

255

Paradoxically, the reverse order is also true. Even though Jesus was divinely conceived and prepared, He was born as a human babe. Because of His connection with humanity, this Child of the Holy Spirit must also be called the Son of Man. His very divinity is inseparably joined with very humanity.

Son of Man

Jesus, the Son of God incarnate, was born from the union of a divine Person with human nature. For this reason, the Son is also spoken of as having laid hold on "the seed of Abraham" (Heb. 2:16). Furthermore, He was known both as the "seed of the woman" (Gen. 3:15), and the "seed of David" (Rom. 1:3).

Since He was physically born of the Virgin Mary, after the natural period of gestation, Jesus Christ personalized human nature. As the person of the Son, who was with the Father from eternity, who became partaker of human flesh and blood, He adopted our human nature in the unity of His person, and He was thus born truly man.

When Jesus was born of Mary, He not only partook of man's flesh and blood; He also assumed the human processes of thinking, willing, and feeling. Consequently, Jesus was susceptible to all the human emotions and sensations that invigorate human life. He is thus said to be made of a woman (Gal. 4:4). And, so far as He partakes of the substance of His mother, Jesus is called the "fruit of her womb" (Luke 1:42).

In a very real sense, Jesus identified himself as a Servant, embracing actual human nature, such as it had become from the fall of man. This is clearly stated in Heb. 2:14, 17: "Forasmuch as the children are partakers of flesh and blood, he also himself likewise took part of the same. . . . Wherefore in all things it behoved him to be

256

made like unto his brethren . . . to make reconciliation for the sins of the people" (KJV).

However, this intimate union of the Son of God with the fallen human nature does not imply the least participation of our sin and guilt. Certainly, we are, by virtue of our conception and birth, unholy, defiled, and guilty as sinners, under the condemnation of hell. But because of the manner of Jesus' conception, He was born "holy, harmless, undefiled, separate from sinners, and made higher than the heavens" (Heb. 7:26, KJV).

Nevertheless, even in His innocence, Jesus was tempted in all things, such as we are. Yet He remained righteous, without sin. "For in that he himself hath suffered being tempted, he is able to succor them that are tempted" (Heb. 2:18). He was "in all points tempted like as we are, yet without sin" (Heb. 4:15). Thus, the scripture definitely affirms true humanity for Jesus as the Son of Man, but it is a unique humanity.

Although Jesus Christ is the Son of Man, it is evident that He is not an ordinary descendant of Adam. He existed before Adam. Jesus was not born passively as we are, for He *took* upon himself the human flesh. Therefore, Jesus does not stand under Adam as His head, but He becomes the New Head of a holy race, as the New Adam, having others under Him. So He says, "Behold, I and the children whom God hath given me" (Heb. 2:13), we will put our trust in God.

Racially, Adam's guilt of sin is imputed to all that should be born after him, for he sinned and fell as our natural and federal head. Our own moral life stands in root relation to his depraved moral life. And as Adam carried us in himself, his fallen state determined our degenerate predicament. Hence, according to the just judgment of God, Adam's guilt was imputed to all his posterity, since they would successively be born by the will of man as his descendants.

However, inherited guilt does not spring from inherited sin. On the contrary, man is conceived and born in sin because he stands in inherited guilt before God. By the stain of this inherited guilt, he is conceived in sin and born in iniquity, in full participation of sin. ("Behold, I was brought forth in iniquity; and in sin did my mother conceive me," was the clear admission of David, Ps. 51:5.) Therefore, our salvation depends upon Jesus, the Son of Man, the New Adam, to be our Mediator before God.

Herein lies the great and necessary expectation since the Fall. We dare not miss it! At last, this wonderful accomplishment is made toward the offering of peace and correspondence between God and man. Both the human and the divine natures are brought together in the unique personality of the Mediator. By this action, Jesus becomes the one qualified Person to lay His hands upon both God and man and provide the means whereby the sins of man could be forgiven and the justice of God could be satisfied.

From the halls of eternity, Jesus Christ came to bring God to be with us, and then, to bring us to be with God. This was the expectation of the patriarchs and the prophets of old. Only such an unprecedented Person, who is both the Son of God and the Son of Man, can open the way to salvation from sin, destroy the works of the devil, and establish man in the kingdom of God. Jesus' birth, then, is God's redemptive answer to the sinful fall of man.

There is one other aspect which should be considered here. Jesus, the Child of the Holy Spirit, is not only the Son of God and the Son of Man, but He is also the firstborn Son. All that might be said of Jesus being both the Son of God and the Son of Man would lose its significance unless He be the "Alpha and Omega," the first and the last, manifested for our salvation. Thus, the advent of Christ breaks into the sinful history of man as the *only* Saviour of the world.

Firstborn Son

Apart from His habitation of eternity, the Scriptures make it clear that Jesus is the Firstborn of Mary (Matt. 1:25). Whatever number of other children Mary may have had during her marriage to Joseph, the birth of this Son is given precedence over them all. No other child was to intervene and challenge the position of His royal lineage, His right to inherit the throne of David. No previous child was to assume the responsibility as elder brother. Since Jesus was the Firstborn of Mary, it likewise confirms the testimony that He was indeed virgin-born.

However, Jesus is not only the Firstborn of Mary, He is affirmed to be the Firstborn of every creature. The New Testament gives a distinct line of thought which connects Jesus Christ with the creation of all things. This conception first occurs in the Prologue of the Fourth Gospel, where we read: "All things were made through him; and without him was not anything made that hath been made" (John 1:3).

Then, in Paul's letter to the Colossians, he wrote what is sometimes called "the great Christology" in Col. 1:15-19. There, Paul indicates the reason of Christ's great inheritance, and why He must be given preeminence in all things. We read:

> *Who is the image of the invisible God, the firstborn of all creation:*
> *For in him were all things created, in the heavens and upon the earth, things visible and things invisible, whether thrones or dominions or principalities or powers; all things have been created through him, and unto him;*

259

*And he is before all things, and in him all
things consist.*

*And he is the head of the body, the church:
who is the beginning, the firstborn from the dead;
that in all things he might have the preeminence.*

*For it was the good pleasure of the Father that
in him should all the fulness dwell.*

This declaration means that Christ not only stands as
the Creator and the Heir of all things, but that He also
takes His place as the Firstborn in righteousness. His
preeminence is contrasted with the fact that all other men
are born in sin, and they must be "born again" of the
Spirit unto righteousness (cf. John 3:1-21). To those who
believe in Him, and who are born again, Jesus is "the firstborn among many brethren" (Rom. 8:29).

Again, in Hebrews, the writer speaks of Him who was
a Son, "whom he [God] appointed heir of all things,
through whom also he made the worlds" (Heb. 1:2). Then,
this concept of Firstborn occurs in the Revelation where
the faithful and true Witness, the risen Christ, is called
"the beginning of the creation of God" (Rev. 3:14). Hence,
Jesus is the Source and Origin of all creation. "In him was
life" (John 1:4). From Christ, both created and recreated
life flow.[20]

To say that Jesus is the Firstborn of creation is certainly to say that the highest place in the universe is His.
Such a title lifts Him above and beyond all created things
and sets Him in the topmost position. But how can this be
true about a man who apparently also came to hang in
shame and agony on a cross? How can anyone believe in
the primacy of this Christ in creation and in the universe?
As William Barclay puts it, there are three lines which
come to focus upon the explanation of Jesus' role as
the Firstborn.[21]

260

1. "Firstborn" was undoubtedly a recognized title of the Messiah. Its use as a Messianic title perhaps comes from the fact that the nation of Israel is called God's firstborn. We recall that Moses was to say to Pharaoh: "Thus saith Jehovah, Israel is my son, my firstborn" (Exod. 4:22). God said to Jeremiah, "I am a father to Israel, and Ephraim is my firstborn" (Jer. 31:9). Again, God says of His faithful Davidic king, "I also will make him my firstborn, The highest of the kings of the earth" (Ps. 89:27). Since this title clearly became a Messianic title, it was inevitably applied to Jesus as He so obviously displayed the characteristics of the Expected One. The immediate meaning attached is that of preeminence and honor.

2. Also, as soon as Jesus was revealed as the Word, the activity of creation was naturally related to Him. In Genesis, chapter one, we see the creative Word in dynamic operation. Accordingly, the Psalmist was moved to declare, "By the word of Jehovah were the heavens made" (Ps. 33:6). Thus, to call Jesus the Word was to positively link Him with creation as the Creator.

3. Then, as Jesus was revealed in terms of Wisdom, the achievement of creation would further relate to Him. Wisdom was with God in the beginning of His work, before the beginning of the earth, taking His place in the operation like a master workman (cf. Prov. 8:22-31). Therefore, once Jesus came to be thought of in terms of Wisdom, He would most certainly be connected with the orderly procedure of all the divine creativity.

But again, it may be asked: How could this crucified Jesus be thought of in terms of being the Messiah, the Word, the Wisdom, the Son of God, the Son of Man, the Firstborn? The answer lies in the Resurrection. Indeed, Jesus was the Firstborn from the dead (cf. Col. 1:18; Rev. 1:5).

We should not ignore the fact that the Resurrection

explains the complete preeminence given to Jesus Christ in time, before time, and in eternity. Nothing is beyond the power of Him whom death was powerless to hold. Hence, even at Jesus' birth, the first place in the universe belonged to Him by right, for He was destined to vanquish death.[22]

Because of His preexistence and His preeminence, Jesus, Child of the Holy Spirit, came to earth the Firstborn of God, and the only begotten Son of the Father. His birth was and is God's first and only gift of a Saviour to mankind. There shall never come another event in time in this world, that a Son will be given, that a Child will be born to save people from their sins. This is the background of truth which enhanced every revelation and every expectation leading up to the birth of Jesus Christ.

The advent of Christ was the divine manifestation to bring man back to God. We must therefore regard the Christ child as the expected Saviour, as the One who is the Heir of all things, "the firstborn among many brethren," "the firstborn of every creature." We look to Him as "God with us," and we also have the privilege of looking to Him as our Elder Brother.

In spite of the humble circumstances of His birth, Jesus was born King of Kings and Lord of Lords, by divine right. No other ruler can properly make such a claim. Jesus Christ is Firstborn in every instance of authority. Thus He clearly takes preeminence over all.

There is yet another aspect of Jesus' birth which should be thankfully regarded. As the Firstborn, the only begotten Son of God, the One sent, He must be viewed as a Child of infinite love. The revelation of the work of Christ in creation establishes the encouraging fact that the same power which created the heavens and the earth is at work redeeming the world. The God of creation and the God of redemption are one, and thus at the foundation of the world there is love.

God gave His all when He sent His only Son to be born of the virgin. He was born as the result of redeeming love. He came to be the Saviour of all men, to be accepted and blessed of men. "For God so loved the world, that he gave his only begotten Son, that whosoever believeth in him should not perish, but have eternal life" (John 3:16). There could be no more gracious motive behind the gift of the Son than divine love for depraved and erring humanity.

What a magnanimous accomplishment, when Jesus was conceived in Mary of the Holy Spirit! This Son of God, Son of Man, the Only Begotten, the Firstborn of the Father, comes to us as the long-awaited Captain of our salvation. He comes to establish a new race in righteousness, for He is the Righteous.

Because He is the Child of the Holy Spirit, Jesus can perform the divine purpose of mankind's redemption. This is the Son which the world had been expecting. The Christ child was born to lead men unto salvation, to reestablish them in the kingdom of God. He alone embodies man's plea for a right relationship with God. The hope of the world is still to look on this Child.

On one bright night this hope was gloriously confirmed by the message of the angels. The Great Expectation, at long last, was to be realized in human experience. The Messiah had come amidst the deep distress of man, amidst the dark despair of His own people. That night was brightened by the joyous tidings of salvation to all people. Will they receive the Truth? The coming and attending message is that of judgment.

Chapter 13

Message of the Angels

And the angel said unto them, Fear not; for, behold, I bring you good tidings of great joy, which shall be to all people.

For unto you is born this day in the city of David a Saviour, which is Christ the Lord.

And this shall be a sign unto you: Ye shall find the babe wrapped in swaddling clothes, lying in a manger.

And suddenly there was with the angel a multitude of the heavenly host praising God, and saying,

Glory to God in the highest, and on earth peace, good will toward men.

(Luke 2:10-14, KJV)

This was apparently the first gospel sermon ever preached in the present tense to humanity. The shining messenger was a heavenly creature—an angel. His sermon was brief and to the point. The extensive and accumulated prophecies of the past are brought to focus on this startling moment. The Expectation and Desire of the ages is now contained in a priceless bundle. The Word of the Covenant is at last made flesh among men.

There could be a no more stunning announcement in message and in song than that which shocked the shepherds' ears. "Unto you is born this day in the city of David a Saviour, which is Christ the Lord." What grander tidings could be given by God in breaking the divine silence, and be heard by mortal ears? What an important day—this day!

The shepherds were on a hillside of Bethlehem, tending their flocks in the chill of the darkness. The usual monotony of their tasks was to be interrupted. Suddenly, a blinding flash of light engulfed them and bathed them in glory. It was amidst this spectacular display that they heard the breathtaking announcement of the Messenger from the heavenly realm.

At first their throats and chests constricted with fear. Then their senses opened to pure, almost unbearable joy. Indeed, it was "Good tidings of great joy . . . to all people . . . a Saviour . . . Christ the Lord." The joyful sound echoed across the Judean hillside, and the keynote of praise was "Christ is born!" The shepherds had been faithfully watching their sheep, but they witnessed what the prophets and sages had expectantly awaited through the centuries of history. The Messiah was born![1]

Amazingly, these men were selected to be the favored audience of the heavenly messenger. This was a case of God choosing the "nobodies" over the "somebodies." In the eyes of society, the shepherds' occupation was a lowly task. The wealthy rulers in Jerusalem—or even the "upper class" in Bethlehem—hardly considered the position of the shepherds as honorable or significant.

We find in the Talmud (treatise "Sanhedrin"), that the shepherds were not even allowed in the courts as witnesses. Then in the treatise "Avodah-Zarah," it is declared that no help should be given to either the heathen or the shepherds.[2] Even so, the mighty angels passed over the earthly aristocracy and brought the blessed message of heaven to crude men of the fields.

One might wonder why shepherds were chosen as the first on earth to hear the glorious news of the holy Saviour's birth. For years, so many had heard and known of the prophecies of old, but who had really listened?

It is obvious that the chief priests and elders of the Jews were totally unprepared to accept a manger-born Saviour. Only the humble and the meek would gladly receive this divine event in faith. Apparently, the low class of the shepherds was selected as a practical illustration of that which God exemplified in men.

Then, we remember that the patriarchs were shepherds, plainsmen dwelling in tents. Abraham, Isaac, and Jacob were all of this occupation, and they were all men of righteous repute. Moses and David were both divinely called from tending sheep to lead and rule God's chosen people. While Moses was keeping the flocks of Jethro, his father-in-law, God gave him special instructions concerning his assigned task of leading the children of Israel out of Egyptian bondage. And, David, the youngest of the sons of Jesse, had to be called in from tending his father's sheep that he might be anointed to be king over Israel.

Seemingly shepherds have always been meditative, accustomed to the thoughtful silence of nature. Apart from the bustle and stir of the city dwellers, they practiced a quiet and simple communion with God in their own hearts.

Moreover, it is possible that these Bethlehem shepherds had been entrusted with a special task. The Mishna (Talmud) tells us that the sheep intended for the daily sacrifices in the Temple were grazed in the Bethlehem pastures.[3]

Perhaps such an involvement with the animals of sacred sacrifice further influenced their thinking and especially fitted them to be the recipients of the glad tidings of Christ's birth. They knew the holy law in the oft-repeated ritual of the Temple. They would also know of the rumors concerning the long-awaited Messiah, and that according to Micah's prophecy, their own Bethlehem, the city of David, was to witness His glorious coming.

Even so, the moment of truth came upon the shepherds unexpectedly. They were not really looking for any personal announcement from heaven. They did not feel worthy of the honor. But "God moves in mysterious ways His wonders to perform." He shocked the shepherds from darkness to light, from fear to joy, and from divine silence to good news. The angelic army of the Lord of hosts shouted, "Glory to God in the highest!" Such praise must surely crumble every wall of oppression, every pinnacle of pride, and every threat of violence. The new age of God's deliverance had at last broken through.[4]

Now, even the lowliest of the world would know that the salvation of God was for all people. The divine fulfillment of promise was not just for the wealthy and the intellectuals. It was particularly for those who would hear the truth in faith. Thus the shepherds were chosen to receive the joy of heaven and the hope of earth.

Good Tidings

It is no wonder that blazing glory attended the announcement of the heavenly messenger. It is no wonder that the shepherds were smitten with awe and fear. The brilliance that encircled them was recognized by the Jews as the "Shekinah," the visible token of the divine presence. No man can behold the glory of the Lord without feeling unworthy. Thus, the terror they felt was the natural awe always experienced by men when they are brought into visible communion with the spiritual and the supernatural. But the wonder of it all was not simply the bright flash of an astonishing experience.

What really mattered was the truth of the message. For the most part, Adam's race had thought that God was far removed from their earthly life. Now, in one spectacular stroke, Adam and Eve's hope was confirmed, Abraham's faith was verified, Jacob's vision was realized, Hannah's prayer and praise were revitalized, and David's trust was justified. The numerous prophecies of the prophets were fulfilled. For the angel to say to the shepherds, "Behold, I bring you good tidings of great joy," was perhaps the understatement of the age of man.

In a sense, it was all unbelievable. Yet, somehow, the glorious announcement of the Messiah's birth that very day also gave birth to the shepherds' faith that the dreary days and weary nights of hopelessness were over. Their lives would never be the same.

This joyous news direct from heaven would continue to bless their lives, and it would transform all those who would receive its saving virtue. One cannot remain neutral upon hearing that the Saviour is born. The prophets had foretold it, and now, at last, He had actually come. But would the people believe it?

As for the shepherds, they would go and see for themselves. The presence of the Babe would prove the message. Then they would tell it abroad to their unknowing countrymen. The privilege the shepherds had in personally receiving the divine tidings also entailed a personal responsibility to not only receive the truth in faith, but to immediately behold its reality. Wonder of wonders, God had chosen shepherds to go and behold His precious Lamb.

But what was the content of the good news? It was that new life had been brought into the world—not just in the form of a newborn babe, but through the birth of the Saviour the source of new life was opened for all of Adam's race. It was the revelation of salvation, full and free, forevermore. It meant a release of mankind from the slavery to sin, and a drawing of the race back to God. The time had come for divine love and mercy to come down and explore the depths of human degradation, to extend its virtues through Christ, and to provide redemption for the vilest sinner.

This was the day when God actually entered human history with His costly gift of salvation. Many times before, God had intervened on behalf of His chosen people. But now the Son is sent to live among men as a mighty Deliverer. His redemption is to reach all creation. He comes as promised, the Only Begotten of the Father, into a rebellious and degraded world, that all people might be saved from the destruction of sin.

Divine guidance and example are now placed in human flesh for all to see and know the will of God for men. The personal and powerful life of the Saviour will provide the means of reconciliation between God and a world of sinners.

According to the fulfillment of prophecy, Jesus Christ was born of the tribe of Judah. Although He was sent amongst the children of Israel, the joy of His birth would bring hope to all nations. All men would share in the godly heritage of His life of righteousness. It is doubtful that the shepherds fully understood all of the implications of the thrilling message of the angels. But it is certain that they understood that the Baby born was sent from heaven.

They also realized that despite their deprived position they were privileged to personally hear the news given by heavenly messengers. And, in their hearing, they were directed to go and see, and worship Him.

The angel proclaimed the birth of the Son of promise in the city of David, in nearby Bethlehem, just as the prophet Micah had foretold (5:2). This was the fore-ordained place of entrance, the point on earth where men would first behold their heaven-sent King. It also fulfilled the divine promise concerning Judah's line (Gen. 49:10), and it was the verification of God's covenant with King David (2 Sam. 7:17). In God's own time, in God's own way, in Bethlehem, apart from the royal palace and the holy Temple of Jerusalem, the mighty Saviour is born.

Such good tidings would have been of little consequence without a sign assuring of actuality. Included in the news was the direction to worship, identifying the Christ child with an unmistakable sign. This was given not only to the shepherds, but to believing men of all time. News of a Saviour is of no benefit to anyone unless it is known where and how to find Him. The Father was faithful to the lost children of men, using the very presence and words of His angelic messenger to direct the shepherds to Jesus.

It is unthinkable that the Son of God should be given for the salvation of men unannounced and unrecognized. The very presence of the heralding angels is certainly a portion of the sign given to men. There is nothing unreasonable about the birth of the Son of heaven here on earth being announced in an unearthly manner by heavenly messengers. Although some may have difficulty in accepting the extraordinary sign pointing to where the infant Saviour lay, there would otherwise be no warranty for men to give acclaim and accept a common, unheralded babe as their Saviour.

Sign of the Saviour

The import of the good tidings was according to heavenly character. The news was given by angels in a glorious and a heavenly fashion. But the sign the angel gave the shepherds was shocking. This sign of heaven was most unheavenly. The clue of the angels given to mark the Lord's birth was this: "Ye shall find the babe wrapped in swaddling clothes, lying in a manger."

No, the Babe was not to be wrapped in princely robes, or found lying in a carved cradle in a palace. The Lord of the angels would be found in a manger, the feed bin for stabled flocks. The sign itself is a scandal. Surely, it is no fit sign for a King. If this is the message, why should angels bring it? Ought not the legions of angels to march on Jerusalem or Rome to prepare Him a throne? What heavenly deliverance could possibly come out of a lowly manger?[5]

Luke (in 2:1-5) is careful to tell us of a further reason how Jesus came to be born in Bethlehem. Augustus Caesar decreed a tax registration. Now, at Caesar's command the royal line of David must be enrolled and taxed by the Roman Empire. But shall the birth of the Lion of the tribe of Judah be determined by the decree of ungodly men? What of God's promise that He would establish David's throne forever? David himself was severely punished for daring to number God's chosen people (2 Samuel 24). Now, shall Caesar dare to even enroll the Lord's anointed? It was allowed. There, on the emperor's list, a name was newly entered: "Jesus, son of Joseph, Son of David—Son of God!"[6]

Although it is true that Caesar decreed an enrollment, that decree served God's purpose. By the severe means of Caesar, God's providence brought Mary and Joseph to David's town so that the word of the Lord might be

271

minutely fulfilled: "Thou, Bethlehem . . . out of thee shall one come forth unto me that is to be ruler in Israel; whose goings forth are from of old" (Mic. 5:2).

Despite the fact that Christ is born in Bethlehem, under Caesar's dominion, the angels ignore the seeming scandal and proclaim praises to God. The heavenly view is that God can withhold His judgment and still proceed with His purposeful work of salvation. In due time, His avenging messengers will carry the mystery of the gospel to all corners of the earth, so that all mankind may know that the Saviour is come. No earthly power can prevent it.

But there is more to the apparent scandal of the Saviour's birth. He is laid in a manger—an unlikely place to pay respects to a King. There is no room for Him in the inn of the city of David. The circumstances seem incredible. This One of royal line was born, of all places, in Bethlehem, and not Jerusalem, in a manger and not a palace. And, of all times, He was born when those who could trace their lineage were gathered by Caesar's edict.

However, the height of the scandal arises from the place of the Saviour's birth. Despite Joseph's desperate efforts, the best Bethlehem could, or would, offer to Mary's maternal needs was only the corner of a stable, where the manger served as a crib. The words of the prophet Isaiah find unimagined fulfillment with vivid irony: "The ox knoweth his owner, and the ass his master's crib; but Israel doth not know, my people doth not consider" (Isa. 1:3).

It is interesting to note the phrase "his master's crib." In the ancient Greek translation of Isaiah, Luke's word for "manger" occurs in this passage, and "master's" is literally "lord's" (kuriou).[7] "The manger of the Lord": the ass knows it, but not "my people"! Again, we are reminded: "He came unto his own, and his own received him not" (John 1:11, KJV).

So, the defaming sign of the manger is given to the

shepherds by the angels. This very act is indeed a scandal to the proud. The wise teachers sleeping in Jerusalem would not recognize it, and the elite in Bethlehem's inn would contemptuously disregard it. Thus, the messengers of heaven bypass every earthly aristocracy to bring the divine blessing to devout men of the fields. In a sense, the manger sign is no more amazing than the "stable men" who are summoned by heaven to the manger of the Lord.[8]

Perhaps still half-blinded by the light, the shepherds go running to Bethlehem. The appeal of the sign is not to the reason of a man, but rather to his faith. The scandal of the manger was no stone of stumbling to the faith of the shepherds. They accepted and believed the message.

In declaring the event, the angel did not propose that the shepherds believe the tidings on the strength of his word alone; he said: "Ye shall find . . ." The angelic proclamation was left open to their personal testing of the sign, to follow heaven's instruction and thereby prove the validity of the announcement. Thus, the shepherds really expected to find the confirmation of their faith.

Actually, this is what God desires of all men. He wants us to give His message a reverent hearing, and then to build our faith according to the signposts that He sets along the way. God has never expected blind faith from humanity. Faith in God is always found to be reasonable when the signs are followed.

But even from our vantage point, there are many who scoff the overtures of God, labelling His works as mythical, imaginary, or superstitious. Yet, we must also give heed to the sign, as did the shepherds. Then we too shall find the Saviour and behold the wonder of His blessed presence in our needy world.

According to the direction of the angel, the shepherds found the Babe in Bethlehem. He was shut out of the inn, but He was not abandoned. He was in a manger, wrapped in swaddling clothes. Apparently, no midwife attended His mother, and she herself had lovingly washed and swaddled her infant son. Her very devotion makes the swaddling clothes a sign also. This is what the shepherds see—the Lord both given and received in a manger.

Perhaps other babies were born in the town that night. But none but the Christ child would be born in a manger. There may have been several mangers in Bethlehem. But, strangely enough, the scripture gives no indication that the shepherds had to search for the one that cradled the Saviour. It has been suggested that the Christ was born in the manger which belonged to the shepherds. According to some authorities, "a manger" (vv. 7, 12, 16), should read "the manger," referring to the manger of the shepherds.[9]

In any event, it seems likely that the manger in which the Saviour was born was the one most familiar to the shepherds. Contrary to popular conceptions, there is no scriptural mention of any guiding star to lead the shepherds to that holy place.

Some have surmised that the same sign in the heavens which guided the wise men also directed the shepherds. But, so far as the scripture states, the shepherds simply had the certain spoken instructions of the angel. By acting immediately on the words of the heavenly messenger, they found the Baby Jesus without any difficulty.

When the shepherds behold the Babe, the further aspect of the angelic sign confronts them. It is the significant apparel of the Infant—His swaddling clothes. Just as Christ's birth was not heralded in lordly guise to priests and princes and the great ones of earth, but rather to obscure shepherds, He is also to be distinguished by the common clothes of humility. His kingly garments had been laid aside to perform the sacrificial office of His saviourhood. The holy Son of God was born in poverty, in the very shadow of death. Thus, His kingship was made all the more remarkable by His condescending humiliation on earth among sinful men.

Perhaps it was not as the shepherds first expected when they were told of the Saviour's birth. They may have at least expected to be sent to the finest dwelling in Bethlehem. Then, wondering at the angel's description, they may have still imagined that they would find the Infant dressed in splendid royal clothes, befitting of His title. Surely, numerous attendants would be present to witness and to identify such a blessed event. Surely, the Child would be lying in some sort of princely state for the many who would come and pay Him homage. But it was all just as the angel said.

However, because of the glory of the announcement, the shepherds were not dismayed by the humble sign related by the angel. And, after they went and saw the stark facts of the message, they were not disappointed. There in the dingy stable they could see the glory of the Lord in the manger. Undoubtedly they were somewhat relieved that such a wonder had occurred in their familiar surroundings.

It was thus the shepherds who received the sign and who saw the Messiah that God had sent. From the fields where young David had harped his praise to God, they came to bow before that Son whom David had in anticipation called his Lord.

Even though the signs of the angelic message lacked luster, the shepherds were convinced. It is evident that one truth dominated their thinking—somehow the glory of the Babe would exceed the glory of the angel and the accompanying heavenly host. In fact, the glory of the tidings, despite the scandalous signs, had convinced them of the more excellent glory of the Saviour. The anthem of the angelic chorus was still ringing in their ears. The shepherds were only satisfied as they stood in the presence of the newborn King.

Glory, Peace, and Goodwill

Not even the manger straw could hide the Christ child's glory. And the fact that He came to the poor and lowly made His coming all the more significant. So, as the rugged shepherds related the reason of their intrusion, telling of the angelic tidings, Mary no doubt remembered the words of the angel Gabriel to her: "The Lord God shall give unto him the throne of his father David: and he shall reign over the house of Jacob for ever; and of his kingdom there shall be no end" (Luke 1:32-33). As the shepherds bowed in worship, Mary knew she had not been forgotten or forsaken of God.

The faithfulness of God had been demonstrated in actual deed. The Messiah—the Expected One to be born of God's promise—had come. And now Mary, the mother, could rejoice in God her Saviour, who scatters the proud, dethrones powerful princes, and exalts those of low degree (cf. Luke 1:46-55). So Jesus was born in the stable because He is the Prince of Salvation to the poor. And He comes in glory to shine upon all who sit in darkness and in the shadow of death.

There, in the manger, the glory of the Lord is truly revealed. The Inhabitant of the manger is an even greater wonder than the birth of any other Davidic king. He is the Lord's Christ (cf. Luke 2:26), but He is more. The angel called Him "Christ, the Lord" (Luke 2:11). For when the virgin conceives and bears a Son, "he shall be great, and shall be called the Son of the Most High" (Luke 1:32). God's ancient and glorious sign, greater than any that man could ever think or ask (cf. Isa. 7:11, 14), has at last been confirmed.

Every sign of God's covenant promise, from the comfort of Eve to the astonishment of Mary, from the arching bow in the clouds to the sign of Jonah in the jaws of death —every sign awaited the glory of the manger. The salvation that God promised is so great that He must come himself to bring it. The human need is so great that only God can provide the remedy. King David could repel the Philistines to deliver the people of God, but David's greater Son must come to overthrow all the powers of darkness, for He must save His people from all their sins.[10]

In days of old, only the Lord, dwelling between the cherubim in His holy place, was the glory of His people Israel. But now the glory was truly present, for the Lord of glory had come. The Word became flesh and tabernacled among us, and "we beheld his glory, glory as of the only begotten from the Father, full of grace and truth" (John 1:14). His glory thus radiates as the light of truth in a misinformed world that has paid more mind to the tempting devices of Satan than to the commandments and promises of God.

It is no wonder that this divine message of truth was too great and marvelous to be voiced by only a single messenger. The heavenly praise to God is coupled with the astounding declaration of the Saviour's birth. Then, the doxology of the heavenly host taught the shepherds and all mankind to give God all glory and honor, especially for the presence of His salvation in the presence of His only begotten Son. This was the heavenly witness of His glory.

Yet it was in the darkness of the manger where the shepherds saw the true Light shine. No angel could take His place here, for His work is beyond even the powerful ability of the heavenly host. Those pure spirits, created but not born, could visit the wrath of heaven upon this rebellious planet, but they could not bring salvation to sin-darkened people. The desperate situation required divine

277

glory from above all the angels. Only then did the manger become a signal of salvation.[11]

The glory of the event of Christ's birth is the glory of God's love—the burning brightness of redeeming grace. "Herein was the love of God manifested in us, that God hath sent his only begotten Son into the world that we might live through him" (1 John 4:9). The Lord himself came, the Son and Sun of love, both the Giver and the Gift. But if He had come in the midst of the angels to the fields of Bethlehem, then no man—shepherd, scribe, or emperor—could have withstood the glory of His presence.

Certainly, other works of God are also for His glory, but the redemption of a sin-cursed world is for His "glory in the highest." It was His infinite wisdom and love that designed and promoted this unmerited favor for impoverished humanity.

Before the foundation of the world the salvation of man was conceived in such a way so that the complete Godhead would be coequally glorified. The Father, Son, and Holy Spirit would share the honor in advancing and reestablishing the kingdom of heaven on earth.

Again, it is no wonder the heavenly host praise God. For this is what the angels celebrate—the invasion of Satan's stronghold to redeem lost humanity for the glory of God. After generations of seeming to allow Satan the upper hand in this contested part of creation, now the divine offensive is launched. This bold and gracious mission of God in sending the Messiah means victory, which redounds to His praise. And, it openly manifests His goodwill towards men.

Had this not been the case, the angelic joy would have been only the solemn triumph of heaven over a world of rebels, for all have sinned and come short of the glory of God. But God's goodwill in giving and sending His only Son to be the Saviour introduced the possibility of peace to this chaotic world. His coming breaks down the barrier of enmity that sin had raised between God and man, and it reestablishes the prospects of a right relationship with God.

Because God has thereby provided peace for all mankind, all peace results as we come to make our peace with Him. There follows the peace of conscience, peace with the rest of creation, and peace among the races of men. This is the peace that the birth of the Christ child brings to all humanity. It indeed means "Joy to the world!" For all divine goodness flows to us from the glorious event of the Incarnation of Jesus Christ, born as God with us in the flesh.

All the hope and happiness that mankind may have is because of God's goodwill. If we are to presently enjoy the comforts and the benefits of divine creation, God must receive the glory. The threatening problems of worldwide pollution and ecological imbalance are the tragic result of man usurping the glory that belongs to God. But the presence of Christ, the Mediator between God and man, rebukes all sin in the flesh, from selfish rebellion against God to the wasteful destruction of His creation. All men, as well as the shepherds, must inevitably bow low before the Saviour and find in Him the answer to their hopeless condition brought about by their own selfishness and pride.

That night the angels proclaimed peace with solemnity, as well as with joy. For the message of the angels points us to a glory beyond the manger—to the glory of the Cross. Indeed, heaven's high glory descends upon the hillside with the angelic host. But the word of the angel directs the shepherds to an even greater glory: to the Lord of the angels who comes to give himself a Sacrifice for sinners. First, at the manger the Mighty God glorified His name; then, at the Cross He glorified it again. When God himself, when the Son of the Highest hallows His name in blood, then the glory of grace and peace is lifted above the heavens.[12]

This glory is offered to all who will hear and receive its saving benefits. As many authorities have translated this portion, it is: "On earth peace among men of goodwill." In other words, there is a definite sense in which the message of the angels was only directed to those who would have goodwill toward God, who would recognize His glory, who were willing to be reconciled to Him by faith in His Son. The heavenly announcement forever puts God on record as revealing His glory, His peace, His goodwill and mercy unto all men, whether they receive it or not.

As for the shepherds, they gladly received the tidings of heaven-sent salvation. As soon as the angels departed, the shepherds said to one another, "Let us now go even unto Bethlehem, and see this thing that is come to pass, which the Lord hath made known unto us" (Luke 2:15). They acted in believing faith by quickly following the directions of the angel. And they found Mary, and Joseph, and the Babe lying in the manger.

Certainly, the reward of the shepherd's faith was not only the realization of the truth of the angelic announcement. They also beheld the glory and experienced the peace and goodwill of God as precious to their own lives. For, when they had seen it, they glorified God; "they made known abroad the saying which was told them concerning the child" (v. 17, KJV).

The message of the angels was not just for the shepherds. It was intended for all men. It is for us today. The vital question is whether we will hear it and receive it in faith, as did the shepherds. Seemingly, all our own seeking for Christ has been fleeing from Him. We have not scaled the heights of knowledge to find Him on our own, but He has pierced the depths of sin-blindedness to find us. The real and living God, expected from ages past, has come. The angels' gospel calls us to the manger to meet Him.

But there is no longer any need to hurry unto Bethlehem to look for a Babe in a manger. He is not there now. The glorious fact remains that He was. And the glory of the message will apply to us just as it did to the shepherds if we will only hear it, hasten to receive it, and believe it as they did. The Saviour was also born unto you and me. Thus, the Light still shines, the Light of the new age, the living, personal Light, Jesus Christ.

Yes, the Expected One has come. He came in accordance with the announcement of the angels. But one day He is coming again with His holy angels to summon the living and the dead to righteous judgment. Men are now expecting His return. Our generation has watched rockets hurtle into the vacancies of space; man has ascended to the mysteries of the moon; but all his journeys have not brought him to Christ.

Rather, our journey must be the soul-transforming journey of accepting Jesus for who He is, the Son of God, the coming King. We have the example of the wise men. They made a long journey for the express purpose of worshiping the King who had come, and their diligence was rewarded. Every divine assistance was given to lead them to Christ. It was particularly by a guiding light in the heavens. Does not the Light of heaven still guide those who look for the King?

Chapter 14

The Guiding Star

> *Now when Jesus was born in Beth-*
> *lehem of Judea in the days of Herod the*
> *king, behold, wise-men from the east came*
> *to Jerusalem, saying,*
> *Where is he that is born King of the*
> *Jews? for we saw his star in the east, and*
> *are come to worship him.*
>
> (Matt. 2:1-2)

The Magi of the Scriptures had the right idea. They had
been looking at the heavens for the sign of the coming
Saviour-King. Apparently, the Great Expectation of One
to be sent of God was not an isolated belief. They knew
that the hope of the world must be heaven-sent and not
humanly arranged. All of the best plans and dreams of the
rulers of mankind eventually ended in total disarray. The

present world domination of Rome was seen to be ineffectual in working out the divine purpose.

Suddenly, a new star penetrated the dark canopy of the night, unexplained and hitherto unknown. Its magnificent brilliance far exceeded all of the other luminaries of the night, and it seemed to hover close to earth. Surely, its outstanding qualities indicated some significant truth, aside from the astonishing wonders of the heavens. Its glowing presence excited unsurpassed study and scrutiny.

This star was so extraordinary that when the wise men saw it, they were convinced that there could be a no more positive sign that the "King of the Jews" had been born. Many before them had watched the heavens for the sign of His coming. It was because of the repeated promise of God, and it had been the clear message of the prophets. Now, indeed the Light pushed back the darkness, revealing the truth of the ages.

A careful study of the Gospels of Matthew and Luke makes it clear that there was a time lag between the experience of the shepherds and the eventual arrival of the wise men where Jesus was. Contrary to popular belief, these were two separate events, probably occurring weeks or months apart. According to the scriptural accounts, the shepherds and the wise men went to two different places to worship the Christ child.

In Luke, according to the message of the angels and the shepherds' response, they found the newborn Baby Jesus in a manger (cf. 2:12, 16). But in Matthew, it is told that the wise men went into the house and saw the young Child with Mary His mother (cf. 2:11). Herod was evidently aware of the possibility of a time lag when he gave his infamous order to slaughter all male babies two years old and under (cf. Matt. 2:16).

It is evident that something strongly motivated the wise men to begin their search from distant lands for the

283

King. The question is: What was it that they saw when they viewed "the star"? It is obvious that their coming and finding Jesus was not accidental. We have a choice of ideas that varyingly involve the natural and the supernatural in their quest.

For example, William Smith views the entire experience of the wise men as the result of the intervention of the supernatural in the realm of the natural realm of this world. He suggests that some supernatural light resembling a star had appeared to these men who were versed in the study of celestial phenomena. This conveyed to their minds a supernatural impulse to go to Jerusalem, where they would find a newborn king.[1]

On the other hand, there is evidence of natural astronomical phenomena recorded in the "Chinese Tables," a document considered accurate by astronomers. These tables report a new star in 6 B.C. and a comet in the year 4 B.C. Seemingly, the light the shepherds saw was of brief duration and within a limited locale. But the star that brought the wise men to Jerusalem was a major event, seen prominently in the heavens for some time. Moreover, it has been astronomically ascertained that such an appearance would be visible to those who left Jerusalem, and that it would point—almost seem to "go before"—in the direction of, and stand over, Bethlehem.[2]

Historically and astronomically speaking, there can be no doubt that the most remarkable conjunction of planets—that of Jupiter and Saturn in the constellation Pisces, which occurs only once in 800 years—did take place no less than three times in the year 747 A.U.C. (*anno urbis conditae,* "in the year of the building of the city" [i.e., Rome, in 753 B.C.]), or two years before the birth of Christ (in May, October, and December). This conjunction is admitted by all astronomers. It was not only extraordinary, but it presented the most brilliant spectacle in the night sky. This would be of special interest to those who watched the heavens with astrological concern.[3]

In the year following, 748 A.U.C., another planet, Mars, joined this radiant conjunction. It was Johannes Kepler, the great Polish astronomer, who is credited with discovering this conjunction by observing a similar one in 1603-4. He noticed that when the three planets came into conjunction, a new, extraordinarily brilliant, and peculiarly colored, evanescent star was visible between Jupiter and Saturn. Kepler thus suggested that a similar star had appeared under the same circumstances in the conjunction which occurred preceding the birth of Christ. He therefore placed the birth date of Jesus in 748 A.U.C. (6 B.C.).[4]

Because of the occurrence of such astronomical evidence, Hans Holzer believes that two of the wise men began their journey to Jerusalem following the first conjunction. They traveled en route to the Arab city of Petra, south of Palestine, where they were joined by the third wise man. It was perhaps there that they noticed the appearance of the strange star overhead, pointing in the direction of Judea. Holzer uses October 3, 747 A.U.C. (7 B.C.), the date of the initial conjunction of the planets, as the actual time of Jesus' birth.[5] He thus presumes that Jesus was over a year old when the wise men found Him.

The actual date of the birth of Jesus does have considerable bearing on our study. All scholars apparently agree that He was not born in the year 1. The so-called Era of the Birth of Christ was not in use until A.D. 532, in the time of Justinian, when it was introduced by Dionysius Exiguus, a Roman monk. His chronology began to prevail in the West about the time of Charles Martel and Pope Gregory II, around A.D. 730. However, it has long been agreed by scholars that Exiguus made a mathematical error in computing the birth date of Jesus, placing it some years too late. The amount of error has been variously estimated at two, three, four, five, or as many as eight years.[6]

It seems to be generally accepted that at least four years were omitted from the Christian calendar because of the mistake. Aside from computations by astronomical events, there is one historically recorded event which helps to determine Christ's date of birth. According to the scriptural record, we know that Jesus was born before the death of Herod. Josephus indicates that Herod died the latter part of March, 4 B.C.[7] Thus, allowing time for the census and the order of Herod to slaughter the male babies of Bethlehem, the birth of Christ apparently could not have occurred any later than the autumn of 5 B.C.[8]

But apart from the spectacular sign of the star, the time of Jesus' birth, the seeming miraculous search and discovery of the wise men, and their presentation of symbolic gifts, we may ask: What is the significance of their pilgrimage? We would again reaffirm that their journey was according to God's holy purpose. It was not accidental. We shall further consider the possibilities by a discussion of: (1) The Identity of the Wise Men; (2) The History of the Star; (3) The Meaning of the Star; and (4) The Mission of the Star.

The Identity of the Wise Men

Aside from considering the occasion of the Nativity, there is also diversity of opinion as to who and what the wise men were. Some take them to be astrologers or sages, while others believe they were magicians. Early references to the word translated "wise men" seem to have Babylonian origin. There, the word primarily meant either "one who is deep whether in power and reputation or in insight, or one who has fullness of power." Perhaps it was first used with special reference to astrologers and interpreters of dreams. And, passing from Babylonia to Media, it became the name of the Median priestly order.[9]

So the Magi among the Persians were their philosophers and their priests. They would not admit anyone to be their king who had not first been enrolled among the Magi. This could support the tradition that the wise men were also kings of the east.

In the Old Testament scripture, in the Hebrew text, the word translated Magi (A.V.) occurs only twice, and then only incidentally. In Jer. 39:3 and 13, we are told of one among the Chaldean officers sent by Nebuchadnezzar to Jerusalem with the name or title of Rab-Mag. This word is interpreted as equivalent to chief of the Magi.[10]

Historically, the Magi are prominent mostly as a Persian religious caste. Herodotus connects them with another people by reckoning them among the six tribes of the Medes (i. 101). They appear in his history of Astyages as interpreters of dreams (i. 120). But in Jeremiah they appear at a still earlier period among the retinue of the Chaldean king. The Magi became a part of "the astrologers and stargazers and monthly prognosticators." It is with such men that Daniel and his fellow exiles were placed. They are described as 10 times wiser than all the magicians and astrologers (Dan. 1:20). Perhaps the office that Daniel was given (Dan. 5:11) was identical to that of Rab-Mag.[11]

However, some think that the Magi, or at least one of them, came from Arabia. Arabians are called men of the east (cf. Judg. 6:3), and they were also noted for their soothsaying (cf. Isa. 2:6). Others are further convinced that there were prophets in Arabia who were of the posterity of Abraham by Keturah, and that they taught the name of God, which they had received in tradition from the religious teaching of Abraham.[12]

According to tradition, there were three wise men, and they are called Caspar, Melchior, and Balthasar. There is no scriptural foundation to support this tradition. However, there is one vital clue in Matt. 2:11, where it tells the respective gifts they offered: "gold and frankincense and myrrh." Gold in the first century came mostly from India. Caspar was supposedly from that distant eastern land, and he was the aging, gaunt man who brought the Christ child gold.

In 1855 an English archeologist, A. Cunningham, wrote in a scientific journal of the period that the Indian King Gundaforus, who is mentioned in the Legend of St. Thomas, a third-century document, was identical with a certain Gondophares, whose name appears on bronze and silver coins of the first century. Moreover, Cunningham showed that this name was later spelled Gadaspar, and eventually during the Middle Ages it turned into the present adaptation, "Caspar."[13]

Furthermore, some coins were found in India which were apparently related to an early era. For some time they were classified as "coins of an unknown king." They bore the Greek inscription "Soter Megas, king of kings," and they remained unidentified for years. However, "Soter Megas" translates as "The Great Saviour," and the portrait on the face of the coins was more likely that of Deity than of a man. Then, on the back of the coins it shows a man on camelback holding a cross. These coins of India were evidently a commemorative issue honoring the visit of their king to Judea to worship Christ.[14]

Hans Holzer claims that the second wise man, Melchior, was identical with a certain Malichus, son of the Arab king, Aretas. The capital city of this kingdom was Petra, located in the desert south of Palestine. Holzer thinks that it was probably here that the three wise men started out together. Traditionally, Melchior is credited with bringing frankincense as his gift. According to the ancients, this aromatic came from a mysterious place called Punt. Investigation indicates that Punt and Petra are names for the same city.[15]

Again, tradition holds that the third wise man, Balthasar, was dark-skinned. Although some scholars had supposed that the name was Phoenician because of the element "Bal" in the word, there is at least one greater probability. After the Italian occupation of Ethiopia in 1936, much new material dealing with ancient Ethiopian history became available. Holzer states that among these documents are the so-called Royal Ethiopian Lists, first published in 1853. Among those listed there is mention of a king named Beese Bazen, and a startling entry: "In the year eight of the reign of Bazen, Christ was born."[16]

It is suggested that the name Beese Bazen turned into Balthasar over the centuries, especially as it sifted through the romance languages in which Beese Bazen would naturally acquire a more euphonic form. Bazen, the Ethiopian king, would have been dark-skinned as has long been thought of the third wise man. Also, this wise man supposedly gave the Child an offering of myrrh. According to William Smith, myrrh was available from Arabia and Abyssinia (Ethiopia), from both sides of the Red Sea.[17] History indicates that at the period of time in question, both sides of the Red Sea were ruled by the king of Ethiopia.

Although there may be much about these men of the East that seems uncertain, there are some things that seem quite definite. Whatever sort of wise men they had been before, the Magi began to be wise men indeed when they commenced their search for Christ.

These men possibly had some knowledge of Jewish prophecy and teaching, even though it is unlikely that any of them were descendants of Jacob. The predominant tone of the Scriptures is that the Jews did not regard Jesus as the Christ. But, significantly, these Gentile men traveled great distance to find the King and worship Him.

Whether the Magi were astrologers, priests, soothsayers, kings, philosophers, prophets, or a combination of these occupations, they were scholars who were willing and anxious to learn of the Messiah. They responded gladly to the radiant sign of the star. They were not satisfied to simply know that a king had been born. They wanted to follow the leading of the heavenly light to worship Him. So, they left their homelands and dominions behind in search of the King above all the kings of earth.

According to some scholars, the journey of the wise men lasted at least seven months.[18] Their destination was the land of Judah, over which the star seemed to hover. The wise men first went to Jerusalem, expecting to find a palace-born king. Instead, they found King Herod, a despotic Idumean, who knew nothing of such a spectacular event. He thus called the chief priests and scribes together to learn where the Messiah should be born. The prophet Micah was quoted as predicting the birth of God's Anointed One in Bethlehem (5:2).

Herod had an immediate and a malicious interest in the purpose of the wise men's pilgrimage. Indeed, he wanted them to find the newborn King, and then to inform him. But his desire was not that he might go and worship Christ. It was rather that he might locate this threat to his throne and kill Him. Herod thus sent the Magi to Bethlehem. When they looked again to the star, it went before them, and they followed it till it came and stood over where the young Child was (Matt. 2:2-10).

Despite the proximity of the several known astronomical incidents which we have previously mentioned, it is extremely difficult to bring the scriptural record and the astronomical record into exact coincidence. There are too many unknowns. Any projection along this line must be viewed in terms of possibility and speculation. It is sufficient to note that the star was certainly used of God.

The long journey of the wise men was over. The star had guided them to the house where the Christ child now lived. There is no scriptural mention of the name of the city where the Magi actually found Him. Jerusalem is ruled out immediately. Mary and Joseph did not return to Nazareth with Jesus until their return from Egypt, following Herod's death. The deciding factor as to where the wise men found Jesus is whether they found Him before or after the flight to Egypt to escape the murderous action of Herod (Matt. 2:13).

The fact that the Magi were warned in a dream by God to return to their own country another way, instead of reporting to Herod, indicates that Herod was still a threat to Jesus. We also know that after the 40 days of purification, following the birth of a male child, Mary and Joseph traveled the six miles from Bethlehem to Jerusalem and presented Jesus in the Temple (cf. Luke 2:22-39). Possibly the warning dream that came to Joseph to flee into Egypt, which Matthew records, occurred while they were in Jerusalem. Therefore, it would seem that the wise men found the little Jesus in Bethlehem sometime during the 40-day period before Mary and Joseph took Him to Jerusalem.

After worshiping the heaven-sent King, the Magi presented Him with gifts of gold and frankincense and myrrh. These were appropriate offerings. Gold was used as an emblem of purity (Job 22:10) and nobility (Lam. 4:1). Frankincense, with its sweet perfume, symbolizes prayer accepted before God (Ps. 141:2). Myrrh is specified in Exod. 30:23 as one of the ingredients of the "oil of holy ointment," and it is typical of the Messiah's graces (Ps. 45:8).[19] These offerings were evidently intended as specimens of the products of their country, and their presentation was expressive of the homage of their people to the newfound King.

In this sense, the Magi may be regarded as the representatives of the Gentile world. Their homage was the first and typical acknowledgement of Christ by those who hitherto had been "far off," and their offerings were symbolic of the world's tribute. The ancient Church has traced in the gift of gold the emblem of Christ's royalty; in the myrrh, of His humanity, and in the fullest evidence of it, in His burying; and in the frankincense, that of His divinity.[20]

All of this was brought about because of the guiding star. It is obvious that the Magi were wise, but we get the definite impression that it was the star that amplified their wisdom. So that we may better understand the motivations of their pilgrimage, we turn now to considering the history of the star.

The History of the Star

It was common practice among the idolatrous peoples to worship the stars as the "host of heaven." This was especially true of the Eastern nations, where the planets were named after their idol gods. Even the Israelites had been guilty of venerating certain stars in connection with their idol worship during the times of their backsliding from their worship of God (cf. 1 Kings 11:33; Amos 5:26).

Although the stars had been misused to lead men away from God, there now comes a time when a particular star is used to lead wise men to Christ. By His star, the gods of pagan peoples are set to nought, and men are directed to the Truth. The created handiwork of God is put in proper perspective, and distant kings are moved to come and worship the only begotten Son of God.

The meaningful occasion of the star's discovery and recognition seems unlikely without some previous enlightenment by teaching, tradition, or prophecy. It is possible that the ancient prophecy of Balaam may have influenced the Magi to be looking for the star. This prophet had also lived to the east of Judea, at Pethor, in Mesopotamia (Num. 22:5; Deut. 23:4). An unusual promise was given of God in the favor of Israel through Balaam, even though he had been hired by Balak, king of the Moabites, to put a curse on Israel. The message of this prophecy is recorded in Num. 24:17: "I shall see him, but not now; I behold him, but not nigh: there shall come forth a Star out of Jacob, and a Sceptre shall rise out of Israel, and shall smite through the corners of Moab, and break down all the sons of tumult (of Sheth)."

This prophecy of Balaam had undoubtedly led to a belief among the Jews that a great star would appear in heaven when the Messiah came. "When the Messiah is to be revealed," says the book Sohar, "a star will rise in the east, shining in great brightness, and seven other stars round it will fight against it on every side."[21] Also, the *Pesitha Sotarta* comments on this prophecy, stating, "A star will rise in the east which is the star of the Messiah, and will remain in the east fifteen days."[22]

Although Balaam's prediction is initially regarded by some as having been fulfilled by the victorious accomplishments of King David, there is the obvious overtone of the coming of a King mightier than David. The preceding interpretations of the prophecy certainly indicate this. The mysterious Person whom Balaam envisions in the undated future, who is to be the King of Israel, is identified as the Shiloh of Jacob's dying prophecy. Since He is the One who is to subdue all the nations, this cannot be David, for his conquests were limited to the surrounding

293

territories adjoining Israel. Yet, it is true that David anticipates Him in many ways.[23]

As for the Messiah, His kingdom shall be universal. He shall reign in righteousness and victory over all competing governments. This was typified by David's victories over Moab and Edom. However, the Messiah, it is prophesied, shall rule over "all the children of Seth"; that is, all the children of men who have descended from Seth, the son of Adam. The descendants of the rest of Adam's sons had been destroyed previously by the Flood.

The Christ, then, shall be King, not only of the children of Israel, but of the whole world. And all the children of Seth (all people born since the Flood) shall either be governed by His golden sceptre or be destroyed. Thus, the Star shall rise to universal rule, possessing all divine power and authority, and put down all people and nations who would unrighteously oppose Him.[24]

This penetrating truth of Balaam's prophecy probably stimulated great interest among the leaders of the Eastern world, even after recognizing its token fulfillment by the conquests of David. Moreover, some believe that Balaam was the founder of the Magi, that he was a rabbi who taught his pupils the black art, and that the Magi, who were his successors, knew his prophecy of the star of the Messiah through the tradition of his schools.[25] Consequently, so far as both the Magi and the Jewish rabbis were concerned, there was more excited expectation at the appearance of the star, than wonder and surprise.

As we have already noted, there is also a definite correspondence between the prophecies of Jacob and Balaam. In the light of Jacob's earlier prophecy, the promise of "a Star" very appropriately connects to the promise of "Shiloh" (Gen. 49:10).

Balaam's prophecy defines the Star as a Ruler of men, for the Sceptre is used in the same sense as it was in the prediction of dying Jacob. Balaam declared: "There shall come forth a Star out of Jacob, and a Sceptre shall rise out of Israel" (Num. 24:17). Previously, Jacob had foretold: "The sceptre shall not depart from Judah, nor the ruler's staff from between his feet, until Shiloh come; and unto him shall the obedience of the peoples be" (Gen. 49:10).

The correspondence of these two messages of promise is threefold. Both vitally concern Jacob and his descendants. Both look to a coming ruler that shall be born from their people, and both designate that His reign shall be over all men. Jewish prophecy, from beginning to end, contemplated the Messiah as the Conqueror, the Subduer, and even the Destroyer of all the heathen.[26]

Incredible as it may seem, the coming of Christ was given the sign of a star even before the sign of the virgin. Although Balaam may not have fully realized it, he was used of God to further proclaim the expected Messiah of Israel, confirming the covenant of a coming Deliverer. Primarily, the sign of the star seemed to be given for the benefit of the Gentiles, although it was also recognized fully by the children of Israel. Then, the later sign of the virgin was given more particularly as a specific witness to the Jews.

The simple fact is that when the star appeared, the Magi immediately recognized its significance, and they expectantly made their way to Jerusalem. The scripture identifies this event in history as happening "in the days of Herod the king" (Matt. 2:1, 3).

As we have already noted, Herod was an Idumean (Edomite), a descendant of Esau, the twin brother of Jacob. He was made king of Judea by Augustus and Antonius, the chief rulers of Rome. In spite of Herod's reign of treachery, he was given the title of "Herod the Great." However, the main implication of the title was simply that those who succeeded him had lesser authority.

History indicates that Jesus was born in the thirty-fifth year of the reign of Herod. This is indeed the prophesied time for Shiloh to come. Matthew Henry calls attention to the fact that by Herod's reign "the sceptre" had thus "departed from Judah," and "the lawgiver from between his feet." Shiloh must now come, "and to him shall the gathering of the people be" (Gen. 49:10, KJV).[27] He who was to come, sent of God to deliver Israel, was also to be the hope of all the peoples of the earth.

This was the evident and firm hope of the Magi. They acknowledged the Star as the symbol of certainty that the heaven-sent King had come. It seems unlikely that any unexpected appearance of a star should give such definite direction to their actions. The star indeed had a history, and the knowledge of the eventual manifestation of such a sign prompted the watchfulness of a few waiting hearts.

To whatever extent the wise men understood the Messianic teachings of the prophets, or received knowledge of the hopes of Israel through social communication, they nevertheless came because of a star, and that star gave them guidance. Without the history of the star, its appearance would not have caused such definite action.

These men of the East came and confronted Herod with a startling question and a positive affirmation. They asked: "Where is he that is born King of the Jews?" Then, they declared, "We have seen his star." Obviously, the history of the star gave understanding to the meaning of the star. Thus, these men who lived in distant lands were brought near to behold its timeless message.

The Meaning of the Star

The star contains meaning because it was the consummation of divine promise. Its beams of light correspond not only with Jacob's vision of Shiloh and Balaam's

Star of Jacob, but it also blends with all other Messianic prophecies and promises. Ultimately, the star means that God is faithful to provide salvation for both the Jew and the Gentile. And it was because of that divine faithfulness that the wise men were led to behold the Saviour.

With the birth of the Christ child, that holy event became the shining light to the Gentiles by the appearance of a heavenly star. Isaiah speaks in terms of such a light of promise, although it is indefinite whether he envisioned the light of a star in the heavens. But, speaking of the Messiah, he records the divine message, which affirms:

> *I, Jehovah, have called thee in righteousness, and will hold thy hand, and will keep thee, and give thee for a covenant of the people, for a light of the Gentiles* (Isa. 42:6).

> *And now saith Jehovah that formed me from the womb to be his servant, to bring Jacob again to him, and that Israel be gathered unto him (for I am honorable in the eyes of Jehovah, and my God is become my strength); yea, he saith, It is too light a thing that thou shouldest be my servant to raise up the tribes of Jacob, and to restore the preserved of Israel: I will also give thee for a light to the Gentiles, that thou mayest be my salvation unto the end of the earth* (Isa. 49:5-6).

Whatever meaning is attached to the star, it of necessity affirms the compliance of God with His previous sacred promises to both the Jews and the Gentiles. In accordance with ultimate events, we may say that the "light to the Gentiles" not only took the form of knowledge or personal example. It became the means of guidance to kneel before the Saviour.

When we take into account the history of the star and its obvious meaning, the fact that the wise men were attracted to the Christ child by the light of the star was no strange coincidence. It was according to the plan of God. And since the Magi had long been cognizant of the light of knowledge, when the star appeared over Judea, it signaled them to look specifically for the expected Messiah, "the desire of all nations" (Hag. 2:7).

Because there had been a star of *promise,* when the star appeared it became the star of *hope.* The Magi left their homeland with deep anticipation, assured by the light of promise and the light of guidance. Although it seemed so fantastic, theirs was more than a hollow hope. An almost irresistible urgency welled in their hearts to literally worship the Child of hope the star symbolized.

At once, the utmost faith of these men became focused on the star. By this light of truth they were constrained to see their hope and faith verified. Any explanation of the reason for their long journey falls short unless it be admitted that the appearance of the star became divinely implanted hope. But both the likelihood and the result of their journey must be considered.

It is true that men, before and since that time, have gone on hopeful conquests. Great and visionary effort has been expended in the building of empires, in searching for riches, in exploring the earth, and now in the conquest of outer space. Some of the attempts were very rewarding, but others met with bitter disappointment and failure.

However, the pilgrimage of the Magi was surely the most hopeful and rewarding of all journeys. It alone was inspired and led by a star of hope. As we have noted, the reason of their travel was to find and worship the newly born King, for they had seen His star (Matt. 2:2). Thus, the star was the present source of hope—a hope enlarged by assurance, a hope certain of realization.

Herod was astounded by their certainty, and he was deeply disturbed. These men of the East supposedly knew of an event in his own kingdom that could bode disruption to his reign. They had come a great distance purposefully and expectantly.

Herod thus called upon the chief priests and scribes of Jerusalem to tell him where such a King as these men were seeking was to be born. They told the king that according to the sure word of the prophet, the Messiah was to be born in Bethlehem of Judea. They quoted Micah, saying: "And thou Bethlehem, in the land of Judah, art not the least among the princes of Judah: for out of thee shall come a Governor, that shall rule my people Israel" (Matt. 2:6, KJV).

When the wise men heard the instructions of King Herod, they departed. The star which they had seen from their homeland appeared and preceded them, "till it came and stood over where the young child was" (Matt. 2:9). As previously noted, the Scriptures make no definite statement as to what city or town the Magi were led to. However, it would seem that if they were led to a place other than Bethlehem, the Gospel writer would have indicated the change as he did concerning the move from the manger, where the shepherds found Christ, to a house where the wise men found Him.

The main issue is not where they found the Christ child, but it is the fact that they found Him. We are impressed with the surety of the star of hope in leading mankind to the Saviour. We are convinced by the results that in spite of competing ideas and advice, if men will follow the star, it will always lead them to Christ.

A further depth of meaning is expressed as the scripture goes on to declare that "when they saw the star, they rejoiced with exceeding great joy" (Matt. 2:10). The star is thus not only a sign of promise and hope, for it also became the object of joy. In every obedient step of the Magi, according to the guidance of the star, the star took on added meaning.

As the journey of the wise men ended in successful completion, *joy* surpassed the previous meanings of *promise* and *hope*. A miracle happened when they beheld the Child. The light of the star illumined His countenance, and all the promise, the hope, and the joy were transferred to His person. Instantly, the wise men realized that the star and the Christ were unified into one magnificent, divine revelation.

Promise and hope climaxed in the joy of their actual fulfillment. And joy culminated in the act of worship with the sublime knowledge, by the divine revelation of the star, that their eyes beheld the King of Kings. The scripture indicates such an experience when it states: "They came into the house, and saw the young child with Mary his mother; and they feel down, and worshipped him" (Matt. 2:11).

This was the ultimate purpose of the heavenly star— that men might be led to the divine Star, the Christ. He is identified as the Star personified. As the star led the Magi to the Christ child, so then shall Christ guide all wise men to the redemption of God. In this manner the meaning of the star coincides with the mission of the star, coming to focus upon the person of Christ.

The Mission of the Star

The wise men had only an inkling of the mission of the star. In the embodiment of the star, as they looked on the Christ child, they were not only aware of His royalty, they were also aware of His saviourhood. The purpose of that bright star of old was to bring the Gentiles into first-hand knowledge of the fact that the Saviour had come.

300

But it is doubtful that the Magi were mindful of the strenuous demands of Christ's mission on earth.

Even now, Jesus Christ appears before men as the Star from heaven, but not all men are conscious of His coming. It was the mission of the Star to be lifted up from the earth, that all men might be drawn unto Him (cf. John 12:32). But the manner of His revelation has caused many to miss both the event and the experience. It is true that His light is no longer a speechless guide, a mere luminary in the sky. Rather, it is the light of truth, the Word of God speaking in audible language through the divine life of Christ in human flesh.

The path of the mysterious star led the wise men to Jesus. But now, the path of the divine Star leads men on to Calvary—to atonement and forgiveness of sin. There is no mistake about where the Star leads, or concerning the nature of His mandate. Men have presumed that Christ came to establish an earthly kingdom, to rule from the throne of David in Jerusalem. However, the initial thrust of His mission erected His throne on the mercy seat of the Cross, there to offer himself a Sacrifice for the sins of the world.

For a time, Christ's kingdom is limited within the hearts and lives of men who will take up their individual crosses and follow Him. At this point, it is not a spectacular display of power and authority. Rather, it is as the light of the star guided the wise men to the Christ child, that now the light of truth continues to draw men unto Him, pointing the world of sinners the way back to God.

According to this unfolding manifestation, it seems obvious that the commission of Christ, the Star, involves three aspects: (1) as Prophet; (2) as Priest, and (3) as King.

As Prophet, we behold in Jesus Christ the very Revelation of God unto mankind. He is a living example of God's

301

will and way. He is the human articulation of divine purpose and love. In every sense, Christ is the Word made flesh, proclaiming in principle and precept, in spirit and in truth, that the salvation of God has come down to sinful men. There can be no doubt as to man's need, the curse upon him, or as to his intended destiny, for the Prophet is faithful to give forth the light of truth to all men.

As Priest, we see Jesus providing atonement for all sinners. Not only does He fill the office as Intercessor, but He offers himself as the one and only sufficient Sacrifice for sin and uncleanness. His priesthood is not of human descent, nor is His sacrifice to be repeated. Christ established an everlasting priesthood, and His sacrifice was once and for all. As Son of God and Son of Man, this Priest is well acquainted with the needs of men, as well as with the remedy of God. So He is able to save from the uttermost to the uttermost, if they will only look to Him.

As King, Jesus Christ must first be crowned, as it were, in the throne room of an individual's life. He must be given supreme allegiance. He must be worshipped as a personal Saviour, and as Lord of all. Initially, His is a spiritual kingdom, for it began in the hearts of men such as the Magi.

This is just the redemptive aspect of His kingdom, however. For even though there may be only a relatively small minority who will accept Christ, and receive Him as King, one day He shall be crowned King of Kings and Lord of Lords. His rule shall then depose all other rulers, and His government shall supersede all others. He shall indeed ascend the throne of His father David, and all people shall call Him Blessed.

We may wonder: Can all of this be the authority of the Star, the little Christ child who was worshipped by the wise men? The answer is unwaveringly affirmative. Although they may not have comprehended His wondrous revelation to the fullest extent, the wise men realized they beheld the salvation of the Lord.

Apparently, the Magi from afar had clearer vision and understanding of the significance of Jesus' birth than did most of His Jewish countrymen who were nearby and well schooled. Whatever truth even those of greatest faith grasped at the time of His coming, the mission of the star was glorious beyond all human expectation.

Even today, we stand amazed at the history, the meaning, and the mandate of the star. By the pure light of Christ, we, as the wise men, are guided to the place where God's great Gift was given. They were led mainly by a light in the heavens. But we are led by the light of His truth. Their expectation was wrapped in the life of a newborn King. Our expectation is wrapped in the everlasting life given by the returning King. Thus, the star has a message for the ages: BEHOLD YOUR KING!

Chapter 15

The King of the Jews

She brought forth her firstborn son;
and she wrapped him in swaddling clothes,
and laid him in a manger; because there
was no room for them in the inn.

(Luke 2:7)

He came unto his own, and his own re-
ceived him not. But as many as received
him, to them gave he power to become the
sons of God, even to them that believe on
his name.

(John 1:11-12, KJV)

And Pilate wrote a title also, and put
it on the cross. And there was written,
JESUS OF NAZARETH, THE KING OF
THE JEWS.

(John 19:19)

In spite of all the prophecies and signs, the world was ill-prepared for the birth of the King. Little did the citizens of Bethlehem realize that right in their village the greatest event in history had occurred. For generations the Great Expectation had been a vague, unlikely hope. Now, what seemed a commonplace night was to affect all generations and all nations. Everyone was so busy working, sleeping, or reveling, that very few were aware of who had come.

The only ones who knew were the ones God specifically told. Simple, humble-hearted shepherds heard the good news from an angel sent direct from God. They went according to his directions, and they found the Babe lying in a manger. Also, the discerning wise men observed His star in the heavens. They followed its light to the house where the young Child lived.

Mary and Joseph carried their astonishing responsibility close to their hearts. It would have been indiscreet for them to have even suggested the import of their heavenly secret. They would have been laughed to scorn.

So, this King was not born in a palace with marble halls and carpeted stairways. Neither was there any luxurious bedchamber prepared for His birth. Likewise, physicians and midwives were absent from the scene. There was no celebration to commemorate His birth: trumpets did not sound, bells did not toll, bands did not play, and earthly choirs were silent. Only the joyful harmony of the heavenly host was heard. The Christ child was born in a stable, and He was laid in a manger.

The King of the Jews was born—but unnoticed by His subjects. The affairs of life went on as usual, for there was no revolution or upheaval announcing the reign of a new Sovereign. Earthly kings and potentates continued to rule as before, assuming their authority to be absolute. This Babe, born of a virgin, whose life was ordained of God to affect the lives of multiplied millions, was born a stranger to His own people.

It was not that the Jews, or the other peoples of the earth, had little need for a Saviour. The whole world was swamped by the murky depths of sin and rebellion against God. Even the chosen people of God, among whom Christ was born, were miserable and despised, having been conquered and suppressed by the mighty Roman Empire.

In the heart of every Jew there was a desperate cry for deliverance. Their great concern, however, was not release from the bondage of sin. Rather, their consuming desire was to be freed from the domination of Rome. This was the human-set goal for the heaven-sent Messiah.

The eyes of the Jews were blind to the promise of the coming of the Anointed One. Their ears had long been stopped to the instructing voice of prophecy. He had been expected as the promised "Seed of the woman," who would bruise Satan's head (Gen. 3:15). Then, He was identified as coming as the "Seed of Abraham" (Gen. 22:18). And, according to the prophecy of Jacob, He was to come from the tribe of Judah (Gen. 49:10). His royalty is established when it is noted that He is also the "Seed of David" (Ps. 132:11; Jer. 23:5). Eventually, the sign of the manner of His coming was given that He was to be born of a virgin (Isa. 7:14).

Generations passed, but there was no sign of certain fulfillment. For years the truth of the prophetic stream seemed indiscernible. There was general confusion as to when the Messiah should come. Already, serious crises had come and eventually dispersed and exiled the chosen people of God. Now, the remnant of Israel, particularly the tribe of Judah, remained. But they were subjected to the iron rule of Rome. How was this time any different than other times which had come and gone with disappointing

306

hopelessness? Indeed, when was the time of Christ's coming?

The Time of His Coming

Along with the other prophecies, it had been foretold that the Messiah, the King, must come at a specified time. In his prophecy, Jacob declared that Shiloh must come before the tribe of Judah lost its tribal identity. He said, "The sceptre shall not depart from Judah, nor a lawgiver from between his feet, until Shiloh come; and unto him shall the gathering [obedience] of the people be" (Gen. 49:10, KJV).

The word "sceptre" in the preceding verse does not necessarily mean a king's staff. The word *"shebet,"* which is translated "sceptre," primarily means a "tribal staff." Apparently, each tribe possessed its own peculiar rod or staff which was their ensign of authority.[1] Thus, the tribal identity of Judah did not pass away—as did that of the other 10 tribes of Israel—until Shiloh (Christ) came.

Even though the kingdom of Judah had been deprived of their national sovereignty during the 70-year period of Babylonian captivity, they never lost their "tribal staff," their own national identity. Furthermore, they always had their own lawgivers (judges) even in captivity (Ezra 1:5, 8).

A similar setup remained when Christ was born. Although the Romans had conquered the Jews, they allowed them their own king. To a large extent, the Jews were governed by their own laws, and the Sanhedrin of the nation still exercised its authority.

However, in the space of a few years, during the year when Jesus was 12 years of age, when He was taken to the Temple (Luke 2:41-52), Archelaus, the king of the Jews, was dethroned and banished. One Coponius was appointed Roman procurator. At this time, the kingdom of Judah, the last remnant of the former glory of Israel, was formally debased into a part of the province of Syria.[2]

For almost another half century, the Jews retained a semblance of provincial governmental structure. Then in A.D. 70, as a consequence of rebellion against Rome, both Jerusalem and the Temple were destroyed by the armies of the Roman general, Titus. After that, no Jewish national sovereignty remained. But it is remarkable to note that Christ (Shiloh) came before Judah lost its tribal identity, exactly as prophesied by Jacob.

It is also interesting to consider that 22 years before Jesus was crucified, the Sanhedrin lost the power of passing the death sentence (cf. John 18:31), when Judea became just another restricted Roman province. Rabbi Rachmon said that when the members of the Sanhedrin found themselves deprived of their right over life and death, a general consternation took possession of them; they covered their heads with ashes and their bodies with sackcloth, exclaiming, "Woe unto us, for the sceptre has departed from Judah and the Messiah has not come."[3] This indicates that the rabbis considered Gen. 49:10 as a Messianic prophecy and that they had a clear concept of its meaning, but they still did not recognize the fact that the Messiah had already come.

Ample prophecy had been given so that the rabbis should have known. It had been prophesied that the Messiah must come while the rebuilt Temple was standing. In Hag. 2:7-9, they had probably often read:

> And I will shake all nations, and the desire of all nations shall come: and I will fill this house with the glory, saith the Lord of hosts. . . . The glory of this latter house shall be greater than of the former, saith the Lord of hosts: and in this

308

place will I give peace, saith the Lord of hosts (KJV).

The prophet Malachi also had confirmed Haggai's prediction by declaring, "The Lord, whom ye seek, will suddenly come to his temple" (3:1). Certainly, neither of these prophecies could have been fulfilled after the destruction of the Temple in A.D. 70. Thus, if God's promise was to be kept, the Messiah had to come before the Temple was destroyed.

Again, a message of the prophet Zechariah apparently implies that the Messiah must come before the destruction of the Temple. This prophecy is viewed as foretelling the betrayal of Christ. "And Jehovah said unto me, Cast it unto the potter, the goodly price that I was prized at by them. And I took thirty pieces of silver, and cast them unto the potter, in the house of Jehovah" (11:13). (This event was apparently fulfilled by Judas, who, after betraying Christ, "cast down the pieces of silver in the temple, and departed, and went and hanged himself" [Matt. 27:5, KJV].)

In Ps. 118:26, the Psalmist prophesies that the people who would welcome the Messiah would say: "Blessed be he that cometh in the name of Jehovah: we have blessed you out of the house of Jehovah." From a Christian viewpoint, this was beautifully fulfilled when Jesus approached Jerusalem for His triumphal entry, and the people cried: "Hosanna to the son of David: Blessed is he that cometh in the name of the Lord; Hosanna in the highest" (Matt. 21:9).

Thus, the public entry of Jesus into Jerusalem and into the Temple, as recorded in the Scriptures, was all in accordance with the plan and promise of God concerning the Messiah. We may readily see that God's Word was perfectly fulfilled when we consider the ministry and message

309

of Jesus of Nazareth. After centuries of waiting and expecting, the Messiah did suddenly come to His temple (Mal. 3:1). But, some years later, God allowed both the Temple and the holy city of Jerusalem to be destroyed, even as Jesus had predicted (Matt. 24:2).

Now on the old Temple site there stands a heathen shrine, the Mohammedan mosque, Dome of the Rock. Surely, Divine Providence is saying, even through this, that the Messiah has come. We are faced with the choice of either accepting Jesus of Nazareth as the true Messiah, or there is no Messiah, no prophecy, no sure Word of God, no God at all, and no objective truth. Jew and Gentile alike should realize that the Saviour has come—that in order to fulfill prophecy, He had to come some 1,900 years ago, before the Temple was last destroyed.

The rabbis and elders of the people were also familiar with the prophet Daniel's timetable concerning the coming of the Messiah. As we have discussed in previous chapter, Daniel makes it very clear that the Messiah will come and be killed before the people of the prince (the Roman armies) come and destroy the city (Jerusalem) and the sanctuary (the Temple) (Dan. 9:26). Daniel's prophecy as to the time of the Messiah is one of the most outstanding predictions in the Bible. It establishes the time of His coming almost 500 years before He actually came.

We need not repeat the various aspects of Daniel's prediction concerning the 70 weeks. However, there is an interesting computation given by Sir Robert Anderson in his book, *The Coming Prince.* His study deals with computing the period "from the commandment to restore and to build Jerusalem" to the coming of "Messiah the Prince." The time span indicated by the prophecy is 483 years.

Anderson starts with the date of March 14, 444 B.C., when Nehemiah went to fulfill the commandment to

310

restore and build Jerusalem, and he ends the period with Jesus' triumphal entry into the city. He believes this was the official presentation of Messiah as "Prince" to Israel (cf. Luke 19:38-40; Zech. 9:9). After careful investigation and consultation with noted astronomers, he made the following computation: From 444 B.C. to A.D. 32 is 476 years; 476 x 365 is 173,740 days; from March 14 to April 6 (the supposed day of Christ's triumphal entry) is 24 days; add 116 days for leap years, for a total of 173,880 days. On the other hand, if the "prophetic year" of the Bible is always 360 days, the 69 "sevens" of this prophecy in Daniel (69 x 7 x 360) also amounts to 173,880 days.[4] Thus, the time given by Daniel "from the commandment to restore and to build Jerusalem" to "Messiah the Prince" (at Christ's triumphal entry) may be computed to the very day.

Certainly, this is a sign that points unerringly to Jesus of Nazareth who was "Messiah the Prince," who was "cut off" (by His crucifixion), but not for himself (who laid down His life for our sins, who was himself blameless). When Jesus began His public ministry, He significantly said, "The time is fulfilled, and the kingdom of God is at hand: repent ye, and believe in the gospel" (Mark 1:15). On the surface, it may have seemed that the Messiah could have been born at any time, during any century, in any year. But after the prophecy of Daniel, there was knowledge revealed as to the exact time of the Messiah's coming.

But the fulfillment of prophecy not only indicated that the Messiah would come at a specific time, it also declared that He must be born in Bethlehem of Judea (Mic. 5:2). As we have previously noted, when King Herod asked the chief priests and scribes where Christ should be born, they told him, "In Bethlehem of Judea; for thus it is written through the prophet, And thou Bethlehem, land of

Judah, art in no wise least among the princes of Judah: For out of thee shall come forth a governor, Who shall be shepherd of my people Israel" (Matt. 2:5-6). It was the seeking wise men who reminded them of a previously known prophetic truth. Nevertheless, the attitude of the people remained unchanged. Only heaven displayed any genuine interest in the consummation of the blessed event of the birth of the King.

Crowded Out at His Coming

The Scriptures tell us that the Christ child was born in a shelter for animals because there was no room to accommodate His birth at the inn. This was not necessarily the fault of the innkeeper. However, it is symbolic of the kind of reception the world would give Him. In spite of the clear message of prophecy, the people were not really looking for Him when He came. Thus, they not only crowded Christ out of their individual lives, they also ignored His royal role in God's redemption plan.

As a babe, Jesus was deprived of the basic comforts of housing at an inn. As a man, He was ultimately rejected and condemned of men to die on a cross. As the Son of God, He was called a blasphemer and labeled insane, as they scoffed His claim to the throne of David. Humanity has not profited from past blunders, nor accumulated much wisdom with regard to the things of God revealed across the centuries. The majority of men still refuse to render homage that is due to Jesus Christ, the King.

Seemingly, from the very first, the Babe was ignored because His own countrymen did not realize who He was. They were not aware, or would not accept, His holy mission, in spite of specific divine revelation through the prophets. Certainly, the people were hoping for and expecting a Messianic deliverer. But they were looking for

One who would release them from the dominion of Rome. They were not particularly interested in the One who was come to deliver them from the bondage and unsightly corruption of their sins.

Mary and Joseph, Christ's earthly parents, undoubtedly had difficulty in comprehending the full meaning of His birth. So, although Jesus was born in the "fulness of the time," the world in general was to remain oblivious to the immediate claims of His gospel. This was simply because men would not receive and believe the truth of God. Instead of grasping the divine gift of the Saviour by faith, it was more convenient for them to just keep looking for the One they thought would surely come to accomplish their selfish desires.

It is very likely that the shepherds were treated with sneering contempt as they tried to tell people of the glorious event. No doubt they attempted to tell the innkeeper of the wondrous circumstances of the Child's birth. He probably cursed them for awakening him, and accused them of being drunk. There is certainly no record of a crowd gathering at the stable to share in the worship of faith. Apparently, people were too busy or too skeptical. Thus, there was no room even in the minds of neighboring men to accept a newborn infant King. He was crowded out of His proper place.

As the Prince of Peace grew to manhood, He was repeatedly rejected by the religious leaders of the people. He was destined to be accused and put to death as a common criminal. In spite of the divine testimony of His remarkable teachings and His marvelous miracles, only a few could find room for Christ in their lives. "He came unto his own, and his own received him not" (John 1:11).

To a great extent, Jesus was followed by the multitudes who wanted free bread, and by those who sought personal benefit, without ever accepting Him as their

313

Lord. Eventually, instead of recognizing His divine authority, they accused Him of blasphemy.

Although the people would freely admit their need and longing for a Saviour, they would not receive Jesus as the Messiah. He was not the kind of Messiah they had come to expect. In the first place, He seemed to be no Deliverer at all. He appeared to be totally insensitive to their frustration and suppression under the Roman rule. Indeed, Jesus displayed no interest at all in destroying their hated enemies. Moreover, He even seemed to condone their authority over them when He said, "Render therefore unto Caesar the things that are Caesar's" (Matt. 22:21).

On the other hand, Jesus manifested all the virtues of an ideal rabbi, applying the Word of God to real-life situations. The manner in which He presented the truth drew crowds and motivated receptive individuals to repent. Contrariwise, Jesus repeatedly punctured their balloon of religious pride by condemning their self-righteousness. It was a sharp barb when He said, "And whosoever shall exalt himself shall be humbled; and whosoever shall humble himself shall be exalted" (Matt. 23:12). The Jews remained unwilling to acknowledge the royal virtue of humility.

Thus, because the Son of God was born in a barn instead of a king's palace, multitudes, by their pride, immediately excluded themselves from receiving Him. From His very birth, humility was the sovereign virtue of Jesus' life. Prideful men could not see how such humility could ever defeat their foes, ascend a throne, and be the Messiah they wanted Him to be. They chose rather to wallow in the muck of sin than to give proper place to the Anointed One of God.

Despite the boundless love manifested by God the Father, His faithfulness in keeping His covenant with them, the people refused the Son He sent. Despite the condescending love of Jesus for a sin-blighted world, and His fulfillment of the divine Word, they put Him on the Cross instead of on the throne. This has been the error of succeeding generations: the rejection of Christ's authority and teachings, as though God did not mean what He said, or was not able to accomplish His purpose. It all amounts to the same thing in the minds of men—Christ is crowded out!

Sin is humanity's sore spot. Strangely enough, men may even recognize their own sinfulness and rebellion against God, and yet they will reject the Christ who came to deliver from all sin. They have confused social and political desires with the purpose of Christ's coming. And when He deals only with their haughty rebellion against God, He is quickly denounced as no Messiah. He is viewed only as a sorry pretender.

Still, man is helpless to cure himself. Everyone feels too self-righteous to humble himself before a suffering Saviour that would redeem him from the fatal destruction of pampered sin. Men have tried almost everything but Jesus Christ in an effort to rid themselves of the certain fate that threatens their lives. They have tried reform, resolution, and revolution, blindly ignoring the salvation offered by the King of Kings.

There was apparently no advantage for a person to be able to behold Him in the flesh, for the majority who saw Him face-to-face could somehow reject Him. Somehow, they could look His love in the eye and call His truth a lie.

Now, after centuries of object lessons, the general attitude of men remains unchanged. Their eyes, their ears, their minds, their hearts are closed to receiving Christ as King. People may still come in direct contact with the love and truth of God in Christ, and yet they may label it as uncertain or as an unbelievable myth. Time has not

315

appreciably changed humanity's attitude toward the heaven-sent King. He remains a stranger in His own domain.

Nevertheless, no matter when or where man is confronted with the claims of the gospel of Christ, he must make a crucial choice. He must either receive Jesus as Lord and Master of his life, or he will crowd Him completely out of his existence. The call of God's Word through the prophets was for the Jews to receive their King.

The call of the New Testament Scriptures as the inspired Word of God is for all humanity to receive their King—to make room for Jesus! All other loyalties must be abandoned. All self-righteousness must be cast aside. All our sinfulness must be confessed in repentance. There can never be room for King Jesus in a sin-dominated life.

Reception of the King

There was one day when it seemed that Jesus' own countrymen might receive Him. It was as He was entering Jerusalem in preparation to observe the Feast of Passover. We may read the scriptural account in Matt. 21:1-11; Mark 11:1-11; Luke 19:28-40; John 12:12-19. This entry into Jerusalem took place on the first day of the last week of Jesus' earthly life and ministry. It was the nation's nearest approach to accepting Him as their King.

As Jesus and His followers approached Jerusalem, Jesus sent two disciples, perhaps Peter and John, with instructions to go into the village nearby (apparently Bethphage), where they would find an ass (a she-ass) tied, and a colt with her. They were to bring these two animals to the Master. And, if anyone protested, they were simply to say, "The Lord hath need of them."[5]

The deliberate preparation for the procession, and the seeming intentional publicity so contrary to Christ's usual

316

habits, can be explained only by the fact that He was fulfilling the character and claims of the Messiah to the ultimate extent. With this one demonstration, He dramatically put himself forward in His true dignity and office as the "King of the Jews." By this display, Jesus affirmed the fact that in Him all prophecy was fulfilled, and that every believing heart might find in Him what all men of faith had long expected and desired.[6]

Matthew makes direct reference to the prophecy, saying that this was come to pass that it might be fulfilled which was spoken through the prophet, saying, "Tell ye the daughter of Zion, Behold, thy King cometh unto thee, meek, and riding upon an ass, and upon a colt the foal of an ass" (Matt. 21:5; cf. Isa. 62:11; Zech. 9:9).

The original passage in Zechariah is even more explicit. It says: "Rejoice greatly, O daughter of Zion; shout, O daughter of Jerusalem: behold, thy king cometh unto thee; he is just, and having salvation; lowly, and riding upon an ass, even upon a colt the foal of an ass."

The prophecy is that a King of their own race, one foretold by all the prophets, was coming to occupy the vacant throne of David and reign forever. Coming as King, Jesus could not walk undistinguished among the crowd; He must ride. To mount a horse would designate Him as the leader of an army or as a worldly potentate. So, Jesus rode upon an ass, an animal used by the judges of Israel, and by chieftains on peaceful errands (cf. Judg. 5:10; 10:4).[7]

Thus, by riding upon an ass, Jesus deliberately fulfilled the prophecy of Zechariah, and so revealed himself to be the Messiah. As we have suggested, the ass was chosen rather than the horse because the ass was the symbol of peace, and the horse, of war. Again, the ass was the symbol of humility; the horse, of pride. It is clear that the Jews fully understood and accepted the Messianic reference of Zech. 9:9. For as Rabbi Salomo has said, "This cannot be interpreted except of King Messiah."[8]

Indeed, the choice of Jesus as their King would be a clear-cut decision. His allusion to Zechariah would mark Him either as an imposter or as the true Messiah. Josephus records the popular belief that the Messiah would appear on the Mount of Olives.[9] And, as the disciples carried out their assignment, the triumphal procession apparently began on the slopes of the Mount of Olives.[10] No King had ever thus come to Jerusalem. Such a circumstance was only predicted of the Messiah. Jesus Christ alone fulfilled it to the letter, showing the nature of His kingdom.

Furthermore, Jerome gives a mystical reason of this unique occasion. He said the ass represented the Jewish people, which had long borne the yoke of the Law. On the other hand, the colt symbolized the Gentiles, as yet unbroken, "whereon never man sat." In this instance, Christ called them both, Jew and Gentile, by His apostles, to submit to His divine authority.[11]

A crowd witnessed this historic scene. It was composed of many pilgrims who were coming to the festival at Jerusalem, and "the whole multitude of the disciples" (Luke 19:37). Their reaction was spontaneous. They stripped off their *"abbas"* (outer garments) and spread them in the way, making a carpet over which the Saviour should ride. This was an extraordinary token of respect, such as was paid to kings and great conquerors (2 Kings 9:13).[12]

We learn from John 12:18 that many people, greatly excited by the news of the raising of Lazarus from the dead, when they heard that Jesus was there, hurried out to meet Him and to do Him honor. Apparently, when they met the procession with Jesus riding in the midst, they turned back and preceded Him into the city. Luke identifies the meeting place as "at the descent of the mount of Olives" (Luke 19:37).

Even the shouts of the people were significant. "Hosanna to the son of David: Blessed is he that cometh in the name of the Lord; Hosanna in the highest" (Matt. 21:9). Mark records them crying: "Hosanna; Blessed is he that cometh in the name of the Lord: Blessed is the Kingdom that cometh, the kingdom of our father David: Hosanna in the highest" (Mark 11:9-10). Luke declares they voiced their praise, saying, "Blessed is the King that cometh in the name of the Lord: peace in heaven, and glory in the highest" (Luke 19:38). Then John records the crowd crying out and saying, "Hosanna: Blessed is he that cometh in the name of the Lord, even the King of Israel" (John 12:13).

On this day, at least for this day, the people were ready to receive Jesus as their King. The language they used was certainly because they identified Him as the Messiah. Notice the terms: "Son of David," "He that cometh," "Blessed is the King," "the King of Israel," "Hosanna." These words all have direct bearing on the fact that at least for these passing moments, the people acknowledged Jesus as the King, the Messiah sent of God.

Again, we should specifically note the meaning of the term *"Hosanna."* It is the opening word of Ps. 118:25, a verse sung and addressed to God in solemn procession round the altar or at the Feast of Tabernacles and on other similar events. The word means "Save now," or "Save, we pray." On this occasion it is probably equivalent to "God save the King!"[13]

Once again the Great Expectation is seen as proceeding from patriarchs and prophets of old anticipating the embodiment of such terms.

During this brief time of acclaim, the people thus acknowledged Jesus to be the Messiah, the promised

Prince of David's line. For the moment they blessed Him whom they presently believed came with divine mission, sent with the authority of Jehovah. But those who were asked concerning Jesus a few days hence, "Who is this?" were to reply much differently. Their words turned from praise to prosecution, from "Crown Him" to "Crucify Him!"

It is an interesting sidelight that those who consider that the day of Jesus' triumphal entry was the tenth day of Nisan see a particular fitness for the event occurring on this day. On the tenth of the month the Paschal lamb was selected and taken up preparatory to its sacrifice four days after (Exod. 12:3, 6). Here, the true Paschal Lamb is now escorted to the place where once and for all the Passover would be sacrificed. Eventually, Jesus was crucified on the fourteenth of Nisan, dying at the hour when the lambs were legally slain.[14]

It was a shameful way for the Jews to receive their King. Their belief on His name was only temporary. Their acknowledgment of His authority was only verbal, for they would not allow the fulfillment of His purpose in their individual lives. But even though their acceptance of Christ was shortlived, this did not discredit His sovereign claim upon the world. Certainly, in this case, the majority was not right. We see that there is always deadly peril in associating ourselves with the mood of the crowd, especially where Jesus is concerned.

The call of the revealed Word, the desire of Christ, was and is for men to receive Him as King and to devote themselves to the cause of His kingdom. However, the difficulty is apparent. Jesus came to establish a spiritual Kingdom in the hearts of men. They were only desiring the Messiah to overthrow earthly kingdoms and empires of their enemies and to ascend the throne of David. How easy it was for them to pray for the destruction of their enemies.

But how difficult it both was and is to surrender one's own authority to the holy King of righteousness.

While His countrymen were crying for deliverance from the idolatrous rule of Rome, Christ was calling for them to cast down the idols in their own hearts. Sin against God was the barrier to their believing on Him. Thus, it is obvious that God cannot have His will done on earth until His kingdom is first established in the lives of men. Only as men believe on the name of Jesus can He be properly received and be crowned King of their lives.

Neither can there be divided loyalties. For Jesus said: "No man can serve two masters: for either he will hate the one, and love the other; or else he will hold to the one, and despise the other. Ye cannot serve God and mammon" (Matt. 6:24). Faith in Christ must be so strong that love for Him takes precedence over all else. If sinful self is on the throne of our hearts, Christ is nailed to the Cross. But to crown Him King of our lives, it is our depraved selves that must be crucified.

Certainly, there is a cost involved if a person is to receive Christ as King. To believe on Him, one must refuse the dominating influence of all else. Every thought and action must be molded by His will. It is human to cry, "I must have my way!" But that is the voice of the idol of self which must yield to Christ the Lord. This was the price the Jews refused to pay to receive Jesus as their King. They would not submit their selfish ambitions to the will of God.

Peter, one of the inner circle of Jesus' disciples, was later moved to write, describing the unpopular role of the Lord:

> *Christ also suffered for us, leaving us an example, that ye should follow his steps:*
> *Who did no sin, neither was guile found in his mouth:*

*Who, when he was reviled, reviled not again;
when he suffered, he threatened not; but committed himself to him that judgeth righteously:*

*Who his own self bare our sins in his own body
on the tree, that we, being dead to sins, should
live unto righteousness: by whose stripes ye were
healed* (1 Pet. 2:21-24, KJV).

The joyous fact that Jesus was born to be the Saviour
of all mankind should have been enough to turn every sin-
sick soul unto Him. But it is not so. "He came unto his
own, and his own received him not"! Moreover, Christ's
manifestation of divinity in the performance of miracles
and the fulfillment of prophecy did not convince them
otherwise. Jesus went to the Cross at their rejection, not to
suffer a martyr's death, but to pay the price for man's
redemption by freely shedding His own life's blood to overcome the curse of sin.

The difficulty of belief in God's plan of salvation is
pointed up by the fact that it is evidently easier to dis-
believe than to believe. Once man has heard the gospel,
his soul becomes a battleground of truth against lies, of
right against wrong, of Christ the Lord and Creator of all
against Satan the usurper and deceiver.

Across the ages, every person has had a part in this
war between the opposing kingdoms. Every man has the
power to place his own will on one side or the other. He
may believe and receive Christ as his King, or he may
reject the royal authority of Christ and remain under the
bondage of sin, enslaved to Satan.

The divine invitation has ever been for all men to
believe on the name of Jesus, to receive their rightful King.
Christ is King by actual "divine right," by virtue of the
fact that He is both man's Creator and Redeemer. He was
specifically King of the Jews because He was born of
David's line, according to God's covenant, and He was sent

to lay claim to the throne of David. But the Jews were to say, "We have no king but Caesar" (John 19:15).

Because the Jews rejected their heavenly King, it may seem that if Christ is King, He is a defeated King, a dead King who lost His domain. However, this is not so. The establishment and growth of the Christian Church prove otherwise.

No matter how few believe on Jesus and accept Him as their Saviour and King, as long as one person does so, Satan is a defeated foe. It was his evil purpose to see the whole human race damned and destroyed, to see the glory of God's creation crumble in ashes. But the fact that multitudes across the centuries have looked for and rejoiced in the salvation of the Lord, Satan's attempt is foiled and the doom of his unrighteous kingdom is sealed.

Whoever believes and receives Jesus Christ as King will not only share in the immediate benefits of His reign, but also in the ultimate and complete victory over the devil's dark domain. The corrupt fruit of his tyranny shall perish, but the extent of Christ's reign shall be forever.

At the time, the Jews, with all the light of prophetic truth, could see no further than the tyranny of Rome. However, the gospel call for men to believe on the name of Jesus and receive Him as King even now remains an invitation to accept a glorious and everlasting relationship with God.

Christ's Claim as King

Whether man recognizes it or not, the divine truth of the invasion of a heaven-sent King is the foundation of all of man's deepest hopes. It is the Great Expectation. There is no real basis for the hope of immortality—life beyond the grave—except by virtue of a vital relationship with the eternal God, the Giver of life.

323

Through the Saviour-King, man is not only delivered from the fetters of sin, but he shall also find release from the finality of the curse of sin, which is death. Thus, one's personal destiny is determined by his decision to receive the Son of God as his King and personal Saviour.

History unfolds the consequences of the Jews rejecting their rightful King. They were scattered and subjected to foreign rule for over 1,900 years, until 1948. Apparently, the dark days of persecution and extermination are over, at least for a time. But now the threat of hostile neighboring nations plagues them. It therefore seems that the ever-present "valley of the shadow of death" for the Jews is but a constant reminder that their pathway continues in the direction that was set when they refused their King.

Jesus unmistakably laid significant claim to the throne of His father David. It seems as though the life of Christ was prewritten in the Old Testament. But Jesus, the Christ of the New Testament, recognized this fully and witnessed to the fact. For instance, in John 5:39, Jesus told the people, "Search the scriptures, for they . . . testify of me." No other ruler in history, or any false Christ, has dared to make that indisputable claim.

According to David Baron, more than 40 false Messiahs have appeared in the history of the Jewish nation. But not one of them ever appealed to fulfilled prophecy to establish his claims. Rather, they bolstered their pretense by promises of revenge and by flatteries which gratified national vanity. And now, except perhaps to a few students of history, the remembrance of their names has perished from the earth, while Jesus of Nazareth, the true Messiah, who fulfilled all the prophecies, is worshiped by hundreds of millions.[15]

Only Jesus could calmly say, "Your father Abraham rejoiced to see my day; and he saw it, and was glad" (John 8:56). Only Jesus could say, "For if ye believed Moses, ye would believe me; for he wrote of me" (John 5:46). (Cf. Gen. 3:15; 12:3; 18:18; 22:18; 49:10; Deut. 18:15, 18.) Then, to show the connection between the Old Testament prediction and New Testament fulfillment, Jesus said in His Sermon on the Mount, "Think not that I came to destroy the law or the prophets: I came not to destroy, but to fulfill" (Matt. 5:17).

Even in the beginning of Jesus' ministry, after reading to the people in the synagogue at Capernaum the identifying Messianic prophecy in Isa. 61:1-2, He declared: "Today hath this scripture been fulfilled in your ears" (Luke 4:21). Then, when talking to Jesus at the well, the woman of Samaria said, "I know that Messiah cometh (he that is called Christ): when he is come, he will declare unto us all things!" Jesus answered, "I that speak unto thee am he" (John 4:25-26). It is important to note that all who were acquainted with the Old Testament Scriptures knew the character of the Messiah.

Again, when Peter confessed his faith in Jesus as the Messiah, saying, "Thou art the Christ, the Son of the living God," Jesus acknowledged the truth of Peter's declaration by answering, "Blessed art thou, Simon Bar-Jonah: for flesh and blood hath not revealed it unto thee, but my father who is in heaven" (Matt. 16:16-17).

Later, in a revealing discussion with the Pharisees, Jesus quoted Ps. 110:1, identifying himself as the "Son of David," an admitted Messianic title, and indicating that David called Him Lord (Matt. 22:41-46).

Also, throughout the ministry of Jesus, He assumed the title "Son of man" (cf. Matt. 16:13; Mark 8:38; Luke 18:8; John 1:51). When Jesus did this, He certainly identified himself with that Messianic title as used in Daniel. The prophet had declared: "Behold, there came with the clouds of heaven one like unto a son of man, and he came even to the ancient of days, and they brought him near before him" (Dan. 7:13).

Such identification is unmistakable in Jesus' declaration at His trial before the Sanhedrin. "Again the high priest asked him, and saith unto him, Art thou the Christ, the Son of the Blessed? And Jesus said, I am: ye shall see the Son of man sitting at the right hand of Power, and coming with the clouds of heaven" (Mark 14:61-62).

Furthermore, by accepting the title "Son of God," as declared by Peter, Jesus identified himself with the Messianic passage of Psalm 2. There, the proclamation is: "Jehovah saith unto me, Thou art my son; This day have I begotten thee" (Ps. 2:7). There can be no mistake. Jesus claimed to be the Messiah, the Son of Man, the Son of God, the Son of David, and the rightful heir to David's throne.

Practically everything Jesus said or did had some direct connection with Old Testament prophecy. His miracles were in fulfillment of Old Testament predictions (Isa. 35:5-6). His ministry was in accord with what Isaiah had foretold concerning Him (Isa. 42:1-4; 61:1-3; cf. Matt. 12:17-21). When praising John the Baptist, Jesus also called attention to the fact that John was His forerunner, even as was predicted in Isa. 40:3 and Mal. 3:1. "This is he [John the Baptist] of whom it is written, Behold, I send my messenger before thy face, who shall prepare thy way before thee" (Matt. 11:10).

As He drew near to the time of His crucifixion, Jesus said to His disciples, "Behold, we go up to Jerusalem, and all the things that are written through the prophets shall be accomplished unto the Son of man" (Luke 18:31). His sufferings and death on the Cross were all in accordance with what had been prophesied (Psalm 22; Isaiah 53).

During the crucial time of Jesus' arrest, He said to Peter (who was attempting to defend his Master with his sword), "Thinkest thou that I cannot beseech my Father, and he shall even now send me more than twelve legions [72,000] of angels? How then should the scriptures be fulfilled, that thus it must be?" (Matt. 26:53-54). And, while suffering on the Cross, Jesus identified himself as the One whose hands and feet were to be pierced (Ps. 22:16), by quoting the first verse of that same psalm, "My God, my God, why hast thou forsaken me?"

At least two other sayings of Jesus from the Cross were also quotations from the Scriptures. In John 19:28, we read: "After this Jesus, knowing that all things are now finished, that the scripture might be accomplished, saith, I thirst." This was in evident fulfillment of Ps. 69:21: "They gave me also gall for my food; and in my thirst they gave me vinegar to drink." The Lord's cry, "Father, into thy hands I commend my spirit" (Luke 23:46), is a direct quote from Ps. 31:5.

After the resurrection of Jesus, His royal claim was reaffirmed. While talking to two of His disciples on the road to Emmaus, Jesus, "beginning from Moses and from all the prophets . . . interpreted to them in all the scriptures the things concerning himself" (Luke 24:27). When meeting with the assembled disciples later, Jesus said: "These are my words which I spake unto you, while I was yet with you, that all things must needs be fulfilled, which are written in the law of Moses, and the prophets, and the psalms, concerning me" (Luke 24:44). Such fulfillment of the Old Testament was not to be surprising because the Word of God cannot fail, neither can it lie. Therefore, the Son of God who fulfilled the Word is Truth indeed.

Nevertheless, the crux of the issue with regard to Christ's claim to be King rests on the answer to the question Jesus put to the Pharisees: "If David then calleth him Lord, how is he his son?" (Matt. 22:46). If Jesus was both David's Lord and his Son as he says, then His claim to be

King is doubly validated. And it is not difficult to see how Jesus could be both David's Son and David's Lord if we consider the manner in which the account of the New Testament harmonizes with the Old Testament.

Jesus was David's Son in that He was a descendant of David after the flesh (cf. Luke 1:32; Rom. 1:3). But Jesus Christ is David's Lord in that the Messiah is called Lord (Jehovah) in Jer. 23:6: "This is his name whereby he shall be called: Jehovah our righteousness." Again, He is called God (Elohim) in Ps. 45:6, "Thy throne, O God, is for ever and ever" (cf. Heb. 1:8). Then, the Messiah is called Lord (Adonai) in Mal. 3:1; "And the Lord, whom ye seek, will suddenly come to his temple." Also, in Ps. 110:1, we read, "Jehovah saith unto my Lord, Sit thou at my right hand."

Thus, such titles are not only Messianic, they are titles of Deity in the Old Testament. The New Testament goes one step further. In Rev. 19:16, Jesus, the Messiah, is ascribed the title: "KING OF KINGS AND LORD OF LORDS." It should therefore be clear that the Messiah is not only David's Lord, but He is Lord of all.

But what of Jesus' actual right to inherit the throne of David as his Son? The Messiah, the Seed of the woman, the Seed of Abraham, of the tribe of Judah, the Seed of David, must also be virgin-born. He must have a legal right to the throne of David despite the fact that Jeconiah (or Coniah), one of Solomon's descendants of the royal line, was blotted out from propagating the right to rule because of his iniquity (cf. Jer. 22:28-30). Also, the right to the throne of Israel was only transmitted through the male line, and Christ must be born of a virgin.

Even so, it is evident that Messiah will inherit "the throne of David" (1 Chron. 17:11, 14; Ps. 132:11; Isa. 9:7; Jer. 25:5; 33:15-17). How, then, will He receive His legal right to the throne of David if He is born of a virgin? How

328

can the obstruction of Jeconiah's sin be circumvented and He still be an acceptable descendant? The prophet answered these questions centuries before. Isaiah said: "The zeal of Jehovah of hosts will perform this" (Isa. 9:7).

The resolution of the seeming impossible is recorded in the New Testament. In Matthew's genealogy of Jesus (1:1-17), His line is traced through Joseph. This shows Christ to be "the son of David," giving Him the right to David's throne. He is also "the son of Abraham," giving Him title to the Land of Promise, to all the territorial possessions given to Abraham and his seed.

Here, in Matthew's genealogy, Joseph is seen to be in the regal line of descent from King David, through Solomon and his descendants. But Joseph was also a descendant of David through Jeconiah. Hence, succession to the throne for Joseph is personally barred. Matthew's record is careful to show that Jesus was not, through Joseph, a direct descendant of David.

In Luke 3:23-38, Jesus' genealogy is given through Mary. (Heli was obviously Mary's father, Joseph's father-in-law, v. 23). In the record of Matthew, it is written that "Jacob begat Joseph," (1:16); that is, Jacob was the actual father of Joseph. However, in Luke 3:23, it is written that Joseph was the son of Heli. We should note that the word "son" is not in the original, but is supplied by the translators. Here, it should be reckoned "son-in-law" instead of "son." The only sense in which Joseph could have had two fathers was that he was born of his father Jacob, and he was the son-in-law of Heli, or the "son" in the sense that he was married to Mary, Heli's daughter. This is in accordance with Jewish custom (cf. 1 Sam. 24:16).[16]

Luke goes on to show that Jesus is a direct descendant of David through His mother, Mary. However, while Mary was in a "royal line" from David, she was not in the "regal lineage," for she was a descendant of King David through Nathan, whereas the throne rights were to come only through Solomon's line (cf. 1 Chron. 28:5-6). In this regard, Joseph's marriage to Mary before the birth of Jesus was an absolute necessity to establish Christ's legal right to the throne.

Thus, through Mary, Jesus Christ obtained His literal descent from King David. And, from Mary's marriage to Joseph, who was also a "son of David," Jesus obtained His legal right to David's throne, for Mary was the espoused wife of Joseph before Jesus was born. As the foster father of Jesus from His birth, this made Joseph His legal father. In this manner, the prophecy concerning Jeconiah was kept in force. For Jesus is not a direct descendant of that accursed king.

Rather, according to the genealogy of Christ given by Luke 3:38, the generation of Jesus is traced back through Heli (Mary's father), to Adam, and to God. This so much as gives Christ a title deed to the whole earth, as "son of Adam" (cf. Gen. 1:27-30; Ps. 8:4-6; Heb. 2:6-9; Rev. 5:1-10), and, as "Son of God," the "heir of all things" (cf. Heb. 1:2).

In view of such amassed scriptural evidence, there can be no doubt that Jesus held (and still holds) rightful claim to the title that was assigned to His cross. When Pilate wrote "JESUS OF NAZARETH, THE KING OF THE JEWS," he may have followed an inspired conviction. But with Christ hanging there, it all seemed in vain. Significantly, when Jesus died, He said, "It is finished," not "This is the end."

Now, more than ever before, we realize that "the end is not yet." All of the fulfillment of prophecy, up to and including the death of Jesus Christ, was not, and is not, in vain. The throne of David still awaits the coming King. Now the Great Expectation is the return of the rejected King. The consistency of Christ in carefully fulfilling the prophecy of old, even through His rejection, still demands that Jesus will surely complete the mission for which He was sent.

The credence of Christ's coming at all now rests upon His coming again. The entire New Testament record banks on it. But neither could we say that the Old Testament account was satisfied unless Christ returns.

Thankfully, the Great Expectation is thrust on by heavenly messengers, declaring at the ascension of Jesus: "This same Jesus, which is taken up from you into heaven, shall so come in like manner as ye have seen him go into heaven" (Acts 1:11, KJV). The next time Christ comes, He comes, not as a babe in a manger, but as Lord of all.

Chapter **16**

Our Returning King

And if I go and prepare a place for you, I will come again, and will receive you unto myself; that where I am, there ye may be also.

(John 14:3)

And then shall appear the sign of the Son of man in heaven: and then shall all the tribes of the earth mourn, and they shall see the Son of man coming on the clouds of heaven with power and great glory.

(Matt. 24:30)

Ye men of Galilee, why stand ye looking into heaven? this Jesus, who was received up from you into heaven, shall so

*come in like manner as ye beheld him go-
ing into heaven.*

(Acts 1:11)

*The kingdom of the world is become
the kingdom of our Lord, and of his Christ:
and he shall reign for ever and ever.*

(Rev. 11:15)

The crucifixion of Jesus Christ did not kill the prospects of
His kingdom. On the third day, He arose from the dead,
victorious over sin and death and hell. This startling event
came as a shock to everyone. Even Jesus' disciples had
not expected it even though He had proclaimed His
resurrection along with the prediction of His death. For
Christ had taught them "that the Son of man must suffer
many things, and be rejected by the elders, and the chief
priests, and the scribes, and be killed, and after three days
rise again" (Mark 8:31; cf. Matt. 16:21-28; Luke 9:22-27).

If the crucifixion had been the final scene of Christ's
life and ministry, and if He had lain in the grave indef-
initely after His death and burial, we would never have
known whether His sacrifice was sufficient to defeat sin.
Death, the curse of sin had to be conquered. When Christ
rose from the dead on the third day, it was evident that
His death for man's sin culminated in triumph over it.
Thus, the resurrection of Jesus climaxed His atoning death
and proved the efficacy of His sacrifice on the Cross. It
broke sin's curse and defeated the intention of Satan to
drag the whole world to destruction.

As Erich Sauer points out, the resurrection of Jesus
also is the seal of the Father on the person and work of the
Son (Acts 2:32). By the Resurrection, Jesus Christ is
demonstrated to be the Prophet and the Son of God
(Rom. 1:4). Thus, the Resurrection is the seal on (1)

333

the testimony of the prophets (cf. Ps. 16:10; Hos. 6:2; the "sign of Jonah"—Matt. 12:39-40; Isa. 53:8-10); (2) the testimony of Jesus to himself (Matt. 16:21; John 2:19-22); (3) the testimony of His apostles (1 Cor. 15:15); (4) the truth that Jesus is the Son of God (Rom. 1:4; Acts 13:33); (5) the kingship of Jesus (Acts 13:34); (6) the full authority of Jesus as universal Judge (Acts 17:31); and guarantees (7) our own future resurrection glory (1 Thess. 4:14).[1]

Even now, because of His glorious resurrection, we have confidence that Christ lives to perpetuate His saving ministry. In Heb. 10:12-13 we read, "But Christ offered for all time one sacrifice for sins, and took his seat at the right hand of God, where he waits henceforth until his enemies are made his footstool" (NEB). When Jesus ascended into heaven, it was reaffirmed that He would come again. The angelic messengers verified what Jesus had already told His followers (cf. Matthew 24; Mark 13; Luke 21; John 14).

Thus, the return of Christ will follow the train of His victorious resurrection and ascension. Jesus' second coming will be in great, irrepressible power and unimpeachable glory. Our expectation joins the Apostle Paul, "Looking forward to the happy fulfillment of our hopes when the splendour of our great God and Saviour Christ Jesus will appear" (Titus 2:13, NEB).

Since the Ascension, we may well ask: Where is Jesus now? What is He doing today? The writer of Hebrews answers, "For Christ has entered, not that sanctuary made by men's hands which is only a symbol of the reality, but heaven itself, to appear now before God on our behalf" (9:24, NEB; cf. 4:14-16). We are told that Jesus is in heaven, seated at the right hand of God, in the position of power (10:13).

This was also the testimony of Stephen as he was being martyred. He saw Jesus and said, "Behold, I see the heavens opened, and the Son of man standing on the right hand of God" (Acts 7:56, KJV). Thus, the first time anyone saw Jesus after the Ascension, He was in heaven, on the right hand of God.

In reply to the question: What is Jesus doing today? the author of Hebrews further says that Christ is "from henceforth expecting till his enemies be made his footstool" (10:13, KJV). So, Christ's present occupation includes sitting in the exalted place by the right hand of the Father "from henceforth expecting." This does not imply an extended period of passive waiting, but rather, continued activity from this exalted post to work out the divine purpose in the world.

However, what is meant by this statement that Christ is "from henceforth expecting"? Herschel Hobbs suggests that a closer examination of this key clause is rewarding. "From henceforth" is translated from two Greek words *(to loipon),* meaning "what remains, hereafter, for the future, henceforth." A. T. Robertson translates the words "for the rest" or "for the future." He calls it an accusative of the extent of time.[2] This obviously refers to the interval between the ascension and the second coming of Christ. The length of time is of uncertain duration. It has already extended for almost 2,000 years. How much longer it will be, no man knows.

Then, the word "expecting" is the participial form of a verb meaning "to look for, expect, wait for, await." The present tense of usage in this scripture expresses the continuing attitude and action of Jesus in this interim time. Thus, we see Jesus seated in the position of power in heaven, and for the period which separates His ascension and His return to earth, He is expecting.[3]

A further question arises: What is Jesus expecting? The answer to this important question may be found as we consider: (1) the success of the divine redemptive plan; (2) the fulfillment of all the promises of God; and (3) the faithfulness of His followers.[4]

First, Jesus is undoubtedly expecting the success of the divine redemptive plan. He entered the arena of battle against sin and Satan with confidence. Even as He died on the Cross, a Sacrifice for the sins of the world, He cried, "It is finished" (John 19:30). At that time, Christ had completed God's will for His incarnation. He successfully finished the role as righteous Example for man as the Son of Man, and at the same time provided the perfect Sacrifice whereby God might justify every sinner that would place his faith in the Son.

Henceforth, God authenticates Jesus' work as He declares Him to be "the Son of God with power, according to the spirit of holiness, by the resurrection from the dead" (Rom. 1:4). Again, the writer of Hebrews emphasizes Christ's expectation of success even at His birth, as he quotes from Ps. 40:6-8:

> *Wherefore when he cometh into the world, he saith, Sacrifice and offering thou wouldst not, but a body didst thou prepare for me; In whole burnt offerings and sacrifices for sin thou hadst no pleasure: Then said I, Lo, I am come (In the roll of the book it is written of me) to do thy will, O God* (Heb. 10:5-7).

The system of animal sacrifices made under the law was temporary. It was ineffective for the redemption of man from evil. So, God abrogated the old covenant that He might establish a new one. The old covenant depended on the priest who "stands performing his service daily and offering time after time the same sacrifices, which can never remove sins" (v. 11, NEB). But Christ, who has become our great High Priest, "after he had offered one sacrifice for sins for ever, sat down at the right hand of God; from henceforth expecting" (vv. 12-13, KJV).

The Son seated at the right hand of God signifies that Jesus both completed and committed to the Father His redemptive work on the Cross to be used to save our sin-shackled world. Christ is confidently expecting that His once-for-all sacrifice (9:28) will suffice for the forgiveness and cleansing of sin to every believer. He is now seated, in the attitude of a finished work. In contrast, the Old Testament priests were never pictured as seated, but always standing in the performance of a futile and an unfinished ministry.[5]

Despite the completion of Christ's redemptive work, this doesn't mean He is now inactive. Rather, we read that He "ever liveth to make intercession for them [us]" (7:25). Elsewhere, Jesus is spoken of as our Advocate before the Father (1 John 2:1). Such passages do not mean that God is praying to God. They simply suggest that the evidence of Jesus' sacrifice is ever before the Father as the surety that the price of man's redemption has been paid (cf. Heb. 9:12, 24-28).

Consequently, the issue of man's salvation rests with his own personal response to Christ's redemptive work already finished. So, Jesus is "from henceforth expecting"— expecting the Father to honor His promise to save all who will believe on Him. And He is expecting those for whom He died to receive the new life thus provided.[6]

In the *second* place, Jesus is expecting the fulfillment of every promise of God. He is "from henceforth expecting till his enemies be made his footstool." This is an obvious reference to Ps. 110:1. There the Psalmist says, "The Lord said unto my Lord, Sit thou at my right hand, until I make thine enemies thy footstool" (KJV). These words give us a glimpse into the eternal council of the Godhead before the foundation of the world, where the Father promised full

337

and final victory to the Son over every kind of evil that would oppose.[7]

The author of Hebrews projects a view beyond the Ascension, where the Son expectantly waits for that promise to be fulfilled. A clearer picture is brought into focus by Paul in 1 Cor. 15:24-25. There we read: "Then [at Christ's second coming] cometh the end, when he shall deliver up the kingdom to God, even the Father; when he shall have abolished all rule and all authority and power. For he must reign, till he hath put all his enemies under his feet."

The two uses here of the word "when" (hotan) refer to condition and not to time. The condition referred to is that of putting down all the forces which oppose the rightful rule of God. The satisfaction of this condition will make possible another in which the Kingdom shall be eventually presented to the Father.[8]

"The end" referred to by Paul is not so much an element of time as it is the goal of God's redemptive purpose which centers in the previous condition. The apostle states that "he must reign" until this condition obtains. Literally, it is ever necessary and binding upon Christ to reign as a King until all of the enemies of God are defeated.[9]

We therefore may ask: When does the reign of Christ begin? It is the New Testament teaching that there is a sense in which He is reigning right now. In 1 Cor. 15:24, "shall have put down" is a constantive aorist tense covering the entire period of conflict from the resurrection of Jesus until the final and complete victory is won. But for all practical purposes, the kingdom of God came when the King was born among men (cf. Matt. 3:2).[10]

While on earth, Jesus saw the earnest of ultimate victory over Satan as the disciples skirmished against evil (Luke 10:17-19). Then, at the time of His death, Jesus himself engaged Satan and his evil forces in mortal combat. Christ was victorious, and He was declared by the Father to be the Son of God with power (Rom. 1:4). He thus continues to reign at the right hand of God until "he hath put all enemies under his feet" (1 Cor. 15:25).

So, in the incarnation of Christ, we see the initial victory of the coming of God's King. The persistent rebellion of sinners brought about His rejection and crucifixion. And, despite Jesus' resurrection, a conflict continues until His return in power and glory. Final victory will be achieved, and the Kingdom shall be delivered up to God the Father. Paul thus declares, "And when all things have been subjected unto him, then shall the Son also himself be subjected to him that did subject all things unto him, that God may be all in all" (1 Cor. 15:28).

This envisions the time when the redemption of man and the world is complete, when all enemies are destroyed, when the universe is reordered, when God's creation is restored to His own glory. It does not mean that the Son and the Holy Spirit shall cease to be in operation. Rather, it emphasizes both the unified purpose and the unified achievement of the Godhead. So Jesus is expecting God to fulfill His promise to the end that He may present a subdued and a restored Kingdom to the Father—that God may be all in all.

The *third* expectation of Jesus is that His followers will be faithful to this end. The propagation of His kingdom largely depends on their loyal service throughout the interval between His ascension and His return. For instance, if we fail to be faithful in our generation, then the eternal purpose of God will not be realized through us (cf. Eph. 3:11).

Nevertheless, God's purpose will not fail. To keep us faithful, Jesus taught that we should live in constant expectancy of His return. From the beginning, numberless believers have died in the faith. So Jesus' expectation that

His followers will be faithful to the end will never be disappointed.

Today, we have an intense responsibility that matches that of the Jews when Christ was born. Most Jews missed the glory of His birth because they doubted the Word of God. They thought it was too fantastic to be true. Despite the many prophecies specifying the lineage of Christ, identifying where He would be born, the sign of His virgin birth, and the meticulous description of His ministry and death, the Jews failed to accept these phenomena even when they transpired before their very eyes. Now, we ourselves must be careful lest we view God's Word as too phenomenal when it tells us to expect Christ's return.

In expecting the return of our rightful King, we would consider: (1) The abiding hope of Christ's return; (2) When He shall come; (3) The reality of Christ's kingdom.

The Abiding Hope of Christ's Return

The abiding "blessed hope" of Christ's coming is necessary. For unless the King returns, God's kingdom on earth remains in dispute. Satan is intent upon the destruction of mankind. But Christ is yet more intent to save us. He will thus come again because of the finite limits of even His most loyal servants to curb the tide of wickedness. He will come to vindicate righteousness for all time.

Indeed, Christ was born among men because of humanity's inability to save itself. The human race has often made attempts at self-redemption, but to no avail. Adam and Eve began the long line of futile attempts when they sewed fig leaves to cover themselves. From that time man has been feverishly trying to extricate himself from the quicksand of depravity resultant from the Fall.

The whole course of history reveals man's tragic failure to meet the perfect standard of a holy God. Because of man's degraded state, God has already intervened on his behalf once, sending Christ to come and die for the sins of the world. He died as the perfect Offering for all sin. Since Jesus died on the Cross, by faith men now go to the Cross to live anew. His seat of death has become the source of life to all who will accept Him as their Saviour. This is certainly God's basic answer to man's individual helplessness.

However, the pages of history also depict that man is also socially helpless and hopeless. In spite of the righteous influence of Christians, there continue to be wars and rumors of wars, nation rising against nation, kingdom against kingdom, race hatreds, class conflicts, and economic struggles. The passing centuries have accounted for no lasting progress.

Seemingly, even the best of man's efforts intensify rather than solve the problems. With all his spectacular use of science, that technical knowledge has complicated as many issues as it has helped. Certainly, science has made the world a neighborhood, but it has not made it a brotherhood. The progress has drawn the world closer geographically, but it has not generated spiritual fellowship.

There is only one solution to our situation which whirls out of control. God must intervene again. His Word teaches that Christ must come again. Only then will every knee bow before Him, and every tongue shall confess that He is Lord to the glory of God the Father (Rom. 14:11). Only then shall the spear be turned into a pruning hook and the sword beaten into a plowshare (Isa. 2:4). Only then shall differences be settled so that even the lamb and the wolf shall feed together (Isa. 65:25). Only then shall the knowledge of God cover the earth as the waters cover the sea (Isa. 11:9). No wonder the closing verse of the Bible is a prayer: "Even so, come, Lord Jesus."

Thus, amidst the present turmoil there remains the

341

living hope that one day the King of Kings will return and set this world aright. The abiding hope of man is not that somehow humanity will progress through reform and negotiation to the point that all evil will be ostracized. A hard look at man's current efforts tells us that for all the brilliant plans and hopes, conflicts between nations still seethe. Evil, deceitful minds and selfish wills of men unceasingly make a shambles of peacekeeping efforts. Despite all human efforts for a "generation of peace," it seems beyond our grasp. We would not scoff at the attempts of man to bring peace, but we must realistically conclude that peace will remain out of reach until the Prince of Peace comes again.

The dubious proposition of peaceful coexistence may be arranged temporarily amongst various political systems. But there can be no permanent peace between sin and righteousness. This twentieth century has seen two world wars, two major "police actions," numerous revolutions, and many destructive struggles. But throughout all time, even between the lulls of the battles among nations, a continuous world conflict has been raging in mortal contest for the lives and minds of men. This earth has been the battleground for the forces of evil and the followers of Christ. Peace cannot reign until righteousness reigns supreme.

Not even the positive action of the Christian Church can warrant any hopes that it will usher a reign of peace into this strife-torn world. This is not necessarily any reflection upon the power of the gospel of Jesus Christ or the dedication of the Church to propagate it. So long as man has the freedom of choice, and so long as wickedness remains unjudged, there will be the wholesale choice of men to do evil rather than good, serving sin and Satan instead of Christ unto righteousness. Thus, so long as the opportunity to choose evil remains, there will be the conflict of right and wrong. Peace cannot reign until evil is destroyed. And only the coming King of righteousness can purge it from His holy kingdom.

So the hope of the world should not be the political peacemaker. Neither should it be placed in consecrated Christians carrying out the evangelistic commission of Christ. Rather, the only true hope for the world is the return of the Lord Jesus Christ. He alone can resolve human history. More specifically, His return is the abiding blessed hope of the Church. It is as the Apostle Paul declares:

> For the grace of God hath appeared, bringing salvation to all men, instructing us, to the intent that, denying ungodliness and worldly lusts, we should live soberly and righteously and godly in this present world; looking for the blessed hope and appearing of the glory of the great God and our Saviour Jesus Christ; who gave himself for us, that he might redeem us from all iniquity, and purify unto himself a people for his own possession, zealous of good works (Titus 2:11-14).

Every believer is thus a member of the body of Christ. As such, he possesses a hope that is peculiar only to those who are of the "household of faith." The Church was first organized as a body of believers at Pentecost, where they united to receive the baptism with the Holy Spirit. God had previously recognized only the distinction of Jew and Gentile, but when the Church came into being, He recognized the Jews, the Gentiles, and the Church (cf. 1 Cor. 10:32; 12:12-28). When anyone becomes a believer in Christ, he ceases to be Jew or Gentile in the sight of God, and is simply regarded as a member of the body of Christ, the Church of the living God.[11]

However, the Church is also called the bride of Christ.

Just as the bride takes the name of her husband, so it is with the Church. She is uniquely seen by the Apostle John as the Lamb's wife, ready for the marriage (Rev. 21:2). Therefore, it is the specific hope of the believer to meet his Saviour at the rapture of the Church, when the Bridegroom returns for His bride (cf. Matt. 25:1-13). This is the first phase of Christ's second coming.

Although the word *rapture* is not found in the Bible, the idea is certainly inherent in the words "caught up," as found in 1 Thess. 4:17. There, the Greek word *"harpazo"* is used in the original, meaning "to snatch," "seize violently," "take by force," "to carry off suddenly."[12] Thus, the primary association of the word *rapture* does not mean ecstacy or delight, but it refers to the sudden transportation of a person (or a body of people) from one place to another.

The Apostle Paul declares the abiding hope of the Church in the aforementioned Epistle. He directs that hope to the coming of the Lord for His own. This involves three wonderful aspects: (1) resurrection, (2) rapture, and (3) reunion. Notice their interrelation:

> *For the Lord himself shall descend from heaven, with a shout, with the voice of the archangel, and with the trump of God: and the dead in Christ shall rise first;* [resurrection]
> *Then we that are alive, that are left, shall together with them be caught up* [rapture] *in the clouds, to meet the Lord in the air: and so shall we ever be with the Lord* [reunion] (1 Thess. 4:16-17).

Jesus had given His followers such a hope in two great discourses immediately preceding His crucifixion and death. The one was given on the Mount of Olives and the other was given in the Upper Room at the Last Supper. In Matt. 24:40-41, 44, He tells us to be ready for His coming, and that He will snatch His own away. Then, in John 14:3, we read some of the most comforting words ever uttered by the Master: "And if I go and prepare a place for you, I come again, and will receive you unto myself; that where I am, there ye may be also."

The abiding hope of the Church, then, is to be caught away (at an undisclosed time) suddenly ("in a moment, in the twinkling of an eye, at the last trump"—1 Cor. 15:52), to the Father's house. Jesus' words "I come again" justify the attitude of the early Christians who lived in constant expectation of His return. Paul's writings particularly reveal that hopeful outlook. He was ready to die and be with Christ, or he was ready to remain and continue to labor for the Master. Meanwhile, he was waiting for the Saviour's return from heaven (cf. Phil. 1:23, 25; 3:20). Thus, Paul taught the early Christians to wait for the return of God's Son, even Jesus whom God raised from the dead, our Deliverer from the wrath to come (1 Thess. 1:10).[13]

Now, our immediate hope should be concerned with an expectant, upward gaze rather than an earthward regard for sign events. The early Christians were watching and waiting for the return of Christ, and not for certain events to take place. It is interesting to recognize the so-called signs of the times, but this should not comprise the hope of His coming again. The abiding hope and expectation of the Church firmly rests upon the fact that Jesus said, "I come again." That single promise verifies and confirms all of the unfulfilled prophecy and promise of God.

As a member of the body of Christ, the basic hope of the believer is to be with Him in heaven. But the rapture also involves "deliverance from the coming wrath," a wrath which particularly befalls the Christ-rejecting people, the Jews (cf. 1 Thess. 2:14-16), along with the world of unbelievers. It is also the hope of the Church to be accounted worthy to escape the great tribulation that will plague the world as evil men are allowed to run the course of their wickedness.

Jesus himself admonished His followers in Luke 21:34-36:

> And take heed to yourselves, lest at any time your hearts be overcharged with surfeiting, and drunkenness, and cares of this life, and so that day come upon you unawares.
>
> For as a snare shall it come on all them that dwell on the face of the whole earth.
>
> Watch ye therefore, and pray always, that ye may be accounted worthy to escape all these things that shall come to pass, and to stand before the Son of man (KJV).

Again, in Rev. 3:10-11, it is directly inferred that the rapture is an escape from the flood of evil that is coming upon the earth because of unbelievers' rejection of the gospel of Christ:

> Because thou hast kept the word of my patience, I also will keep thee from the hour of temptation, which shall come upon all the world to try them that dwell upon the earth.
>
> Behold, I come quickly: hold that fast which thou hast, that no man take thy crown (KJV).

Though the abiding hope of the Church particularly involves resurrection, rapture, and reunion, our primary consideration has been of the rapture, for it seems to be the focal point of Christ's return for His own. This does not detract, however, from the wonderful preliminary action of the resurrection of those who have died in Christ. In fact, deceased believers will have priority in that resurrection. Paul declares, "The dead in Christ shall rise first" (1

Thess. 4:16). Those who die in the faith before the return of Christ have no less part in the hope or the joy of His coming.

In a sense, the present age is Easter time. Our era begins with the resurrection of Christ, our Redeemer, and ends with the resurrection of the redeemed. Running between these two events lies the spiritual "resurrection" of those called from being dead in sin, and raised unto life (cf. Rom. 6:1-11; Col. 3:1-4).

We now live between two Easters, as those who have been raised between two resurrections, as burning and shining lights (Phil. 2:15) between two brilliant outshinings *(epiphaneiai)* of the Eternal Light (cf. 2 Tim. 1:10; Titus 2:13). And, in the power of that first Easter, we, as followers of Christ, go to meet the last Easter. Confirming every hope, Christ's resurrection as the Head of the Church guarantees the resurrection of the members of His body.[14]

This resurrection is not a general, simultaneous raising of the dead. Rather, it is a resurrection "out of the dead" (Mark 12:25), "from among the dead" (Luke 20:35-36), leaving the unrighteous dead to await the resurrection of judgment (John 5:29), at the "great white throne" (Rev. 20:12-15). So we are told: "Blessed and holy is he that hath part in the first resurrection" (Rev. 20:6). This resurrection is unto life everlasting. It therefore belongs to the glorifying of Christ as the Head that the members of His body should share in a special resurrection, one like His own, a "resurrection out of the dead" (Luke 20:35).

The third aspect of the abiding hope of the Church is that of reunion. Immediately we consider this to be the reuniting of loved ones previously separated by death. This joyful event will occur when the believers who are alive are caught up together with the dead in Christ that

347

have been resurrected, to meet the Lord in the air (1 Thess. 4:16-17). What a great reunion that will be!

Even so, the main event concerning the reunion is that of the bride (the Church) with her Bridegroom (Christ). We have noted that this picture is presented in one of the last parables of Jesus (Matt. 25:1-13). Paul also expresses this concept in Eph. 5:25-27:

> Husbands, love your wives, even as Christ also loved the church, and gave himself for it; that he might sanctify it, having cleansed it by the washing of water with the word, that he might present the church to himself a glorious church, not having spot or wrinkle or any such thing; but that it should be holy and without blemish.

The role of the Church as the bride of Christ is both important and glorious. It requires certain preparation and continual watchfulness to be ready when the Bridegroom comes. The meeting in the air is but the preliminary phase of the reunion. If this figure is valid, then the further revelation of Revelation also applies. It declares:

> Let us be glad and rejoice, and give honour to him: for the marriage of the Lamb is come, and his wife hath made herself ready.
>
> And to her was granted that she should be arrayed in fine linen, clean and white: for the fine linen is the righteousness of the saints.
>
> And he saith unto me, Write, Blessed are they which are called unto the marriage supper of the Lamb. And he saith unto me, These are the true sayings of God (19:7-9, KJV; cf. Isa. 25:6-8).

During Jesus' earthly ministry, at the Last Supper, He said, "I will not drink henceforth of this fruit of the vine, until that day when I drink it new with you in my Father's kingdom" (Matt. 26:29, KJV). Also, in Luke 22:

348

29-30, Jesus declared to His followers: "And I appoint unto you a kingdom, as my Father hath appointed unto me; that ye may eat and drink at my table in my kingdom."

Although both the Old and New Testaments seem to refer to the marriage of the Lamb, there are differences of opinion as to where it falls in the sequence of end-time events. It seems apparent that the Bridegroom is Christ, and that the bride at least includes the Church. Even the Old Testament body of believers is represented as betrothed to God, anticipating a glorious reunion with Him in due time. Psalm 45 unmistakably refers to this subject. Also, the Song of Solomon must be understood as referring to Christ and His bride.[15]

It seems logical, therefore, to associate the marriage supper of the Lamb with the initial reunion that takes place at the rapture. This period of feasting is conceived as running concurrently with the time of great tribulation that engulfs the earth following the snatching away of the bride of Christ. So the certain and abiding hope of the Church is to escape the oppression of Satan and be delivered to rejoice in the salvation of God through Jesus Christ our Lord.

Significantly, there is a total absence in the New Testament Epistles of any directions to the believer as to his preparing either for death or the great tribulation. He is not told what to do in either eventuality. There is no such word as "Set thine house in order," or "When ye see . . . flee." But everywhere the eye is turned upward, and the hope of the Lord's return is presented as the abiding comfort and stay.[16]

This has been the hope of the Church across the centuries. Paul, in writing to the Romans, says, "We ourselves groan within ourselves, waiting for our adoption, to wit, the redemption of our body" (Rom. 8:23). "We with patience wait for it" (Rom. 8:25). The believers at Corinth are said to be "waiting for the revelation of our Lord Jesus Christ" (1 Cor. 1:7). The Galatians are encouraged to "wait for the hope of righteousness" (Gal. 5:5). The Philippians are waiting "for a Saviour, the Lord Jesus Christ: who shall fashion anew the body of our humiliation, that it may be conformed to the body of his glory" (Phil. 3:20-21).

We have already noted that Paul wrote to Titus about "looking for the blessed hope and appearing of the glory of the great God and our Saviour Jesus Christ" (Titus 2:13). The writer to the Hebrews declares that Christ shall appear a second time, "apart from sin, to them that wait for him, unto salvation" (Heb. 9:28). James exhorts Christians, "Be patient therefore, brethren, until the coming of the Lord" (Jas. 5:7). Then, Peter admonishes believers to give heed to the prophetic word "until the day dawn" (2 Pet. 1:19).[17]

From the time of the ascension of Jesus, when the angels promised His return "in like manner," the abiding hope of the Church has been the expectation of that glorious event. The cry of every believer still is *"Marana tha"* ("Our Lord, come!") (1 Cor. 16:22).

When He Shall Come

If an angel from heaven would appear before us to answer any question we might ask, our first question would probably be "When is Christ coming?" But it would not be the first time this has been asked. A form of this question is recorded in the Bible five times—twice in the Book of Daniel, and once in each of the Synoptic Gospels of Matthew, Mark, and Luke.

Certainly, things are not recorded in the Scriptures without a definite purpose. It should therefore be expected that such questioning is provided with an answer. The amazing thing, as we examine the answers given, is that in all five instances reference is made to the same two events as signs of the end of the age.

The gist of the question is first asked in Dan. 8:13. The prophet had just been shown a vision of the rise of the Gentile kingdoms and their dominion down to the close of history. The vision started with the fall of the Babylonian Empire, the rise of the Persian Empire (the ram, vv. 2-3), its defeat by the Grecian Empire (he-goat, vv. 5-8), which, after the death of Alexander, was broken up into four distinct parts: (1) Macedonia and Greece; (2) Asia Minor; (3) Syria; and (4) Cyrene (Egypt, North Africa).

One of these kingdoms is identified as a "little horn" which becomes great. Scholars generally agree that his immediate identity is Antiochus Epiphanes, the ruler of the Syrian domain. His invasion of Egypt included a brutal assault on Jerusalem in 170 B.C. (cf. vv. 11-12). Because of this ravaging destruction of the Holy City, Antiochus is at least noted as a type of the Antichrist.

However, Daniel's vision provoked a question about how long "to give both the sanctuary and the host to be trodden under foot" (8:13). Apparently "the sanctuary" is in Jerusalem in the Temple area. The angel answers that after "two thousand and three hundred days; then shall the sanctuary be cleansed" (v. 14, KJV).

This gives rise to a further question: How are we to consider this stated period? Jerome, one of the early church fathers, gives a primary interpretation:

> If we read the books of the Maccabees and the history of Josephus, we shall find there recorded that . . . Antiochus entered Jerusalem, and after wreaking a general devastation he returned again in the third year and set up the statue of Jupiter in the Temple. Up until the time of Judas Maccabaeus . . . Jerusalem lay waste over a period of six years, and for three of those years

the Temple lay defiled; making a total of two thousand three hundred days plus three months.[18]

However, it seems that this is not the only applicable interpretation, for in verse 17 the angel tells Daniel that this vision is for "the time of the end." Obviously, the end did not take place some 2,000 years ago. Time still goes on.

Adam Clarke, a noted commentator who wrote in the early nineteenth century, indicates that here and elsewhere in Daniel, "days" may mean "years," and the period most likely means 2,300 years. He began the numbering of these years with the first event described in the vision. This was the decisive victory of Alexander the Great (the he-goat of Greece) over the Persians (the ram) at the Granicus River in Asia Minor. This battle was fought about the first week of June, 334 B.C.[19]

Computing 2,300 years from that date (remembering that the year 0 is absent from the calendar), leads to the expectation that the first week of June, 1967, would see the end of Gentile dominion over Jerusalem. That this did happen shows that Adam Clarke, writing in 1825, made a valid interpretation. On the third day of the six-day blitz of Israel against the Arabian confederacy, Moshe Dayan led the Israeli troops to the Wailing Wall, the only remnant of the Old Temple, and said, "We have returned to our holiest of holy places, never to leave her again." Although Israel had been a self-governing nation since 1948, this was the first time she had control of the ancient part of the Holy City.[20] Remember, the angel identified this event as "for the time of the end" (v. 17).

The question is then framed in a little different form: "How long shall it be to the end of these wonders?" (Dan. 12:6). The answer given in verse 7 is translated in awkward English in the King James Version. It is "when he shall have accomplished to scatter the power of the holy people, all these things shall be finished." The original language simply says, "When the Dispersion is ended." In either case, the meaning is the same. It refers to the end of the scattering of the Jewish nation (the "holy people" in the Old Testament). Thus, when Israel became a nation again, providing a homeland for God's chosen people, that would also be a sign of the approaching end. This actually occurred in 1948.[21]

The remaining three references to this question about the end are in the Gospels of Matthew, Mark, and Luke. Matthew 24:3 is representative, where the disciples ask: "When shall these things be? and what shall be the sign of thy coming, and of the end of the world?" Here the disciples ask for both the time and a sign. The ensuing account of Jesus' response indicates that He gave an intelligible answer in both respects. Indeed, in the discourse that followed, Jesus gave many signs, but twice He gave a definite sign.

The first sign was one which the whole world would recognize, and it is related in Luke 21:24. There, Jesus clearly refers to Daniel's prophecy that Jerusalem would be under Gentile dominion until the last days. He reminds the disciples that "Jerusalem shall be trodden down of the Gentiles, until the times of the Gentiles be fulfilled." This must mean that in 1967, when Israel captured the Jordanian portion of Jerusalem (the old city), it was the closing of the "fullness of the Gentiles" (cf. Rom. 11:25-26).

The second definite sign is that of the fig tree. The fig tree is generally recognized by Bible scholars as representing Israel. Apparently, to symbolize God's rejection of Israel for their rejection of Him, Jesus had cursed a fig tree the day before because it had no fruit. He then speaks of the Jewish nation (the fig tree) coming to life again after it had been dispersed throughout the nations of the world. In Matt. 24:32-34, we read:

Now learn a parable of the fig tree; When his

353

branch is yet tender, and putteth forth leaves, ye know that summer is nigh:

So likewise ye, when ye shall see all these things, know that it is near, even at the doors.

Verily I say unto you, This generation shall not pass, till all these things be fulfilled.

Israel, the fig tree, does not yet have any fruits of righteousness. These will come only after they look upon Him "whom they have pierced" (Zech. 12:10), the Messiah, at His second coming. Therefore, the reference must directly refer to the national, not spiritual, reviving of Israel, which occurred in our own time, 1947-48.

The "when" part of the question is apparently answered by the words, "This generation shall not pass, till all these things be fulfilled." Since the time of the disciples, many generations have passed away, so "this generation" cannot refer to the one that was living then. Rather, it must be that Jesus is indicating that a generation will not pass from the occurrence of the sign given (the rebirth of Israel, 1948).

A further question must now be considered: How long is a generation? In some respects it may be used to signify an indefinite period of time. Its terms of years is variously recognized. For Abraham it was 100 years (Gen. 15:13, 16). In Job's time it was 35 years (Job 42:16). Perhaps another way of computing the length of a generation is to consider that Jesus' generation lasted only 33 years. At any rate, civilized nations have generally recognized a generation to span 30 to 40 years. This gives ample reason to declare that many now living may indeed behold the return of the King.

These two signs, the rebirth of the nation of Israel and the Jewish capture of Jerusalem, are the same two signs given in answer to Daniel's questions about the end.

On seeing these signs, Christians have every right to believe that their redemption is near (Luke 21:28).

Whether believers are ready for the return of the King must be determined beforehand. Many scriptures teach that the rapture, God's first judgment, comes suddenly, without warning, as a thief in the night. In this vein, Jesus declared: "Watch therefore: for ye know not on what day your Lord cometh" (Matt. 24:42).

In order to more fully understand the scriptural teaching of the second coming of Christ, we must make a distinction between the aspects of the rapture and the revelation at His return. We have noted that the rapture is the abiding hope of the Church. On the other hand, we must recognize that the full purpose of Christ's return is not accomplished until He actually comes to earth again to rule in kingly glory. This is called the revelation, for then every eye shall see Him.

We said that the rapture means to be caught up when Christ comes for His own. The revelation *(apokalupsis)* means "appearing," or "shining forth," or "manifestation" (Rom. 8:19), when Christ reveals himself to the whole world. The rapture occurs when the Church is caught up to meet Christ in the air (1 Thess. 4:14, 17). The revelation occurs when Christ comes, with His saints, to end the tribulation, by the execution of His righteous judgment upon the earth (cf. 2 Thess. 1:7-10; Jude 14-15).[22]

At the time of the rapture, Christ comes in the air for His own (John 14:3). At the revelation, He comes back to the earth with them (1 Thess. 3:13). Obviously, He must come for them before He can come back with them. Again, at the rapture, Christ comes as the Bridegroom (Matt. 25:10) to take unto himself His bride, the Church (Eph. 5:25-32). But at the revelation, He comes with His bride to rule the nations of the world (cf. 2:26-27; 5:10; 19:15).[23]

Thus, at the rapture Christ comes only to meet His own in the air (1 Thess. 4:17). At the revelation He actually returns to earth (Acts 1:11), and His feet shall stand upon the same Mount Olivet from which He ascended (Zech. 14: 4-5). At the rapture, the Church, like Enoch, is taken out of the world (Acts 15:13-17). But at the revelation, the Millennial Kingdom is begun (cf. preceding reference).[24]

So, in Luke 21:28, the rapture is referred to as occurring at the beginning of the tribulation. "But when these things begin to come to pass, look up, and lift up your heads; because your redemption draweth nigh" (cf. Rom. 8:23). In Luke 21:31, the revelation is referred to, saying, "Even so ye also, when ye see these things coming to pass, know ye that the kingdom of God is nigh."[25]

Such distinctions between the rapture and the revelation should be made if one is to understand when Christ will come. Generally, the scriptural signs pointing to His return ultimately focalize upon the revelation. These signs may be divided into two categories: (1) the international conditions, and (2) the religious conditions.

Many of the international conditions which are signs of Jesus' soon return have been in evidence for generations. They are nevertheless important to the expectation of the Lord's coming again. The Scriptures tell us that there will be: constant rumors of war (Matt. 24:6); increasing world conflicts accompanied by famine, pestilence, and earthquakes (Matt. 24:7; Isa. 13:4-5); economic perils such as the world has never known (Matt. 24:21-22; Dan. 12:1); the hearts of people failing for fear (Luke 21:25-26; Isa. 24:17-18); perilous conditions in general (2 Tim. 3:1-5); the restoration of Israel as a nation (Matt. 24:32); increased persecution of Christians and Jews (Matt. 24:9; Dan. 7:21-22); the attempt by Russia and the Northern countries to defeat Israel (Ezekiel 38—39), the formation of a world government (Rev. 13:1-18; Dan. 2:40-45; 11:36-39, 41-42), and a time of awful trouble for the Jews (Jer. 30:7; Dan. 9:27).

A number of religious conditions in our world have also long pointed to the necessity of Christ's return. They are of increasing importance to us today as we consider their ultimate effect on the affairs of men. For example, the Scriptures declare that there will be ridicule of the very teaching of Christ's return (2 Pet. 3:3-4), that organized atheism will mock Christianity (Jude 18), that true religion will wane and iniquity will abound (Matt. 24:12, 38), that many will not endure sound doctrine (2 Tim. 4:3-4), that most religion will become a matter of form (2 Tim. 3:5; Rev. 3:16-17), that the occult practices such as astrology and spiritualism will increase (1 Tim. 4:1-3; 2 Pet. 2:1-3), that deceit and iniquity shall discipline the Church (Matt. 24:12-13), that many shall come pretending to be Christ or His prophet (Matt. 24:5, 11), that the man of sin will be revealed (2 Thess. 2:3-4), that there will be a world religious federation contrary to the purpose of God (Matt. 24:24; Rev. 13:11-18), and that before Jesus comes, the gospel shall be preached to all nations (Matt. 24:14).

Our world today is almost blinded by the floodlight of truth that shines through the signs of Christ's coming. With the Lord's two definite signs, and the other numerous scriptural signs, we must surely say that the coming of the Lord is at hand. Indeed, the rapture may occur at any moment (Matt. 24:42). There is not one word of prophecy that "needs" to be fulfilled before Christ comes for His own.

On the other hand, regarding the further aspect of the revelation, we may say that Christ's actual return to earth will be at the time appointed. It will occur in accordance with the signs given by prophecy. It will be as God has

357

foreordained. God is in charge of this world's destiny, and everything will happen at the appointed time.

Throughout history, God has dealt with His people at the times appointed. In fact, both Daniel and Habakkuk were told that their prophetic visions dealt with "the appointed time of the end" (cf. Dan. 8:19; 11:27, 29, 35; Hab. 2:3). Also, the seven feasts God commanded Israel to keep annually, beginning with the Passover in Egypt, have direct reference to the divine time schedule. Each of the feasts were appointed for a very special purpose and for a definite time.

The *Passover* (cf. Exodus 12; Lev. 23:4-5) was divinely instituted on the first month, Abib (or Nisan), on the fourteenth day, around 1441 B.C. This, according to the old Jewish calendar, is equivalent to April 14. It is the beginning of the year 1 for Israel as a nation. This feast meant salvation from the judgment of God as the final plague fell on Egypt alone. It also signified that the previous covenant of God with His chosen ones was verified in bringing about the deliverance of their children from bondage.

As the blood of an unblemished lamb, placed on the lintels and doorposts, guaranteed protection from the angel of death, it symbolized every aspect of the salvation of God. This Old Testament feast was fulfilled when Jesus ate the last Passover with His disciples and instituted the New Testament of salvation by the shedding of His own blood.[26]

The second feast appointed was the *Feast of Un-leavened Bread* (cf. Exod. 23:15; Lev. 23:6-8). This occurred the day after Passover began, and the people were to eat unleavened bread for seven days. It signified the casting out of sin, for leaven is viewed as a type of sin. Thus, the Feast of Unleavened Bread was complementary to the Passover, indicating not only the deliverance of Israel from Egyptian bondage, but denoted the people as holy unto the Lord. Again, we see that this feast was fulfilled as Christ became sin for us, dying in our stead, breaking the hold of sin upon us.[27]

The third feast instituted was that of the *First Fruits* (Lev. 23:10). It was also joined to the Feasts of Passover and Unleavened Bread, following on the third day of the Passover. This was to teach the Israelites that salvation and even life itself was from the hand of God, and not of their own doing. This feast is fulfilled by the resurrection of Jesus Christ from the dead. The Gospel indicates that His resurrection took place on the very day of the feast. Paul makes the connection: "But now hath Christ been raised from the dead, the first-fruits of them that are asleep" (1 Cor. 15:20).

The fourth feast, the *Feast of Pentecost,* was to be 50 days after the Feast of First Fruits, on the fifth day of Sivan (June). This was to be the occasion of a harvest offering. In type, Jesus likened himself (John 12) to "a grain of wheat," His death to the planting of that grain, and the fruits of His passion and death to the products growing from it.

Because of that holy harvest the Church was established. In Acts 2, we read of the fulfillment of this feast: "And when the day of Pentecost was fully come . . . they were all filled with the Holy Ghost" (vv. 2, 4, KJV). Thus, the offering of our lives to receive the Holy Spirit fulfills the kind of harvest God desires.

The fifth feast is the *Feast of Trumpets,* set on the first day of the seventh month, Tisri (October 1). This was the festival of the new year, with the sounding of trumpets from morning till evening. Since the organization of God's purpose of salvation had typically been completed through the previous feasts, testimony is now given for the world to hear. From the day of Pentecostal outpouring, the joyful sound of gospel tidings has gone forth. However, this feast of good news can only be fulfilled when the Lord of Harvest shall return to take away His own in the secret rapture of His second coming.

The sixth feast is the *Feast of Redemption,* or the Day of Atonement, on the tenth day of Tisri. It was an ordered time of affliction for Israel's sins, a day of penitence and soul-sorrow. A scapegoat was turned loose, symbolizing their sins being carried away, and a bullock and a goat were offered up in sacrifice. So, this day of reconciliation with God was appointed for the seventh month.

Seven is the symbol for completeness. According to Gal. 4:4-5, "When the fulness of time was come, God sent forth his Son, made of a woman, made under the law, to redeem them that were under the law, that we might receive the adoption of sons." Apparently, this appointed time will be fulfilled in Christ at His return to close the tribulation of Israel, after the rapture of the "first-fruits," to make an end of sin for Israel (Matt. 24:29-30; Dan. 9:23-24).

The seventh feast is the *Feast of Tabernacles* (Lev. 23:33-37), appointed for the fifteenth of Tisri, lasting seven days. It was an occasion of rejoicing in all the things God had done for Israel. During this time they also lived in temporary shelters. It indicated a period of waiting for the complete fulfillment of God's purpose, both in this life and throughout eternity.

This feast will evidently be fulfilled in the final phase of Christ's second coming to reign over all the earth. Indeed, the Feast of Tabernacles will be consummated when at last the King of Kings actually comes to dwell with His people and rule the kingdoms of earth (cf. Dan. 7:13-14; Zech. 14:4; Matt. 24:27-30; 25:31-34; Rev. 19:15-17).

The corresponding relationship of the coming of

Christ and His earthly life and ministry, to the appointed Old Testament feasts, seems beyond dispute.

The Reality of Christ's Kingdom

The kingly rule of Jesus Christ on earth is the ultimate goal of salvation's history. The final defeat of Satan and his evil forces must take place right here where his deceptive power held sway for so long. This battleground must be transformed by the Prince of Peace, and the people must learn to do the will of God. So the victorious reign of Christ has ever been the prophetic expectation.

For instance, Zechariah says, "And the Lord shall be king over all the earth: in that day shall there be one Lord, and his name one" (14:9, KJV; cf. Dan. 2:44-45; 7: 24-27). It was foretold that "a king shall reign in righteousness" (Isa. 32:1; Jer. 23:1-6), "upon the throne of David" (Isa. 9:7; cf. Luke 1:32-33), "in Jerusalem" (Jer. 3:17; Zech. 14:16). Thus, speaking of the kingdom of Israel, the Lord God says, "I will overturn, overturn, overturn it, and it shall be no more, until he come whose right it is; and I will give it him" (Ezek. 21:27).

Previously, in chapters 5 through 7, we dealt at length with the Old Testament expectation in terms of "The King Messiah," "The Everlasting Kingdom," and "The Ideal King." The prophetic foresight of Hannah and David, in this regard, definitely viewed the divine establishment of a physical kingdom on earth with strong anticipation. Furthermore, the continued New Testament revelation verifies such a literal expectation of the coming kingdom of Christ.

Perhaps we seldom think of the Lord's Prayer in this manner, but when Jesus taught His disciples to pray, they were taught to pray for the coming of His kingdom on earth. They were told to say, "Thy kingdom come, Thy will be done, on earth as in heaven" (Matt. 6:10, NEB). Apparently, when Jesus gave this instruction, He was referring to the Kingdom predicted through the prophets, to the time when "the earth shall be full of the knowledge of Jehovah" (Isa. 11:9).

In Matt. 19:28, Jesus included His apostles in the exercise of His kingdom, saying, "Ye who have followed me, in the regeneration when the Son of man shall sit on the throne of his glory, ye also shall sit upon twelve thrones, judging the twelve tribes of Israel." Then, Rev. 5:10 says that the Lord makes the redeemed "a royal house, to serve our God as priests; and they shall reign upon earth" (NEB).

A key question is whether prophecy should be interpreted literally or allegorically. One's answer to that question will be reflected in the type of reality he assigns to the coming kingdom of Christ. Throughout our consideration of the prophecy of the first coming of Christ, we have noted how every word literally came to pass. Since this great body of prophecy has thus been fulfilled, we have a demonstration of the manner in which unfulfilled prophecy may be expected to come to pass.

We believe that we have a "sure word of prophecy," spoken by "holy men of God" as they were "impelled by the Holy Spirit" (cf. 2 Pet. 1:19, 21, KJV, NEB). Indeed, such belief leads one towards an understanding of prophecy in the literal sense, "which alone," as Martin Luther said, "is the substance of faith and of Christian theology."[28] This was a return to the foundation of faith laid by the early church fathers.

Generally, the early leaders of the Church, from the first to the third century, held belief in the literal fulfillment of prophecy, looking for the visible kingdom of God on earth. These included Papias, Justin, Tertullian, Irenaeus, and Hippolytus. Apparently, with the political establishment of Christianity in the Roman Empire, and the rise and growth of the Roman Catholic hierarchy, this doctrine was lost, as by Clement and Origen (about A.D. 250), and by Augustine (around A.D. 400).[29] Even so, the coming earthly kingdom of Christ is one of the basic themes of the Bible, and it remains an integral part of the Great Expectation.

Obviously, the basic issue is not merely "Shall we literalize or spiritualize prophecy?" Before that question, we must answer: "Does God really keep His promises?" If we maintain that God does keep His Word, then we must consider the manner in which He has kept His Word in the past. Thus, since God brought about the literal fulfillment of the birth of Christ, we find a firm foundation to believe that God will similarly be faithful and exact in the prophetic fulfillment of our Lord's return.

Despite the doubts and confusion of many, the original Christian hope and expectation of the earthly reign of Christ rests upon a firm base of five pillars. They are: (1) A literal Kingdom is the only adequate confirmation of God's truthfulness and faithfulness to His covenant promises; (2) A literal interpretation of Old Testament Messianic prophecy is the only logical and practical one; (3) The historical reality of Christ's kingdom is the only explanation of the ending of time which agrees with the declarations of the Lord and His apostles; (4) The establishment of such a kingdom is the only complete conclusion of divine self-justification in the history of redemption; (5) Christ's reign on earth is the only and necessary means of moving human history from its present stage on to its ultimate goal in the eternal kingdom of the Father.[30]

1. We expect the literal reality of Christ's kingdom because *its coming provides the only sufficient proof of*

God's truthfulness and faithfulness to His promises. For example, the actual birth of Isaac was the only means whereby God could prove to Abraham that His covenant was valid. Again, the only way the truth of the covenant and the faithfulness of God could be shown was for God to deliver the children of Israel out of Egypt. The fact is that the validity of God's covenant with Abraham, Jacob, and David all depend upon the literal fulfillment of the coming kingdom of Christ.

2. *The literal interpretation of Old Testament Messianic prophecy seems to be the only logical one.* It is evident that the Old Testament expectation of the Messiah was kept alive because the people found God's word dependable. Looking back from our vantage point, we see that God did literally fulfill His word with regard to the Son that was sent. When we consider that the promises of Christ's second coming often stand in the same setting along with those of His first coming, it would be illogical to spiritualize the one aspect while accepting the other literally (e.g., Luke 1:31-33).

If we believe the Bible, we must admit that Jesus was born of a virgin as specified by the prophet Isaiah (7:14). He was literally born in Bethlehem as foretold by Micah (5:2). He was anointed with the Spirit as indicated by Isaiah (11:2). Christ literally rode into Jerusalem on an ass (Zech. 9:9), was literally betrayed for 30 pieces of silver (Zech. 11:12), and His hands and feet were literally pierced on the cross (Ps. 22:16). Literally His bones were not broken (Ps. 34:20), and literally His side was pierced by a lance (Zech. 12:10). He died and was buried literally (Isa. 53:8, 9, 12) and He also literally rose again on the third day (Ps. 16:10; Hos. 6:2).[31]

Therefore, it would be absurd to evaporate the predictions of Christ's coming again in glory into mere metaphors. God did not figuratively scatter His chosen people among all nations (Deut. 4:27). They are now more than metaphorically without king, without prince, without sacrifice, without altar, without ephod, and without sanctuary (Hos. 3:4). It would thus be incorrect to assume that when God by the prophets repeatedly asserts that He will gather the people of Israel out of the nations of the world and bring them again into the land of their fathers (e.g., Jer. 16:14-15; Zech. 10:8-9; Isa. 27:12-13) that all of this was figurative speech.[32] The events of recent history deny this. Jews are still returning to their homeland by the thousands.

We must admit, of course, that the prophets often used poetic metaphors. Certainly, the earthly kingdom of Christ is a typical forecast of eternity. And, in a sense, this Kingdom has given the Church a spiritual fulfillment. Thus, "spiritualizing" should not totally be rejected; indeed, with eternity in view, it has great significance.[33]

But there is no precedent to indicate that we may interpret the Jews as representative Christians, Jerusalem as standing for the Church, or that Canaan is heaven. Certainly, the "throne of David" has never stood in heaven (Luke 1:32). Neither has "this" land and Lebanon, and the land of Gilead, where God said He would replant His people (Jer. 32:41; Zech. 10:10) ever been anywhere but here on earth—in the Middle East. The "spiritualizing" of such prophecies pointing to the actual establishment of Christ's kingdom is a dangerous circumventing of the simplest meaning of the Scriptures. So in view of the literal prophetic fulfillment concerning the first coming of Christ, it is arbitrary and illogical to consider God's Word concerning the Second Coming any differently.[34]

3. We hold that *the historical reality of Christ's earthly kingdom is the only explanation of the ending of*

365

time which agrees with the testimony of Jesus and His apostles. The kingdom of the Lord Jesus is not *of* this world (as to its origin or character, John 18:36), but it is certainly *for* this world.

Jesus himself told His disciples, "Ye who have followed me, in the regeneration [i.e., in the time of the rebirth of the earthly creation in the visible kingdom of God] when the Son of man shall sit on the throne of his glory, ye also shall sit upon twelve thrones, judging the twelve tribes of Israel" (Matt. 19:28). After His resurrection, when His disciples asked: "Lord, dost thou at this time restore the kingdom to Israel?" (Acts 1:6), He did not rebuke them for their fleshly view or give any denial of the coming of such a Kingdom in the visible sense which they implied. He only said, "It is not for you to know times or seasons, which the Father hath set within his own authority" (Acts 1:7). But it is this very prophetic expression "times or seasons" which indicates that the kingdom of God will someday actually be set up (cf. Matt. 8:11; 26:29).[35]

The Apostle John further testifies to this coming Kingdom of glory in his Book of the Revelation. It is the only book of the Bible which expressly speaks of the "thousand years" (Rev. 20:2-7) in connection with that Kingdom. The placing of this period of time after the account of the appearing of Christ and the utter defeat of the Antichrist (Rev. 19:11-21) implies that this "thousand years" is to be reckoned from the return of Christ and will transpire between the "first" resurrection and the "great white throne" judgment (Rev. 20:11-15).[36]

The Apostle Paul testifies to such a coming Kingdom. He does so because he foresees a time when Israel will turn to their Christ (2 Cor. 3:14-16). Moreover, his concept of the bodily resurrection of the dead (1 Corinthians 15) anticipates an earthly kingdom of Christ. In a special

366

section (vv. 22-24), Paul speaks of the times of the stages and the order of the resurrections: (1) Christ the First-fruits, (2) "Then, those that are of Christ, at his advent [parousia]," and (3) "Then, the end, when he gives over the kingdom to God the Father."[37]

Paul also looks for a kingdom of Christ between the resurrection of the dead in Christ and the general resurrection at the end. Because the latter coincides with the "great white throne" judgment and the destruction of the old earth (Rev. 20:4-13), Paul's view supports the kingly reign of Christ on the old earth. Only after this time of earthly glory does history run into eternity.

Such testimonies at once touch the question as to the meaning of this coming Kingdom. Several questions arise: To what purpose is such a visible Kingdom? Why did God give such promises to Israel in particular? What is the meaning of this coming Kingdom period in His plan of redemption?

4. The answer is found in the fact that *the visible kingdom of Christ is the only complete conclusion of divine self-justification in the history of salvation.* This means that God is under obligation to give His anointed King the opportunity to prove himself to be the best Lawgiver, Judge, Regent, and World Ruler, the only One qualified to direct world affairs. Since Satan has for thousands of years deceived the peoples of the world unto vile corruption, should not God reveal how He, in Christ, can bless, save, and bring peace to this troubled planet?

This same earth which has seen the shame of the rejection of God's Son must also view His glory. This same world which participated in the spilling of Christ's blood must also yet participate in His redemption. God's very righteousness demands this. Right here, where Satan seemingly triumphed, Jesus must be crowned King of Kings and Lord of Lords.

Not only will God prove that a righteous Kingdom is still possible on this old earth, but by it He will prove that it was not the fault of circumstances and elementary powers that peoples could not live in peace. Rather, it was the sin of man and the corruption wrought by Satan.

What happens at the end of this Millennial Kingdom shows how deeply the stain of disobedience has soiled man's nature. For what does mankind do after this 1,000 year period of perfect divine government? It rebels against King Jesus, as armed millions take the field of battle against His rule (in the battle of Gog and Magog, Rev. 20:7-10). This final test shows that unless men will receive Jesus Christ as their Lord and Saviour, they are hopelessly lost in their wickedness.[38]

In spite of the most ideal economic and political conditions, the maximum of proofs of the grace of Almighty God, and the direct rule of Christ himself, the nations will have learned so little that they will rush headlong into the most fearful of human revolts (Rev. 20:8). It will thus become clear that not only is man unable to create ideal conditions, but even when they exist, they cannot hold him.

This most brilliant period of human history will offer the most catastrophic proof of the lost condition of the sinner. It will irrefutably prove that God was right when, in the matter of human redemption, He absolutely excluded man's own ability. At this point the summit and conclusion of divine self-justification is reached. It is publicly proved before all the world that there could be only one way for mankind to find peace—by the grace of God alone, so freely given through Christ at Calvary.[39]

5. *The visible kingdom of Christ at the conclusion of*

history is the only means of carrying human history forward from its present stage on to its ultimate goal in the eternal kingdom of the Father. Out of its present hidden character, the kingdom of God will at last be revealed unto the world. "He [the Son] must reign, till he hath put all his enemies under his feet" (1 Cor. 15:25). This is the Kingdom which will finally be manifested, the consummation of all things visible (as we know the term) on earth, and the most splendid period of its history.[40]

The Son is not the Father, but the Effulgence of His glory (Heb. 1:3), the Image of the invisible God (Col. 1:15). In the person of Jesus Christ the image of God is therefore present on earth in the visible kingdom of God. There remains, however, the need of a historical transition which transfers the history of the kingdom of God to the Father himself. This is the chief and deepest meaning of the Millennial Kingdom. The kingly activity of Christ in the earthly Kingdom carries the history of revelation over from this last preparatory stage into the holy of holies, into direct fellowship with God the Father.

Bible prophecy discloses two chief victorious advances of the coming kingdom of God, and two chief exhibitions of power which stand in special relation to the two divine persons of the Son and the Father. First, there is the appearing of the kingdom of the Son at the beginning of Millennial Kingdom, with the old earth as its scene. Then, there is the final manifestation of the kingdom of the Father in the triumph of the consummation in the new heaven and on the new earth (2 Pet. 3:12-13).[41] (Cf. Revelation 21—22.)

The Great Expectation began in the garden of God, which man lost through sin. Mankind then looked for a Saviour, even a Son sent of God. Prophets long foretold His coming. Even so, many missed Christ's manger birth. The

369

"hopes and fears of all the years" were plunged to deep despair when unbelieving people crucified Him. But before Jesus went to the Cross, He said, "I will come again." Death was not the victor, for Christ rose from the dead. While He was ascending into heaven, the disciples were told once again, "This same Jesus . . . shall so come in like manner."

The expectation of the Old Testament was indeed that Christ, the Messiah, would come. The expectation of the New Testament is that Christ will return. The promise of His first coming was gloriously fulfilled, even though Calvary was a part of His mission.

Our present expectation is that Christ will come again. This coming shall be even more glorious. It will unite the redeemed of all the ages. It will break the dominion of Satan, and it will reestablish the kingdom of God on earth.

But the ultimate expectation is the restoration of all things, even unto the Father. We therefore "look for new heavens and a new earth, wherein dwelleth righteousness [only]" (2 Pet. 3:13).

When King Jesus returns for His own, our Great Expectation shall be rewarded. In the meantime, knowing that Christ the Saviour is born, that He died for our sins and rose again, that He ascended into heaven, we await His coming again. Just as surely as Jesus was born according to the word of the prophets, He will come again as He promised. His word of testimony rings true down to us, "Yes, I am coming soon!" May our expectant reply ever be, "Amen. Even so come, Lord Jesus!"

Reference Notes

CHAPTER 1:

1. Cf. George Foot Moore, *History of Religions* (New York: Charles Scribner's Sons, 1919), 2:69-70.

2. William Barclay, *Jesus as They Saw Him* (New York: SCM Press, 1962), p. 95.

3. *Ibid.*, pp. 95-96.

4. A. B. Davidson, *The Theology of the Old Testament* (New York: Charles Scribner's Sons, 1917), p. 367.

5. *Ibid.*, pp. 367-68.

6. *Ibid.*, p. 371.

7. Cf. Barclay, *Jesus as They Saw Him*, p. 93; William Smith, ed., *A Dictionary of the Bible* (Hartford, Conn.: The S. S. Scranton Co., 1905), p. 551.

8. *Ibid.*

9. Cf. *Ibid.;* H. Wheeler Robinson, *The Religious Ideas of the Old Testament* (New York: Charles Scribner's Sons, 1915), p. 199.

10. Alfred Edersheim, *The Life and Times of Jesus the Messiah* (New York: Longmans, Green, and Co., 1905), 1:168.

11-17. Davidson, *Theology of the OT*, pp. 205-25.

18. Cited in *Ibid.*, p. 309.

19-24. Edersheim, *Jesus the Messiah*, 1:162-68.

25. Smith, *Dictionary, loc. cit.*

CHAPTER 2:

1. Sigmund Mowinckel, *He That Cometh*, trans. by G. W. Anderson, (New York: Abingdon Press, 1954), p. 11.

2. Edward Hartley Dewart, *Jesus the Messiah* (Cincinnati: Cranston & Stowe, 1891), p. 90.

3. *Ibid.*, p. 91.

4. Cited in *Ibid.*, p. 92.

5. Arthur E. Bloomfield, *The Genealogy of Christ* (Butler, Ind.: The Higley Press, 1951), pp. 6-8.

6. Cf. James M. Gray, *Synthetic Bible Studies* (New York: Fleming H. Revell Co., 1906), p. 10.

7. Smith, *Dictionary*, p. 490.

8. *Ibid.*

9. W. B. Godbey, *Commentary on the New Testament* (Cincinnati: Revivalist Office, 1896), 1:88-89, 134.

CHAPTER 3:

1. Cf. Matthew Henry, *Commentary on the Whole Bible* (New York: Fleming H. Revell Co., n.d.), 1:74-77; H. D. M. Spence and Joseph S. Exell, eds., *The Pulpit Commentary* (Grand Rapids, Mich.: Wm. B. Eerdmans Publishing Co., 1958), 1:148-51.

2. *Ibid.*

3. Charles L. Feinberg, ed., *Focus on Prophecy* (Westwood, N.J.: Fleming H. Revell Co., 1964), p. 16.

4. Cf. *Ibid.*, pp. 15, 19.

5. Cited in John Fleetwood, *Life of Christ* (Philadelphia: Bradley & Co., 1868), p. 16.

6. Gray, *Synthetic Bible Studies,* p. 13.

7. Adam Clarke, *Commentary on the Holy Bible* (New York: Hunt & Eaton, n.d.), 1:90.

8. Cf. Henry, *Commentary,* pp. 84-85.

CHAPTER 4:

1. Dewart, *Jesus the Messiah,* p. 97.

2. Spence and Exell, *Pulpit Commentary,* 1:525-26; cf. *Ibid.*

3. *Ibid.*

4. Dewart, *Jesus the Messiah,* p. 98.

5. *Ibid.*

6. Smith, *Dictionary,* p. 892.

7. *Ibid.;* cf. *Beacon Bible Commentary* (Kansas City: Beacon Hill Press of Kansas City, 1969), 1:161.

8. Mowinckel, *He That Cometh,* p. 13.

9. Cf. *BBC, loc. cit.*

10. Gray, *Synthetic Bible Studies,* p. 16.

11. Spence and Exell, *Pulpit Commentary, loc. cit.*

12. *Ibid.*

13. Robert N. Pfeiffer, *Introduction to the Old Testament* (New York: Harper and Brothers, Publishers, 1948), p. 276.

14. Henry Law, *The Gospel in Genesis* (London: The Banner of Truth Trust, 1961 reprint), p. 180.

15. Fleetwood, *Life of Christ*, p. 17.

16. G. Campbell Morgan, *The Analyzed Bible* (New York: Fleming H. Revell Co., 1911), 1:270.

Chapter 5:

1. Robert Jamieson, A. H. Fausset, and David Brown, *Commentary on the Old and New Testaments* (Hartford, Conn.: The S. S. Scranton Co., n.d.), 1:176.

2. *BBC*, 2:217.

3. Spence and Exell, *Pulpit Commentary*, 4:31-32.

4. *Ibid.*, p. 28; *BBC, loc. cit.;* cf. Otto F. Baab, *Theology of the Old Testament* (New York: Abingdon-Cokesbury Press, 1949), pp. 115-55.

5-8. *Ibid.*, pp. 28-29.

9. *BBC*, 2:232-33.

10. Spence and Exell, *Pulpit Commentary*, 4:33, 35, 38.

11. *Ibid.*

12. Cited in *Ibid.*, p. 34.

13. *BBC*, 2:214, 238.

14. Spence and Exell, *Pulpit Commentary*, 4:38.

15. Cf. *BBC*, 2:254-55.

16. Cited in Spence and Exell, *Pulpit Commentary*, 4:34.

Chapter 6:

1. William G. Blaikie, revised by Charles D. Matthews, *A Manual of Bible History* (New York: The Ronald Press Co., 1940), p. 170.

2. Henry, *Commentary*, 2:483.

3. Clarke, *Commentary*, 2:326.

4-7. *Ibid.*, pp. 326-27.

8. Henry, *Commentary*, 2:480.

9-13. Clarke, *Commentary*, 2:326-28.

14. Cf. Spence and Exell, *Pulpit Commentary*, 4:184-86.

Chapter 7:

1. W. Graham Scroggie, *The Psalter* (London: Harper &

Brothers Publishers, n.d.), 1:xxxi-xxxii; *BBC*, 3:132; cf. James M. Gray *Christian Workers' Commentary* (New York: Fleming H. Revell Co., 1915), p. 216.

2. Mowinckel, *He That Cometh*, pp. 11-12.

3. *BBC*, 3:143.

4. Both quotations cited in *BBC*, *loc. cit.*

5-9. Scroggie, *Psalter*, *loc. cit.*

10. Cited in *BBC*, 3:373.

11. Spence and Exell, *Pulpit Commentary*, 8:28.

12. Mowinckel, *He That Cometh*, pp. 96, 98.

13. Spence and Exell, *Pulpit Commentary*, 8:28-29.

14. Clarke, *Commentary*, 3:580.

15. *Ibid.*, pp. 580-81.

16-22. Cf. *Ibid.*, p. 585; Spence and Exell, *Pulpit Commentary, loc. cit.;* Henry, *Commentary*, 3:659.

23-25. *BBC*, 3:374.

26-30. Clarke, *Commentary*, 3:586-87.

31. Cf. *BBC*, 3:375; Spence and Exell, *Pulpit Commentary, loc. cit.*

32. Henry, *Commentary*, 3:661.

33. *Ibid.*, p. 662.

34. Spence and Exell, *Pulpit Commentary, loc. cit.*

35. *Ibid.*, pp. 29-30.

36. *BBC, loc. cit.*

37. Henry, *Commentary, loc. cit.*

38. Clarke, *Commentary*, 3:587.

CHAPTER 8:

1. Ross E. Price, "The Virgin—in Prophecy and Fulfillment," (*Nazarene Preacher*, Dec. 1967), p. 42.

2. Dewart, *Jesus the Messiah*, pp. 119-20.

3. Cf. Spence and Exell, *Pulpit Commentary*, 10:129.

4. *BBC*, 4:457.

5. *Ibid.*

6-10. Spence and Exell, *Pulpit Commentary*, 10:129-30.

11. Dewart, *Jesus the Messiah*, pp. 124-25.

12. Cited in *Ibid.,* p. 118.

13. *Ibid.,* p. 122.

14. *Ibid.,* p. 126.

15. Cited in *Ibid.*

16. Spence and Exell, *Pulpit Commentary,* 10:128.

17. Cited by Louis Matthews Sweet, *The Birth and Infancy of Jesus Christ* (Philadelphia: The Westminster Press, 1906), p. 36.

18. *Ibid.,* p. 37.

19. Cited by Dewart, *Jesus the Messiah,* p. 128.

20. Sweet, *Birth and Infancy of Christ,* p. 170.

21. *Ibid.,* pp. 171-72.

22. *Ibid.,* p. 178.

23. *Ibid.,* pp. 184-85.

24. Cf. *Ibid.,* p. 150.

25. As quoted by Hugh C. Benner in *Herald of Holiness,* Dec. 25, 1963, p. 1.

26-30. *BBC,* 4:62-64.

CHAPTER 9:

1-8. Dewart, *Jesus the Messiah,* pp. 165-70.

9. Arthur E. Bloomfield, *The End of the Days* (Minneapolis: Bethany Fellowship, Inc., 1961), p. 58.

10-11. *BBC,* 4:671-72.

13-14. Bloomfield, *End of Days, loc. cit.*

15. Henry, *Commentary, loc. cit.*

16-17. Bloomfield, *End of Days,* p. 60.

18. Henry, *Commentary,* 4:1094.

19-22. Bloomfield, *End of Days,* pp. 60-62.

23-25. *BBC., loc. cit.*

26. *Ibid.,* 4:622; cf. Harold H. Rowley, *Jewish Apocalyptic and the Dead Sea Scrolls* (London: Athlone Press, 1957), pp. 17, 23; Millar Burrows, ed., *The Dead Sea Scrolls of St. Mark's Monastery* (New Haven: American Schools of Oriental Research, 1950), pp. 28, 63.

27. *Ibid.,* 4:673.

28. Dewart, *Jesus the Messiah,* p. 171.

29. *BBC,* 4:673-74; cf. Edward J. Young, *The Prophecy of*

Daniel (Grand Rapids, Mich.: Wm. B. Eerdmans Publishing Co., 1949), pp. 192-94.

30. Cited in *BBC*, 4:674.

31-33. Dewart, *Jesus the Messiah*, pp. 172-73.

34-38. *BBC*, 4:674-76.

39. Dewart, *Jesus the Messiah*, p. 174.

40. *BBC, loc. cit.*

41. Cf. Bloomfield, *End of Days*, p. 65.

42. Jamieson, Fausset, and Brown, *Commentary*, 1:641.

43. Bloomfield, *End of Days*, p. 65.

44. *Ibid.*

45. Cf. Jamieson, Fausset, and Brown, *Commentary, loc. cit.*; Spence and Exell, *Pulpit Commentary*, 13:274-75.

46. Bloomfield, *End of Days*, p. 66.

47. Charles Lee Feinberg, ed., *Prophecy and the Seventies* (Chicago: Moody Press, 1971), p. 58.

48. *Ibid.*

49-51. Hal Lindsey, *The Late Great Planet Earth* (Grand Rapids, Mich.: Zondervan Publishing House, 1970), pp. 34-35.

CHAPTER 10:

1. Henry, *Commentary*, 4:1481.

2. Jamieson, Fausset, and Brown, *Commentary*, 1:739.

3. Clarke, *Commentary*, 4:805.

4. Cited in *BBC*, 5:429.

5. Jamieson, Fausset, & Brown, *Commentary, loc. cit.*

6. Cited in *BBC*, 5:428.

7. Clarke, *Commentary, loc. cit.*

8. Jamieson, Fausset, and Brown, *Commentary, loc. cit.*

9. Flavius Josephus, trans. William Whiston, *History of the Jews* (New York: A. L. Burt Co., Publishers, n.d.), 2:452 (*Antiquities*, Book XVIII, 5:2).

10. Cf. Smith, *Dictionary*, p. 422; F. N. Peloubet, *Bible Dictionary* (Philadelphia: The John C. Winston Co., 1925), p. 323.

11-13. Cited in *BBC*, 6:42-45.

14. Henry, *Commentary*, 4:1492.

15-18. *BBC,* Vol. 5, *loc. cit.*

19. Spence and Exell, *Pulpit Commentary,* 14:39.

20. Jamieson, Fausset, and Brown, *Commentary,* 1:740.

21. Henry, *Commentary, loc. cit.*

22-24. *BBC,* 5:429-30.

25. Spence and Exell, *Pulpit Commentary, loc. cit.*

26. Cf. Henry, *Commentary,* 4:1493.

27. Jamieson, Fausset, and Brown, *Commentary, loc. cit.*

28. *Ibid.*

29. Spence and Exell, *Pulpit Commentary, loc. cit.*

30. *Ibid.*

CHAPTER 11:

1. Moore, *History of Religions,* 2:72.

2-5. Barclay, *Jesus as They Saw Him,* pp. 422-44.

6. George Barker Stevens, *The Theology of the New Testament* (New York: Charles Scribner's Sons, 1914), p. 579; cf. Edersheim, *Jesus the Messiah,* pp. 46-47.

7. *Ibid.*

8. *Ibid.,* cf. pp. 279-80.

9. Charles Bigg, *The Christian Platonists of Alexandria* (Oxford: The Clarendon Press, 1886), pp. 16-17.

10. *Ibid.*

11. Harry Wolfson, *Religious Philosophy, Philo* (Cambridge, Mass.: Harvard University Press, 1947), 1:230-31.

12-14. Bigg, *Christian Platonists, loc. cit.;* cf. Wolfson, *Ibid.,* pp. 236-37, 243-44.

15-22. *Ibid.,* pp. 18-22; cf. Wolfson, *Philo,* pp. 259-60.

22. Moore, *History of Religions,* 2:61.

24. *Ibid.*

25. Arthur S. Peake, *A Critical Introduction to the New Testament* (New York: Charles Scribner's Sons, 1916), p. 201.

26. *Ibid.,* p. 202.

27. Stevens, *Theology of NT,* p. 580.

28. *Ibid.,* pp. 584-85.

29. Andrew Martin Fairbairn, *The Philosophy of the Christian Religion* (New York: Hodder and Stoughton, 1911), p. 454.

CHAPTER 12:

1. Karl Barth, *Church Dogmatics, 1936-39* (Naperville, Ill.: Alec Allenson, 1969), 2:176.

2. Clarence E. MacCartney, *Things Most Surely Believed* (Nashville: Cokesbury Press, 1930), pp. 37-38.

3. Spence and Exell, *Pulpit Commentary,* 16:70.

4. Josephus, *History of the Jews,* 1:4.

5. Spence and Exell, *Pulpit Commentary, loc. cit.*

6. Macartney, *Things Believed,* p. 41.

7-10. Spence and Exell, *Pulpit Commentary,* pp. 71-72.

11-14. Macartney, *Things Believed,* pp. 43-45.

15. Cf. Barclay, *Jesus as They Saw Him,* pp. 46-47.

16. *Ibid.*

17. Cf. George C. Berkouwer, *The Work of Christ* (Grand Rapids, Mich.: Wm. B. Eerdmans Publishing Co., 1965), pp. 111-13.

18. *Ibid.*

19. Sweet, *Birth and Infancy of Christ,* p. 282.

20. Barclay, *Jesus as They Saw Him,* p. 398.

21. Cf. *Ibid.,* pp. 401-2.

22. *Ibid.,* p. 402.

CHAPTER 13:

1. Edmund P. Clowney, "The Lord of the Manger," *Christianity Today,* (Dec. 5, 1969), p. 3.

2. Spence and Exell, *Pulpit Commentary,* 16:38.

3. *Ibid.*

4-8. Cf. Clowney, *Christianity Today,* pp. 3-4.

9. George Williams, *The Student's Commentary on the Holy Scriptures* (Grand Rapids, Mich.: Kregel Publications, 1956), p. 744; cf. George Ricker Berry, *The Interlinear Greek-English New Testament* (Grand Rapids, Mich.: Zondervan Publishing House, 1950), pp. 151-52.

10-12. Cf. Clowney, *Christianity Today,* p. 5.

CHAPTER 14:

1. Smith, *Dictionary,* pp. 918-19.

2. Cf. Edersheim, *Jesus the Messiah,* p. 213; cf. Hans Holzer, "The True Story of the Three Wise Men," *Family Weekly* (Dec. 15, 1968), p. 8.

3. *Ibid.*

4. *Ibid.*

5. Holzer, *Family Weekly,* p. 8.

6. John Kitto, *History of the Bible* (Hartford, Conn.: The S. S. Scranton Co., 1904), p. 510.

7. Josephus, *History of the Jews,* 2:401-406 (Antiquities, Book XVII, cc. 6—8); cf. Edersheim, *Jesus the Messiah,* p. 212.

8. *Ibid.*

9. Spence and Exell, *Pulpit Commentary,* 15:30.

10. Smith, *Dictionary,* p. 501.

11. *Ibid.*

12. Henry, *Commentary,* 5:10-11; Clarke, *Commentary,* 5:43.

13-16. Holzer, *Family Weekly,* pp. 8-9.

17. Smith, *Dictionary,* p. 919.

18. Cf. *Ibid.,* pp. 296, 592; A. R. Fausset, *Bible Cyclopaedia* (Hartford, Conn.: The S. S. Scranton Co., 1903), pp. 236, 491.

19. Edersheim, *Jesus the Messiah,* p. 214.

20. Cunningham Geikie, *The Life and Words of Christ* (New York: D. Appleton and Co., 1890), 1:148.

21. *Ibid.,* pp. 148-49.

22. Spence and Exell, *Pulpit Commentary,* 2:319.

23. Cf. Henry, *Commentary,* 1:685-86.

24. Geikie, *Life and Words,* 1:148.

25. Spence and Exell, *Pulpit Commentary,* 2:317.

26. Henry, *Commentary,* 5:10.

27. *Ibid.*

CHAPTER 15:

1. James Strong, *Exhaustive Concordance of the Bible* (New York: Abingdon-Cokesbury Press, 1947), "Hebrew and Chaldee Dictionary," p. 111.

2. Cf. Josephus, *History of the Jews,* 2:429-31 (*Antiquities,* Book XVII, 13:1-5).

3. Cited in Fred J. Meldau, *Messiah in Both Testaments* (Denver: The Christian Victory Publishing Co., 1967), p. 30.

4. *Ibid.*, p. 34.

5. Spence and Exell, *Pulpit Commentary*, 15:312.

6. *Ibid.*

7. *Ibid.*, p. 313.

8. J. R. Dummelow, ed., *A Commentary on the Holy Bible* (New York: The Macmillan Co., 1945), p. 693.

9. Josephus, *History of the Jews*, 3:165-66, (*Wars*, Book II, 13:5).

10. Cf. *BBC*, 6:190.

11. Spence and Exell, *Pulpit Commentary*, 15:132.

12. Dummelow, *Commentary*, p. 693.

13. *BBC*, 6:191.

14. Spence and Exell, *Pulpit Commentary*, 15:315, 513.

15. Cited in Meldau, *Messiah*, p. 12.

16. Cf. *Ibid.*, p. 50; *BBC*, 6:464-65.

Chapter 16:

1. Erich Sauer, *The Triumph of the Crucified* (Grand Rapids, Mich.: Wm. B. Eerdmans Publishing Co., 1957), p. 41.

2-10. H. Leo Eddleman, comp., *The Second Coming* (Nashville: Broadman Press, 1963), pp. 80-83.

11. E. W. Rogers, *Concerning the Future* (Chicago: Moody Press, 1962), p. 51.

12. Berry, *Greek-English New Testament Lexicon*, p. 14.

13. Cf. Rogers, *The Future*, pp. 56-57.

14. Sauer, *Triumph of the Crucified*, p. 101.

15. Arthur E. Bloomfield, *All Things New* (Minneapolis, Minn.: Bethany Fellowship, Inc., 1959), p. 287.

16. Rogers, *Concerning the Future*, p. 60.

17. Cf. *Ibid.*, pp. 60-61.

18. Cited in *BBC*, 4:664-65.

19. Clarke, *Commentary*, 4:600.

20. Cf. Rodger Young, "When Is the End?" *Nazarene Preacher*, Feb., 1968, p. 13; Lindsey, *Late Great Planet*, p. 55.

21. Cf. *Ibid.*

22-25. Wm. E. Blackstone, *Jesus Is Coming* (New York: Fleming H. Revell Co., 1908), pp. 75-77.

26. Cf. Smith, *Dictionary,* pp. 580, 692.

27. Cf. J. A. Seiss, *The Gospel in Leviticus* (Grand Rapids, Mich.: Zondervan Publishing House, reprint, n.d.), pp. 352-53.

28. Cited in Blackstone, *Jesus Is Coming,* p. 23.

29-41. Sauer, *Triumph of the Crucified,* pp. 144-53.